Interviewing Practices for Technical Writers

Earl E. McDowell

Baywood's Technical Communications Series
Series Editor: JAY R. GOULD

Baywood Publishing Company, Inc.

AMITYVILLE, NEW YORK

Library of Congress Catalog Number: 90-28479
ISBN: 0-89503-073-X (cloth)
ISBN: 0-89503-072-1 (paper)

Library of Congress Cataloging-in-Publication Data

McDowell, Earl E.
    Interviewing practices for technical writers / Earl E. McDowell.
      p.   cm. -- (Baywood's technical communications series)
    Includes bibliographical references and index.
    ISBN 0-89503-073-X (cloth). -- ISBN 0-89503-072-1 (paper)
    1. Technical writing--Examinations, questions, etc.
2. Interviewing in journalism. I. Title. II. Series : Baywood's
technical communications series (Unnumbered)
T11.M363 1991
070.4'3--dc20   90-28479
                                       CIP

ACKNOWLEDGMENTS

Acknowledgment is given for permission to reprint: "The Interview" *The Journalism Bulletin*, pp. 13-18, 1924; "An Investigation of the Interviewing Practices of Technical Writers in Their World of Work," *RPI Proceedings, 35*, pp. 1-21, 1987; and "Exit Interviews: Don't Just Say Goodbye to Your Technical Communication Students," *ITCC Proceedings, 35*, pp. RET 51-53, 1988.

Preface

In 1924 Edward Bell likened skillful interviewers to the great portrait painters of the world [1]. Whereas, the role of painter was to create lifelike reproductions of physical lineaments, he observed, the role of the interviewer was to provide a faithful picture of the human mind and soul. Though today, interviewers may be regarded in less metaphorical and more substantive terms, interviewing remains an important form of human communication with wide application in the workplace. In addition to providing a means for selecting potential employees, interviewing is a highly useful method for giving information, gathering information, appraising employees, solving people-and-work-related problems, and persuading in the business world.

Unfortunately, limited attention has been devoted in the technical communication journals and technical writing textbooks on types of interviewing. Leslie Levine reported in the *Journal of Technical Writing and Communication* that technical writers are likely to discover that their jobs require them to be expert interviewers because good interviewing is often the key to good documentation [2]. In this same article, David Carson, editor of the *Journal of Technical Writing and Communication,* asserted that interviewing often plays a larger role in documentation processing than does writing and editing, that some technical writers spend approximately 75 percent of their time gathering information, and that a significant amount of this time is spent interviewing [2, p. 55].

During the past ten years over 700 technical communication majors enrolled in a graduate level course in interviewing taught in the Department of Rhetoric, University of Minnesota, have interviewed technical writers to learn how they function in the workplace. The results reveal that a majority of writers engage in interviewing quite often—probably an average of once a day. In some cases they interview other writers, while in other cases they interview subject matter experts. Other research indicates that interviewing skills extend beyond the completion of written projects as technical writers must often depend on customer interviews and surveys to gauge the success of a project; therefore, writers need to develop interviewing skills for the collection and analysis of feedback in a systematic and formal manner.

With the above information in mind, this book is written to help technical writers be competent interviewers. The fact that writers participate almost daily in a variety of different types of interviews as both interviewers and interviewees does not mean they are effective. In fact, most students who enroll in my interviewing course have never heard of such terms as interview guide, directive and nondirective approaches, question sequences and question types. A knowledge of the fundamentals of interviewing and a knowledge of specifics pertaining to various types of interviews in both interviewer and interviewee roles are essentials to be effective communicators in the workplace.

Interviewing Practices for Technical Writers is designed for students who are majoring or minoring in technical communication, professional technical writers who have a degree in technical communication, and subject matter experts (SME) who work as technical writers. The contents also are applicable for graphic designers and subject matter experts. Part 1 focuses on the *fundamentals of interviewing*. Chapter 1 introduces interviewing terminology, types of messages, relationship and situational variables and the listening process. Chapter 2 focuses on developing an interview guide, structuring the interview, developing questions and also introduces different types of openings and conclusions.

Part 2 focuses on *informational interviews.* Chapters 3 and 4 focus on information-gathering and information-giving interviews. Chapter 3 introduces various types of information-gathering interviews. The primary focus is journalistic and survey interviews. In a journalistic interview open questions are used the majority of the time, while in the survey interview closed-ended questions are used most of the time. This book will discuss how these types of interviews might be used by the technical writer. In Chapter 4 the purposes of orientation interviews and their importance for technical writers are discussed.

In Part 3 *employment cycle interviews* are discussed. Chapters 5, 6, and 7 focus on hiring, assessing performance, and exiting interviews. Specifically, Chapter 5 focuses on the resume, job description, types of questions, roles of interviewers and interviewee. In Chapter 6 the tell-and-sell, tell-and-listen, problem-solving, and management-by-objective types of appraisal interviews are discussed. Chapter 7 focuses on voluntary and involuntary exit interviews.

Part 4 focuses on *internal and external interviews.* In Chapter 8 problem-solving interviews such as counseling and disciplinary are discussed. In Chapter 9 on-the-job and external persuasive interviews are discussed. Finally, in Chapter 10 the roles of interviewers and interviewees for the types of interviews and the relationships among the types of interviews for the technical writer are discussed.

Part 5 contains several articles that reinforce and add to the overall content of the book. With the exception of Bell's article all others are targeted toward the types of interviewing in the technical writer's "world of work." Bell's article provides the reader with some insight about the importance of interviewing. Please read this article before reading Chapter 1.

Overall, *Interviewing Practices for Technical Writers* will provide writers with the necessary content to build interviewing skills which are essential to be effective technical writers.

I am grateful to Elaine Knight and Jay Lieberman for their significant contribution to Appendix A and to Joseph Schuld for proofreading the manuscript. I also wish to thank Emmie Ingram and Laurie Gardner for typing the articles in Part 5 of the book. I also wish to thank several undergraduate and graduate scientific and technical communication students and professional technical writers for their comments. I especially want to thank Dr. Jay Gould for his comments over the past two years.

Most of all I wish to thank my wife, Carlene, for her proofreading, scholarly comments, support, and love, and my daughters, Beth Ann and Leann for their constant encouragement.

REFERENCES

1. E. P. Bell, The Interview, *The Journalism Quarterly,* pp. 13-18, 1924.
2. L. Levine, Interviewing for Information, *Journal of Technical Writing and Communication, 14,* pp. 55-58, 1984.

Table of Contents

PART 1: FUNDAMENTALS OF INTERVIEWING

PART 2: INFORMATIONAL INTERVIEWS

PART 3: EMPLOYMENT CYCLE INTERVIEWS

PART 5: ARTICLE REVIEW

List of Tables

List of Illustrations

Part 1
FUNDAMENTALS
OF INTERVIEWING

CHAPTER 1

The Interviewing Process

OBJECTIVES

On completion of this chapter you should be able to:
    Define interviewing
    Explain relationship variables
    Describe verbal and nonverbal communication skills
    List types of interviews
    Participate in role playing exercises

Mary arrived early for her employment interview for the position as a software writer for a small computer firm. She felt confident as she waited for the interview to begin. After all she had thoroughly prepared for the moment—she'd researched the company, developed questions about the position and the company, and had put on her navy blue dress for success suit. In the next office Brian, a computer programmer, sat patiently, awaiting his annual appraisal interview. This year Brian's supervisor had told him to complete a self-evaluation about a week prior to the interview and to be prepared to talk about his personal objectives for the upcoming three-month period. Two doors down from Brian was Bill, an electrical engineer, who a week earlier had turned in his resignation. The Director of Personnel would be arriving shortly to conduct an exit interview. Bill was somewhat apprehensive about this as he had never participated in an exit interview and was uncertain about its purpose.

Other interviews were being conducted in the company that same day. Terri and Belinda, two junior technical writers, had been working on a new computer manual and discovered they needed to talk to a subject matter expert (SME) and graphic designer to clarify some of the documentation. Since they had already interviewed the SME several times, Terri decided that a few closed-ended questions would be adequate to get the job done. Meantime, Belinda would develop several open-ended questions for the graphic designer, for she needed quite a bit of information to put together some complex diagrams in the manual.

Good news! Mary was hired and now is participating in an information-giving interview. This orientation session is designed to provide information about the company and answer any questions that the supervisor did not cover. **Good news!** Brian received an excellent performance rating. Bill decided to disclose that his main reason for leaving the company was his desire to be a writer rather than an editor. Terri was in the final stage of completing her manual. Belinda was having some difficulty with the graphic designer who was arguing about page design. As tactfully as possible she explained that the format had been determined by the project director. While she was trying to persuade him to keep the format, he was trying to persuade her that the format needed changing. They compromised and decided to conduct usability testing.

In each of the preceding examples, the parties involved were using purposeful, planned communication. For example, Mary wanted to "sell herself" to the company by stressing her skills as a technical writer. At the same time, her interviewer was "selling" the company as a desirable employer. In the appraisal interview, Brian was concerned with creating a favorable impression of his performance over the past three months and gave himself a good self-assessment. The interviewer also wanted to create a supportive climate for the interview and to determine Brian's responsibilities and objectives for the next three-month period. In the exit interview both Bill and the interviewer tried to create favorable lasting impressions. The interviewer also wanted to discover the true reasons Bill was leaving the company. Other interviews were being conducted to gather and give information, persuade the other interview party, and, perhaps, to counsel and discipline employees of the Good Writers Company.

These examples demonstrate that writers probably are more involved with interviewing than they think. They use the interview to hire, to appraise, to exit, to motivate, to discipline, to gain information, to give information, to persuade, and to counsel.

DEFINITION OF INTERVIEWING

Many definitions of interviewing are available. Stewart and Cash, authors of one of the best selling interviewing textbooks, provide a definition that is similar to the one in this book. *Interviewing is defined as a dyadic, relational communication process which involves two parties with a definite purpose designed to interchange behavior by speaking and listening to one another and involves the asking and answering of questions.* This definition is similar to that of Stewart and Cash's definition which is cited frequently in interviewing textbooks [1, p. 3]. The definition suggests that interviewing is a transactional process as both the interviewer and interviewee communicate their attitudes and values through various messages. In face-to-face interviews nonverbal, vocal, and verbal messages are exchanged, while in telephone interviews vocal and verbal messages are exchanged. The following characteristics apply to both face-to-face and telephone interviews.

Dyadic, Relational Communication Process

The word "dyadic" refers to a two-persons/parties context. Most of our conversations occur in a two person context. In addition, most interpersonal communication in an organization occurs between a two-person context through various types of structured and unstructured interviews. The term "relational communication process" denotes an interpersonal connection between the interviewer and interviewee. The relationship between the two parties is influenced by the following dimensions: inclusion, control, and affection.

Inclusion — This term refers to the degree to which each party desires to take part in the interview and each party's perceptions of the other party. Both the interviewer and interviewee must determine the roles that they will play in the interview. For example, Mary might be very excited to be interviewed for the position as a technical writer, but the interviewer might have already interviewed several candidates and made a decision to hire another person. In contrast, Mary might want the technical writing position but is very apprehensive about the interview because she heard through the grapevine that the interviewer is very extroverted and dominates employment interviews.

Control — This dimension refers to the power each party has to determine the outcome of the interview. Position in the organization will determine who holds power in the interview situation. For example, the lead writer will generally have more control to determine the final content of a manual than do the other writers working on the project. Control, however, might be determined by the relationships that exist between the lead writer and subordinates. An open-minded lead writer might be more concerned with the final product rather than dictating to subordinates. Obviously, control plays a significant role in all types of interviews. In an appraisal interview, the interviewer, for example, needs to create a cooperative climate in order to persuade the interviewee to be less redundant in writing directions.

Affection — The degree of affection, or the interpersonal closeness each party feels for the other, is referenced in this dimension. The degree of interpersonal closeness will determine the willingness of participants to disclose their actual feelings and attitudes during the interview. A high level of trust facilitates the movement to maximum self-disclosure. Sometimes individuals do not self-disclose as they feel it might lead to negative evaluation and rejection. The *Johari Window Model*, developed by Luft and Ingham, provides a framework for examining the willingness to share oneself with another person [2]. The model consists of the following four windows:

1. **Free area**—Information known to both parties in an interview. Information and feelings that the interviewee is willing to share with the interviewer and information and feelings that the interviewer is willing to share with the interviewee refer to the free area. For example, Mary might be willing to

disclose her feelings about various topics that are relevant to the writing position.

2. **Blind area**—Information which others know about you which you do not know about yourself. This area consists of both verbal and nonverbal messages, that is unintentional information that the interviewee discloses to the interviewer. For example, an interviewee might be a passive listener and unintentionally convey little feedback when the interviewer is talking. As a result, the interviewer might think that the interviewee lacks interest in the topic. In addition, the interviewee might dress inappropriately for the interview. In a screening interview, this could be the difference between being asked to come back for a second interview or being cut from the list of applicants.

3. **Hidden area**—Contains information which you know about yourself, but you keep hidden from others. For example, a technical communication major interviewing for a writing position might not disclose that he received a "D" in a technical editing course or that he was fired as writer for a well known writing company.

4. **Unknown area**—Neither you nor others know the information. The unknown area should be rather small if members of interviewing parties disclose to each other. On-going contact between the two parties should help both to understand each other.

The Johari Window Model, Figure 1, can be used by the interviewer and interviewee to determine the trust that each party has for the other party.

The willingness of both parties to self-disclose will promote good will. Although this should occur in all interviews, people are different, and different levels of self-disclosure will occur based on the relationship and personalities of the two parties in the interview. For example during a counseling interview much self-disclosure might occur, but during a disciplinary interview or involuntary exit interview limited self-disclosure might occur.

	Known to Self	Not Known to Self
Known to others	OPEN	BLIND
Not known to others	HIDDEN	UNKNOWN

Figure 1. Johari Window Model.

The Johari Window Model can be applied to all forms of interpersonal communication. The amount of disclosure will depend upon the relationship between the two parties. For example, in some cases the interviewing parties might focus on a project. That is, if two writers focus on the document rather than on who has more control over the final product, they are depersonalizing the situation and the final product should be better. By doing this both parties are increasing the size of the open window and decreasing the sizes of the hidden and blind windows. Here is how Gus depersonalizes the situation:

> **Gus**: Gene, we have been working on this manual for three months, and it is now complete. However, there is some disagreement concerning the contents of the tutorial. I think the present tutorial does a good job of introducing the user to how to use the manual, but the testing we have done seems to indicate that an advanced organizer would help novice users at the beginning of the program. Let's look at the comments of the users to see if we can create a more personal advanced organizer. (Gus maintained excellent eye contact with Gene.)
>
> **Gene**: I think you are right, Gus. I was uncertain about the clarity of the tutorial. I will follow the users' suggestions to create a better introduction.

Definite Purpose

The interviewer has a definite or specific purpose for the interview. The purpose might be to gather information, give information, persuade, discipline, counsel, or perhaps to solve a problem. The interviewee may share these same purposes.

Interchange Behavior

The interchanging of behavior refers to the verbal, nonverbal, and vocal messages that occur between the interviewer and interviewee during the interview. Both parties speak and listen during the interview. Participants play both sender and receiver roles during the interview. Both have perceptions of themselves in both of these roles. For example, Bill might feel comfortable as a source of information but not as a receiver of information. In other words, he might be apprehensive about listening to why he should remain with the Good Writers Company. To maximize the effectiveness of the communication, interviewers need to:

- develop the ability to concentrate;
- use questions to help you to remember;
- listen for central ideas;
- listen to nonverbal and voice messages; and
- provide feedback to the other party in the interview.

The percentage of time that each person talks will vary based on the purpose of the interview. For example, during the first information-gathering interview between a writer and technical expert, the writer might ask primarily open-ended questions. In this case the writer might listen 80 percent of the time. After writing a draft of the document, both parties might speak and listen 50 percent of the time. During the final phases of a project the writer might speak 80 percent of the time and listen 20 percent of the time.

Asking and Answering of Questions

Questions are termed the "tools of the trade." It is essential for the interviewer to prepare questions for all types of interviews. The interviewee may find it beneficial to prepare questions for situations such as employment, appraisal, and counseling interviews. Remember Mary, our aspiring technical writer, first researched the company and then developed questions based on the job description and the results of her research. By developing questions the interviewee will better understand the purpose and the roles played during the interviews. Chapter 2 will focus on different types of questions and their uses in various types of interviews.

CODES OF COMMUNICATION

The codes of communication are verbal cues and nonverbal cues. To be an effective communicator in a face-to-face interview, writers need to use each code.

Verbal Cues

Language is the medium of ideas. Writers develop questions that will provide the necessary information. The writer's objective is to use clear, accurate, simple, appropriate, and concrete language to transfer messages to users. During an interview the interviewee might use examples, explanations, statistics, active verbs, and transitions to answer the technical writer's questions. The interviewee also might ask questions that call for the interviewer to give examples, explanations, and other verbal messages. Chapter 2 will focus on the importance of structuring and questioning to obtain information.

Nonverbal Cues

Nonverbal communication plays a significant role in the content and outcome of interviews. When we meet someone for the first time, we generally shake hands and observe the physical appearance of that individual. The distance between the interviewer and interviewee, the seating arrangement, the sex and age of each party, the amount of eye contact, posture, hand gestures, and body gestures, all confirm or disconfirm the verbal messages. For example, during an appraisal interview the interviewer might say to the interviewee, "we need to complete our project on time." This message might be reinforced with direct eye contact, serious facial expression, open hand gestures, and serious vocal inflection.

Nonverbal cues also might substitute for verbal cues. In a persuasive interview, the interviewer might point to a book that supports why the plan is the most workable. In a disciplinary interview the interviewer might point toward the door indicating that the interview is over. Obviously, the nonverbal greeting is important to create a favorable first impression, and the nonverbal closing is important in creating a lasting impression. Below is a list of research findings about nonverbal communication in interpersonal communication situations:

1. Direct eye contact tells the others that you are interested in them and what they are saying.
2. Leaning slightly forward shows more interest in the other party as opposed to slouching in the chair which shows disinterest.
3. Sitting with arms and legs uncrossed communicates openness, while crossed legs and arms might communicate defensiveness and/or a closed mind.
4. In our society a distance of about three or four feet between participants is the optimal "comfort zone" for conducting an interview.
5. Appearance, including body shape, clothing and grooming, sends strong messages about self-image and attitude.
6. Sitting across the desk from the interviewer implies a subordinate-superior relationship as in an appraisal interview, while sitting kitty-cornered creates a peer relationship. Sitting side-by-side creates an intimate relationship as in a counseling interview.
7. Persons who tend to fidget, shift, or change posture frequently create a feeling of distrust, stress, and tension. A relaxed posture, with much eye contact creates a feeling of trust and friendliness and should lead to much discourse in the interview.

Table 1 shows the types of nonverbal cues used in various face-to-face communication situations. How important are each of these cues in your interviewing success?

Obviously, the type of interview and the relationship the interviewer and interviewee have established with the other party will determine the type of nonverbal cues to be used during the interview. Below is a list of nonverbal cues that an interviewer or interviewee might use during an interview. What types of attitudes do they communicate? Which ones have you used during your interviews? Which ones would be appropriate for your future interviews?

fistlike gesture	leaning forward
arms crossed	pointing index feature
open hands	clearing throat
smiling	"whew" sound
tilted head	playing with paper clips/pen/pencil
pinching flesh	unbuttoned coat
peering over glasses	biting fingernails or cuticles

Table 1. Nonverbal Cues

Category	Example
Proxemics (study of space) might be three feet apart	Employment interview parties
Intimate distance—Up to 1.5 feet	
Personal distance—1.5 to 4 feet	Disciplinary interview parties might
Social distance—4 to 12 feet	be seven or eight feet apart
Public distance—more than 12 feet	
Kinesics (study of body movement)	Eye contact between interviewer and
Eye contact	interviewee in a persuasive
Smiling	interview
Facial expressions	
Gestures	Posture can reveal confidence of
Body movement	interviewer and interviewee
Posture	
Paralanguage Cues (the study of the voice)	A slower rate will be used in problem solving. The rate and force of the
Rate	interviewee are very important in
Pitch	influencing the interviewer in an
Force	employment interview.
Quality	
Articulation	
Appearance (the study of external cues)	Dressing appropriately helps build a favorable first impression.
Body shape	
Skin color	
Smell	
Hair	
Clothes	
Accessories	
Haptics (the study of touch)	Physical closeness might occur in
Handshake	counseling interview. Handshake is
Arms around person	important in building a favorable first impression

COMMUNICATION PROCESS

Earlier in the chapter interviewing was defined as a face-to-face, two-way communication process in which the interviewer and interviewee are in close proximity and send and receive messages. In order for the communication to be effective both the sender and receiver must understand the various messages that are being sent and received. The elements of the communication process include *source, messages, channel, receiver, noise, encoding, decoding,* and *feedback.*

Elements of the Communication Process

Source — The source (either the interviewer or interviewee) is the originator of the verbal, vocal, and nonverbal messages. The source creates messages based on knowledge, past experiences, attitudes, feelings, emotions, and values. A number of other variables, such as the sex, age, and height, can affect the verbal and nonverbal messages of the interviewer and interviewee.

Messages — The three types of messages are *verbal, vocal,* and *nonverbal.* Each message type is important for both the interviewer and interviewee. Remember these messages can be intentional or unintentional. Intentional messages are planned, whereas unintentional messages occur without the source being consciously aware of them. Verbal messages include language used by both parties. Vocal cues refer to the sound of the voice. Nonverbal cues, such as eye contact and facial expressions, are difficult to control.

Channel — The channel refers to the methods used to transfer messages. For example, words are delivered by the voice to the receiver by air waves, and nonverbal messages are delivered by light waves.

Receiver — Just as the sender generates verbal and nonverbal messages based on past experiences, attitudes, feelings, emotions, and values, the receiver decodes the messages based on the internal states of feelings and attitudes.

Noise — External and internal interferences are the two basic types of noise. *External noise* refers to background noise, people passing outside a door or window, body odor of the person sitting next to you, or an uncomfortable room. *Internal noise* consists of daydreaming, positive or negative reactions to your interviewing partner, and a lack of motivation to listen.

Encoding — This element refers to transferring a message into a code; that is, putting it into verbal, vocal, and nonverbal messages that can be understood by the receiver. To understand this process think of the brain as a computer program. Each person has stored information on various persons, topics, and situations. Through the selective process interviewing participants retrieve from their "storehouse" information, encode the information, and share it with their interviewing partner.

Decoding — This refers to translating the messages of their interviewing partner based on the "storehouse" of knowledge. Through the selective process interviewers and interviewees interpret the various verbal, vocal, and nonverbal messages of the sender.

Feedback — Effective feedback occurs between the interviewer and interviewee when both parties understand and interpret accurately the messages of each other. Brooks provides the following guidelines to help individuals increase effectiveness as communicators [3, p. 178]:

1. Use both positive and negative feedback.
   The graphics you did on this project look very professional, but you need to include more white space
2. Effective feedback is descriptive rather than evaluative.
   Descriptive: Colorful bow ties are nice, but you need to select attire that will be accepted by our clients as appropriate.
   Evaluative: I really think that your attire is inappropriate for this position. You dress like a clown.
3. Immediate feedback is more effective than delayed feedback.
   Immediate: I just read the manual and it seems easy to follow the directions, but I am uncertain about the connection between visual 1 and visual 2. Let me explain.
   Delayed feedback: Yea! I read the manual. As I recall I had some difficulty with linkage of the visuals. Please redo the visuals.
4. Effective feedback is constructive rather than destructive.
   Constructive: I asked several users to read your directions. They indicated that you need to use bar graphs as well as numbers for them to understand the product.
   Destructive: Eddy, you apparently were not thinking when you did the statistics. Don't you know these people don't understand the parametric statistics? Redo the statistics. Use graphs.

INTERVIEWING MODEL

Several ways can be used to visualize what occurs in the interviewing process. For example, an employment interviewer (source) develops an interview guide and series of questions to interview applicants for a technical writing position. The interviewer uses his/her knowledge, past experiences, attitudes, beliefs, and values to prepare for the interview. Specifically, the interviewer sorts the various messages and encodes them into verbal, vocal, and nonverbal messages and sends them to the interviewee (receiver) by light waves and air waves. The interviewee decodes the messages, selects and sorts information based on personal knowledge, past experiences, attitudes, beliefs and values. The interviewee (source) selects and sorts information, then encodes messages, and sends messages by air waves and light waves back to the interviewer (receiver). The interviewer and interviewee continue to send and receive messages throughout the interview.

Interviewing should be viewed as a transactional process between an interviewer and interviewee in which both parties play the roles of interviewer and interviewee (see Figure 2). The model indicates: I (source) talk (messages) to you (receiver) who listens and gives feedback, and then you (source) answer (messages) while I (receiver) listen. While talking, I am receiving your nonverbal messages. Thus, I am sender and receiver at the same time. Remember that many situational factors can affect the interview. We have already mentioned that the

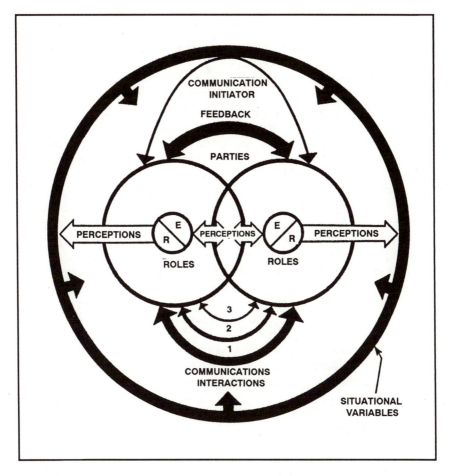

Figure 2. The Cash-Stewart Model of Interviewing.
From Charles J. Stewart and William B. Cash, Jr.,
Interviewing: Principles and Practices, 5th ed. Wm. C. Brown Publishers,
Dubuque IA, p. 14, 1988. Reprinted by permission of Wm. C. Brown Publishers.

relationship variables will affect how each party will view each other. In addition, the type of interview will affect the interviewing climate. Other factors, such as the time of day and day of the week, where the interview takes place, and specific events that precede or follow the interview might influence the level of success of the interviewing parties. For example, a technical writer might want to know what the best times are to conduct information-gathering interviews with subject matter experts. Research indicates that Tuesday, Wednesday, and Thursday mornings are the best times to conduct these interviews.

LISTENING

Listening is an important part of the interviewing process for both the interviewer and the interviewee. Rankin concluded that college students are engaged in listening more than any other communication activity [4]. Werner's study shows that employees spend about 25 percent of their time talking and 55 percent listening [5, p. 26]. A survey completed at the University of Minnesota indicates that former graduates believe that listening is the communication area in which they need the most help [6, p. 14]. Another survey by DiSalvo, Larsen, and Seiler indicates that listening is the number one communication activity in the professional's "world of work" [7, p. 270].

Lundsteen defines listening as "the process by which spoken language is converted to meaning in the mind" [8, p. 9]. Ehninger, Monroe, and Gronbeck's definition is more specific as they indicate that listening is the "whole interpretative process whereby your body makes sense out of the communication process" [9, p. 36]. This definition would include possible stimuli from all the senses. For example, as you listen to the interviewer's voice, you will be decoding not only the words but the paraverbal messages as well as nonverbal messages. You also might be influenced by the smell or color of the room or the smell and appearance of the interviewer. In addition, the room might be hot which might impede processing the various messages.

Barker developed the listening process model [10, p. 47]. It consists of the elements of the listening process which are hearing, seeing, attending, understanding, and remembering. These elements are presented in Figure 3 and are discussed below.

Elements of Listening

Hearing — This element refers to sound waves that stimulate the senses of the ear. This is purely a physical response to the words and voice of the interviewer or interviewee. Even if you do not understand the language, interviewing participants still experience this phase of the listening process.

Seeing — This part of the listening process refers to the light waves that stimulate the eye, such as the appearance of the other party in the interview. Except for individuals who are blind this sense is important to the listening process.

Attending — Your ability and willingness to tune in and concentrate on the messages presented by the other party in the interview is the focus of this element. Attending is the first state of the mental process where the messages must be decoded.

Understanding — This element concerns both parties' abilities to assimilate various messages based on knowledge, past experiences, attitudes, values, and

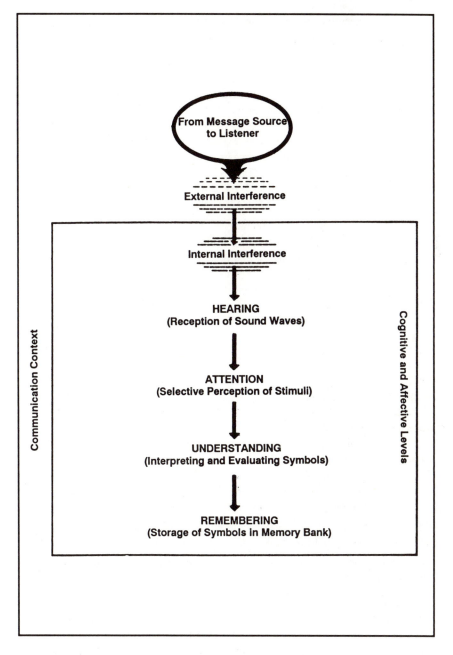

Figure 3. Barker's listening model. Barker, L., *Communication*.
Prentice-Hall, Inc., Englewood Cliffs, N.J., p. 47, 1978. Reprint by permission
of Prentice-Hall, Inc., Englewood Cliffs, N.J.

beliefs. The objective of this phase of the listening process is to interpret the intended meaning of messages created by other members of the interviewing party.

Remembering — Both short-term and long-term memory are considered in this phase. It involves the ability to recall information. Active listening is essential for both short-term and long-term memory.

Listening Problems

As you prepare for an interview you need to prepare for your role as a listener during the interview and to avoid the listening pitfalls. For example, Barker lists nine common listening problems [11, pp. 61-65]:

1. viewing the topic as uninteresting;
2. criticizing the other party's communication delivery;
3. becoming over-stimulated or emotionally involved;
4. listening only for facts;
5. preparing to answer questions before fully understanding them;
6. faking attention;
7. listening only to what is easy to understand;
8. allowing emotionally laden words to interfere with listening; and
9. permitting personal prejudices or deep-seated convictions to impair comprehension.

Much could be written about each of these problems in reference to various types of communication. How do you relate to each of these pitfalls based on your interviewing experiences? For example, when writers are gathering information about a new topic, they might try to write down too much information and miss some of the significant material. In addition, if you are the interviewer in a disciplinary interview, it would be difficult to avoid becoming over-stimulated.

The good listener will respond by clarifying questions and answers, by using reflective and probing questions, by listening for critical content and main ideas, and by processing answers before asking the next question. The good listener will respond with empathy by paraphrasing information presented by the interviewee.

> **Jim:** I think I performed as well as I could under the circumstances. After all, I had to share the computer with two other writers.
> **Tom:** You feel that you did well because you did not have your own computer.

Listening is complex and difficult. It demands that you follow the elements of the listening process and become aware of your barriers to effective listening. To be an effective listener Keltner suggests that you do the following [12, pp. 135-137]:

1. Develop habits beyond what you expect a situation to produce.
2. Develop habits of focusing attention on the other party.

3. Prepare to listen.
4. Examine the role and purpose of the communication with the other party.
5. Determine how you wish to relate to the other party.
6. Deliberately attempt to perceive the relevant stimuli of the communication situation from as many different viewpoints as possible.

Remember that listening is a selective process; thus, you will need to select various vocal, nonverbal and verbal messages, decode the messages, and encode messages for your interviewing partner. You will remember the messages that are important to you in the interviewing situation.

SEVEN TYPES OF INTERVIEWING

This textbook focuses on seven different types of interviewing: information-gathering, information-giving, employment, appraisal, problem solving, persuasion, and exit. These types of interviews are common in most organizations. The focus will be on why and how these interviews are important for technical communicators. Each interview type will be developed. Table 2 provides a list, description and example of each of the types of interviews.

These types of interviews are used by technical communicators in a variety of different ways. For example, informal information-giving interviews occur between writers, between writers and subject matter experts, and between personnel directors and writers. In fact, technical writers could probably generate a long list of the times they conduct information-giving and information-gathering interviews, as well as informal problem-solving and appraisal interviews on the job.

DIRECTIVE AND NONDIRECTIVE APPROACHES

Earlier in the chapter interviewing was discussed as a transactional process between the interviewer and interviewee in which inclusion, control, and affection determine the relationship between the two parties. Based on the purpose and relationship variables, the interviewer must decide whether to use a directive or nondirective approach or a combination of both to conduct the interview.

The directive approach is used in information-gathering and information-giving interviews, as well as persuasive and employment interviews. When using the directive approach, the interviewer establishes the purpose, controls the interview, and plays a highly dominant role by the types of questions posed to the interviewee. In contrast, when using the nondirective approach, the interviewer allows the interviewee to control the interview and plays a less active role. A journalist will use this approach to provide the interviewee with an opportunity to share detailed information about events. Technical writers might use this approach to gain background information on a new project.

Table 2. Types of Interviews

Type	Description	Example
Information gathering	Parties gather facts, opinions and suggestions from each other	Writer clarifies key information with engineer Writer gathers information about electronic publishing
Information giving	A form of instruction	Interviewer giving facts about company benefits Graphic designer explaining use of graphics for a manual
Employment	Exchange information on which to make an employment decision	Technical writing recruiter meets with technical communication graduates
Appraisal	Interviewer reviews performance	Senior writer gives evaluation of each of the writers on a project
Problem solving	Both parties attempt to solve cause of work problems	Writing supervisor and graphic supervisor identify and try to solve differences between writers and designers in terms of the final project
Persuasion	Parties attempt to influence each other's attitudes and ultimate decision	Writer wants word processors with desktop publishing capabilities
Exit	Determine reasons interviewee is leaving company	Personnel director wants to find out the real reasons the writer is going to another company

Both approaches have advantages and disadvantages. For example, when interviewing a subject matter expert (SME) for the first time, the writer might decide to use the nondirective approach when the primary purpose is to gather information. By using this approach the writer is giving the interviewee an opportunity to tell, to explain, and to amplify in his/her own way. The nondirective method also is used in counseling and problem-solving interviews. When using the nondirective approach the interviewer relies primarily on open-ended questions. This method is interviewee-centered.

The directive approach is used in all types of interviews. In the employment interview, the interviewer might want all candidates for the position to answer certain questions. Likewise, in a persuasive interview, the interviewer wants to persuade the interviewee toward his viewpoint using primarily closed-ended questions. This method is interviewer-centered.

INTERVIEWER AND INTERVIEWEE ROLES

This chapter concludes with a list of roles that interviewers and interviewees play. These roles are linked to part of a larger process in a sequence of events. Thus, Mary's employment interview is a stage in the process of determining if she will be hired as a software writer. Both interviewer and interviewee should plan for the interview. Keltner suggests that the interviewer should [12, pp. 276-278]:

1. anticipate the nature of the interviewee;
2. anticipate the interviewee's perception of the interview;
3. determine the degree of psychological proximity with the interviewee that will be most appropriate for the specific interview occasion;
4. focus the direction of the communication process toward the specific purpose;
5. create a trusting relationship to maximize self-disclosure;
6. understand emotional stress and pressure;
7. develop skill in timing of questions and providing transitions;
8. listen carefully; and
9. use feedback frequently and effectively.

Likewise, Keltner indicates that the interviewee has several responsibilities before and during the interview [12, pp. 280-282]:

1. be willing to communicate;
2. be willing to deal with specific as well as general ideas;
3. avoid discussing information that is not relevant to the interview;
4. provide clear and specific responses; and
5. correct apparent misunderstandings on the part of the interviewer and request feedback in order to be sure that messages are interpreted accurately.

SUMMARY

This book began with key information about the interviewing process. As you complete this chapter, you should review the definition of interviewing. We have discussed a definition of interviewing, codes of communication, the communication process, the interviewing model, types of listening, types of interviews, directive and nondirective approaches, and the roles of interviewers and interviewees. We also have indicated that interviewing is a planned process in which the interviewer and interviewee should attain a sense of mutuality and interdependence. The focus of this chapter has been on the role of interviewing in the technical writer's "world of work." Face-to-face interviewing is an important way to communicate with others. Now go to Part 5 and read the article, "Interviewing for Information," which cites several examples of the importance of interviewing for the technical writer.

QUESTIONS

1. Generate a list of interviews in which you have participated. What roles did you play? How effectively did you play these roles?
2. Pick a recent interview and assess your performance in terms of the relationship variables: inclusion, control, and affection.
3. Watch an interview on television and assess the interviewer/interviewee in terms of the codes of communication. Use the interview evaluation to evaluate both parties.
4. Contact a technical writer and ask him/her to assess his/her last information-gathering interview in terms of his/her success as the interviewer/interviewee.
5. During the first class students could participate in an impromptu employment interview. Students should generate a list of questions and interview a partner, and then the partners should interview them.
6. Keep a record of your interviewing experiences for this quarter or semester. If you are employed as a technical writer, keep a record of your job-related interviews for the next three months. Assess yourself and your partner on a scale of 1 to 5:
   (1=poor to 5=excellent) on listening, nonverbal communication, verbal communication, feedback, and interviewing approach.

REFERENCES

1. C. J. Stewart and W. B. Cash, Jr., *Interviewing: Principles and Practices*, Wm. C. Brown Publishers, Dubuque, Iowa, 1988.
2. J. Luft, *On Human Interaction*, National Press Book, Palo Alto, California, 1969.
3. W. Brooks, *Speech Communication*, Wm. C. Brown Publishers, Dubuque, Iowa, 1981.
4. P. Rankin, The Importance of Listening Ability, *English Journal, 17*, pp. 623-630, 1928.
5. E. Werner, *A Study of Communication Time*, M.A. thesis, University of Maryland—College Park, 1975.
6. V. Winkler and E. McDowell, *A Communication Assessment Study of Former Graduates from the Colleges of Agriculture, Forestry and Home Economics*, University of Minnesota, St. Paul, 1983.
7. V. DiSalvo, D. Larsen, and W. Seiler, Communication Skills Needed by Persons in Business Organizations, *Communication Education, 25*, pp. 267-270, 1976.

8. S. Lundsteen, *Listening: Its Impact on Reading and Other Language Arts*, National Council of Teachers of English, Urbana, Illinois, 1971.

9. D. Ehninger, A. Monroe, and B. Gronbeck, *Principles and Types of Speech Communication*, Scott, Foresman and Company, Glenville, Illinois, 1978.

10. L. Barker, *Communication*, Prentice Hall, Inc., Englewood Cliffs, New Jersey, p. 47, 1978.

11. L. Barker, *Listening Behavior*, Prentice Hall, Inc., Englewood Cliffs, New Jersey, pp. 61-65, 1971.

12. L. Keltner, *Interpersonal Speech-Communication Elements and Structure*, Wadsworth Publishing Company, Inc., Belmont, California, 1976.

CHAPTER 2

Fundamentals of Interviewing

OBJECTIVES

On completion of this chapter you should be able to:
Develop various types of openings
Develop interview guides and schedules
Understand question types
Develop question types
Understand question sequences
Develop question sequences
Develop various types of closings

While Chapter 1 introduced you to the interviewing process, this chapter will focus on fundamentals of interviewing. Past research indicates that only 25 percent of technical writers have had any formal training in interviewing while 75 percent of writers operate primarily on intuition. Writers need to have a knowledge of the fundamentals of interviewing.

This chapter will provide the "tools of the trade." Specifically we will focus on the types of openings, body, types of closings, types of questions and question sequences. As we begin this chapter think about your past interviews in which you played the role of interviewer and about your past interviews when you played the role of interviewee. How organized were you in these roles? How satisfied were you with the other party's performances? How effective were the openings? How effective were the closings? What types of organizational patterns did you use? Did you develop interview guides? Did you develop interview schedules?

OPENINGS

The two basic purposes of the opening are to establish *rapport* and to *orient* the interviewee. Interviewers can establish rapport in a variety of ways. For example, when you are meeting the other party for the first time, rapport might be enhanced by a firm handshake, direct eye contact, smiling, overall attentiveness, and a friendly voice. The nonverbal cues can be reinforced by personal inquiry.

First impressions are established during the rapport building phase. Both parties are drawing inferences about their partner. An expression of interest and concern for the other party tends to build trust and good will which will influence the level of self-disclosure that will occur during the interview. For example, in Chapter 1, Mary applied for a position as a software writer and was hired. During the rapport building stage, she obviously used good nonverbal cues and engaged in small talk. Likewise, the interviewer was trying to create a favorable first impression and used supportive nonverbal communication and showed interest in Mary.

In many informational interviews the rapport building stage can be omitted if both parties know each other well. Instead, participants will move directly into the orientation phase of the opening. The interviewer will generally control this part of the interview by establishing the purpose, by indicating the topic areas, and by stating the procedures that will be followed. Several types of openings can be used to start an interview.

Types of Openings

1. *Summary of the problem* — This method is used when the other party is not aware of the problem. Generally, the two parties know each other so the interviewer will move directly to the problem. For example, a lead writer might tell the graphic expert the following:

> Since we purchased our desktop publishing word processors, we have received 500 percent more complaints from users. Our manager has asked me to interview each graphic designer using a specific set of questions. I'm here to gain your insight into how we can improve the quality of our graphics. First, I would like to ask you . . .

2. *Explanation of how the problem was discovered* — This method explains how you learned about the problem and reinforces the summary of the problem opening and adds to the impact:

> Yesterday, I was reviewing letters of complaint that we have received during the past six months and discovered a problem. I shared this information with our manager (state summary).

3. *Statement of incentive or reward for taking part in an interview* — Perhaps, you have received a telephone call in which the interviewer indicated that if you are willing to listen to a speech on why people are buying land in the desert, you could win a free car. This type of incentive is a very powerful method of persuasion, but interviewers need to avoid making it sound like a sales pitch and should create trust and sincerity. Below is an example of how a vendor might use this method to sell technical publications:

> Good morning! I'm Georgia Toogood; I know you are interested in increasing your sales. I would like to discuss with you ways you can increase your sales by

improving the quality of your advertisements. This can be done by better writing and illustrations. I would like to talk to you about how we edit, rewrite, and illustrate various advertisements.

4. *Request for advice or assistance* — Requesting advise is probably the most common type of opening and might occur several times when working on a project. It might occur when dealing with co-workers, subject matter experts, graphic designers, as well as others who are part of a team working on a project.

> John, I'm concerned about the first three pages of our instructional manual. I don't feel the large type size leaves breathing space which makes it hard to find information on the page. I need your advice on what visuals we might use to make the instructions less difficult.

5. *Refer to interviewee's position* — This method might occur when the two parties disagree on how to solve a problem, so the interviewer tries to create "common ground" with the interviewee. Obviously, if you use this method you must analyze how you feel the interviewee will respond. Be tactful when using this approach.

> Leann, I understand you feel we need fewer visuals as it creates a "band-aid" approach. Would you please review with me how we might increase the readability of the first three pages by using type sizes, bullets, and dingbats?

6. *Refer to the person who sent you to the interview* — This method might be used during the various phases of developing documentation. The interviewee knows the person who recommended that the interviewer discuss something with the interviewee. The interviewer should assess the relationship between the known person and the interviewee prior to developing this opening.

> Bill suggested I check with you concerning several terms in our manual. Basically, we want to make sure we are using the terms accurately.

7. *Refer to the company, organization, or group that sent you* — This method is used for various types of interviews. Initially, we need to state our name and the company we represent. Gallup polls and sales organizations are two examples of how this opening is used. For example, here is how a sales representative introduces himself and company to the president of an insurance company.

> Mr. Smith, I'm Jerry Wright and I represent the XYZ Corporation. I'd like a few minutes of your time to discuss our new laser printers with you.

8. *Request a brief amount of time* — This method probably would be used by various individuals throughout the cycle of developing a document. In one situation a writer might be the interviewer and in another situation the writer might be the interviewee. When using this method, make sure that you request a realistic and specific period of time.

> Jan, do you have five minutes to discuss the visuals we are using on the first two pages of the employment procedure manual?

9. *Ask questions* — A common way to begin an interview is to use a question. Both open-ended and closed-ended questions might be used. An open-ended question might be used as a transition from the rapport building stage to the orientation stage.

> Open-Ended: Why have you chosen the advance organizer as a tutorial?
> Closed-Ended: Which tutorial method do you prefer?

We will discuss the use of questions later in this chapter.

The opening of the interview helps to build rapport and to orient the interviewee and should be planned in advance. Prior to developing the opening, the interviewer needs to analyze the interviewee in terms of knowledge, motives, and attitudes. The opening might be developed after the interviewer has developed the body or content elements of the interview.

BODY

Unlike a speech, the body of an interview consists mainly of asking and answering questions. Before developing questions, the interviewer should develop an interview guide. Stewart and Cash indicate that *an interview guide is an outline or lists of topics or subtopics that will be discussed during the interview* [1, p. 44]. The guide should provide the interviewer with the structure of the interview. The *interview schedule consists of the questions that are developed based on the contents of the guide* [1, p. 46]. Gordon indicates that types of schedules will determine the organization of the interview [2, p. 49].

Types of Sequences

As we indicated in Chapter 1, the directive approach is highly structured, while the nondirective method is unstructured. Interview guides can be developed around topical, time, space, cause to effect, and problem-solution sequences. Below is a brief description of each and how they might be used by technical communicators:

1. *Time sequence* — This sequence focuses on the chronological order of events. For example, an employment interviewer might use this method in discussing the employment history of an interviewee.

> **Mary,** I see that you did an internship at IBM, have worked two years at 3-M, and a year at Honeywell. I would like you to describe your specific duties at each of the corporations. First, describe your duties as an intern at IBM.

2. *Topical sequence* — This follows natural subject matter divisions and, in some cases, has become standardized over time. In the beginning phases of a

project, the lead writer might be concerned about answering questions of what, when, where, who, how, and why. Before assigning a writer to work on a project, the lead writer might interview several writers to assess their levels of competence for specific assignments. Specifically, the lead writer might ask the following questions:

> How much training have you had with this software package?
> How much reading have you done on the topic?
> Describe your experiences in working on a project of this type.

3. *Spatial sequence* — The focus in this sequence is on the physical arrangements of something. Examples might include east to west, left to right, top to bottom, etc. The spatial sequence might be used to discuss how an office is organized and reasons for the arrangement. Another example is how to arrange visuals in manuals. This sequence could be used during an information-gathering interview to discover whether the interviewee understands page design.

> Okay, we need to decide where to use the various type sizes and white space. Research indicates that more white space should be at the top of the screen than at the bottom. How do you feel about moving some of the visuals to the middle or bottom of the pages so that we have more white space at the top of the pages?

4. *Cause-to-effect sequence* — This sequence might move from an analysis of causes to consideration of future effects or from an analysis of present conditions to an analysis of specific causes. A manager of a technical publication firm might interview clients to discover why they have not renewed their subscriptions to a technical magazine. The following questions might be used:

> Why haven't you renewed your subscription?
> Are there other reasons? cost? quality of illustrations? personal problems? other?

5. *Problem-solution sequence* — Generally, the purpose is to identify the problem and generate possible solutions. More specifically, the interviewer might attempt to identify the problem, investigate the causes, specify the goals and criteria, generate possible solutions, select the best solution, implement the solution, and evaluate the results. Although this arrangement can be used in all types of interviews, it is especially appropriate for counseling, disciplinary, appraisal, and persuasive interviews. In the cause-to-effect sequence example, the manager might have discovered that the quality of the illustration and page design were primary reasons for a decrease in sales of the technical magazine. As a result the manager arranges a series of interviews with the president of the company, technical writers, and graphic designers to discuss specific problems and possible solutions. Through a series of interviews they decide on changes in page design.

Schedules

As indicated in the introduction to this section, the interview guide is an outline or blueprint of the main parts of the interview. The specificity of the interview guide is determined by the purpose and the relationship with the interviewee. For example, if you are just starting a project, your interview guide might consist only of the major topics. the interview schedule consists of questions you develop to complete the purpose of the interview. That is, after a personal assessment of your level of knowledge on the topic, you might have decided you would allow the interviewee to dominate the interview. In this case you would be using a non-scheduled interview which provides you with an opportunity to probe. The major disadvantage is that it requires a highly skilled interviewer because you will need to ask questions, listen carefully, and record information accurately.

In some interviews the interviewer can develop major questions and probing questions in advance. For example, a writer who has been working on a manual on an on-going basis with a scientist for a period of time might develop a short opening and proceed with a series of questions. The purpose of the interview would be to check on the accuracy of information, as well as to find out what information is missing. For example, the writer might ask the scientist the following questions:

How do you feel about the way I have covered this topic?
What is needed to make this area more understandable?
Is there anything that I should add here?

In contrast, if you are conducting a survey of the level of satisfaction of users, you would use a highly scheduled interview guide. Although you might ask some open-ended questions, you probably would use mostly closed-ended questions.

Is the manual easy to understand?
· Do you enjoy using the latest software?
How satisfied are you with the overall product?—1. very satisfied; 2. satisfied; 3. uncertain; 4. unsatisfied; or 5. very unsatisfied.

The major advantages of the highly scheduled interview are that it is easy to replicate and it takes less time, while the major disadvantage is that the interviewer does not have the freedom to probe. Remember that different schedules can be used for different parts of the interview. At the beginning a highly non-scheduled approach might be used, while in the middle a moderately scheduled approach, and at the end a highly scheduled approach. The type of schedule will depend upon the purpose, the interviewer's level of knowledge on the topic, the interviewee's perceived level of knowledge on the topic, as well as the relationship between two parties. The following is a sample interview guide and schedule that could be used to conduct an informational interview with a technical writer.

INTERVIEW GUIDE

I. Educational and Employment Background
   A. Technical communication program
   B. Career history
II. Current Employer
   A. Departmental Information
      1. Name
      2. Number of employees
      3. Types of documents
   B. Personal Employment Information
III. Advice for Technical Communication students

Using these topic areas the interviewer would develop the interview schedule. The schedule would consist of several questions under each topic area. For example, the interviewer might ask some of the following questions under each of the topic areas.

INTERVIEW SCHEDULE

I. Educational and Employment Background
   A. When did you graduate?
   B. What courses in your technical communication program have prepared you to be a technical writer?
   C. What specific knowledge did you bring with you to this organization?
   D. What other organizations did you work for?
II. Current Employer
   A. Departmental Information
      1. What is the name of the department in which you work?
      2. Approximately how many employees work in the organization?
      3. How many employees work in your division?
      4. What are some of the documents that you produce?
   B. Personal Employment Information
      1. What suggestions do you have to improve our present Technical Communication Program?
      2. How important are the various competency areas?

QUESTIONS

Questions are the "tools of the trade." Effective questions are clear, non-threatening, capable of being answered, relevant to the purpose, free from unintentional bias, and simple. Writing good questions takes practice. When developing the interview schedule, the interviewer should take into account the length of the question. Questions should be limited to twenty words.

The following guidelines should be used in developing questions:

1. Question clarity seems to diminish as the question grows longer.
2. Specificity refers to how well the interviewee can provide the information.
3. A question should focus on a specific dimension—*unidimensionality*. For example, how would a user respond to this question: Do the graphics and text provide a clear understanding of the process?
   The interviewee might feel that the graphics clearly explain the process, but feels that the text is somewhat confusing. The interviewer needs to develop two questions to obtain accurate responses.
4. The interviewer should word each question so that it is understood by the interviewee.
5. Each question should have a specific purpose.

Questions have three functions: *gain information, motivate the interviewee to respond,* and *reveal information about the questioner*. In this section we will discuss open-ended, closed-ended and various types of probing questions.

Open-Ended Questions

The open-ended question provides interviewers and interviewees with freedom to determine how they will respond to the question. A list of advantages and disadvantages is reported in Table 3.

Generally open-ended questions are broad and unstructured and provide the respondents with an opportunity to structure the answer the way they see fit. Although they can be used effectively throughout the interview, open-ended questions are most effective at the beginning of the interview, as they help establish rapport and can be used in all types of interviews. Obviously, they would be used in employment screening information-gathering, appraisal and exit

Table 3. Advantages and Disadvantages of Open-Ended Questions

Advantages

1. Provides the interviewee with an opportunity to have his/her say.
2. Is non-threatening to the interviewing parties.
3. Enables the interviewer to gain background information on a topic.
4. Elicits a wide variety of responses.
5. Provides background for interpreting results.

Disadvantages

1. Responses might consume a great deal of time.
2. The responses are not quantifiable.
3. Interviewer must be more skilled; otherwise, the interviewee might digress from the topic area.

interviews where the interviewer is interested in the knowledge, opinions, feelings, and suggestions of the interviewee.

Questions might vary in terms of their level of openness. Some questions are highly open such as:

Tell me about yourself.
How should graphics be used?
What are your feelings about desktop publishing?
What are your feelings about the workbook concept?

Other questions might be moderately open:

Tell me about your internship experience.
How should graphics be used on the first three pages of this manual?
What do you think of our desktop publishing capabilities?
What are your feelings about the workbook approach for this project?

Closed-Ended Questions

Closed-ended questions also may be used throughout an interview. The interviewer, for the most part, has determined in advance the range of responses to a question. Closed-ended questions are used extensively in survey and persuasive interviews. A list of advantages and disadvantages is reported in Table 4. The following forms of closed questions will be discussed: direct, classification, and two-alternative (yes/no) type.

1. *Direct questions* — These direct questions seek a specific type of information or data. For example, at the beginning of a survey interview the interviewer might request some biographical information from the interviewee. In an employment interview, the interviewer might ask the following question: What was your grade-point average? In an informational interviewer, a graphic designer might

Table 4. Advantages and Disadvantages of Closed-Ended Questions

Advantages	
1.	Are interpreted more uniformly by interviewees.
2.	Need less interviewing skill to ask closed-ended questions.
3.	Can eliminate some problems of definition and vocabulary.
4.	More questions can be asked in a shorter period of time.
5.	Are easier for most respondents to complete.
Disadvantages	
1.	Answers might be incomplete.
2.	Interviewers talk more and might bias the responses of interviewees.
3.	Questions might be biased.

ask: On what date do you need the illustration? Direct questions might be used throughout an interview. Questions should be well planned and pretested, and those that appear threatening should be avoided because they might create defensiveness between the interviewer and interviewee.

2. *Classification questions* — These questions differ from direct questions since they provide categories, and the respondent generally selects one of the response categories. Typically a 5-point interval scale from "strongly agree" to "strongly disagree" or from "very satisfied" to "very dissatisfied" is used. For example, users might be asked to indicate their level of agreement with the following statements:

The tutorial provides enough detail for me to understand how to initialize a disk.
_____ strongly agree
_____ agree
_____ uncertain
_____ disagree
_____ strongly disagree

The tutorial in the manual makes it easy to learn the various tasks.
_____ strongly agree
_____ agree
_____ uncertain
_____ disagree
_____ strongly disagree

The use of classification questions enables the interviewer to compare a large group of respondents. The interviewer needs to practice reading the questions many times. In informational interviews this type of question should be used with open-ended and other closed-ended questions so that the interviewer is certain that the interviewee has the expertise to answer the question.

3. *Two-alternative (yes/no) questions* — These questions have been labeled a dichotomous, bipolar questions and are, perhaps, the most common types of questions. The interviewee is forced to respond either "yes" or "no" and does not have an opportunity to provide other information. This type of question frequently is used to evaluate products. For example, a sales representative might ask users to answer several questions about a new software package. Here are some typical questions that might be asked:

Are the directions clearly stated?
Do the visuals support the verbal message?
Are you satisfied with quality of the software?

The yes/no question is frequently overused. The interviewer needs to decide whether the question requires a definition or an explanation rather than a simple yes or no. A manager might want to know if a desktop publishing system improves the efficiency of writers. The manager might decide to ask several writers to respond to one or both of the following questions: Has your writing improved by using the new desktop publishing system? If yes, in what way have you become more efficient by using the desktop publishing system?

The yes/no question can be used effectively with open-ended questions. Interviewers need to determine if they want the interviewee to respond either yes or no. In most informational interviews, interviewers want the interviewees to amplify on their responses. Thus, open-ended questions should be used when more information is needed. After several interviews with a SME, the interviewee might use the yes/no question to confirm the accuracy of the information. In persuasive interviews the yes/no question is used frequently to lead the interviewee to purchase a product.

Primary and Secondary Questions

1. *Primary questions* — These independent queries introduce new topics and are the core questions in an interview. After completing an interview guide the interviewer will develop an interview schedule. The schedule will include the primary questions in an interview. These questions can stand alone and make sense. The various questions listed under open-ended and closed-ended are primary questions.

2. *Secondary questions* — Additional information about a topic is revealed in secondary questions. Respondents might not answer the primary questions as thoroughly as the interviewer wants, so secondary questions would be asked to obtain the needed information. These questions are often referred to as probes. Probes can be both verbal and nonverbal. For example, if interviewees are asked to list their strengths as writers, they might be somewhat hesitant, but if the interviewer smiles and remains silent, they might respond. If the interviewers feel interviewees are not providing enough information, they might use a *nudging* probe, a question calling for additional information, such as the following: Go on; Tell me more; Really, I see; and Explain in more detail.

In contrast, the interviewee might provide detailed information, but some of the information appears to be inaccurate. For example, a graphic designer might have said the type of graphic capabilities would increase the price of the software package by $2,000.00. In this case, the interviewer might ask a *reflective* question: Do you mean $200.00 or $2,000.00?

The *mirror* or *summary* question is closely related to the *reflective* probe as the interviewee summarizes a series of answers to determine the accuracy of the previous responses to a series of questions. A technical writer might want to check on the accuracy of notes taken during the interview by summarizing them.

Okay, Bridget, you indicated that I should use a diagram to explain the subroutine, use the engineering terms, but provide definitions in a glossary, and add the additional information on page six after the second paragraph.

A *hypothetical* probe might be used. This type of probe is designed to force interviewees to respond to "what if" questions. This type of question can be used in all types of interviews and is especially effective in employment and problem-solving interviews. Here is how it might be used in an employment interview: What if you were the lead writer on the project I just described, how would you handle the graphic problems? In a problem-solving interview the interviewer might ask: What if we were to change these directions, would this lower the level of difficulty? What other problems might surface?

Reactive probes might be used to seek the interviewee's reaction to a specific statement as well as to gain insight into the interviewee's views on important issues. The interviewer might ask the following: As you know, some writers are very happy with their jobs, while others are very unhappy. What types of working conditions make you happy? What types of working conditions make you unhappy?

Finally, *clearinghouse* probes are used to determine if we have obtained all the necessary information. Unlike the *mirror/summary* probe, the *clearinghouse* probe seeks maximum self-disclosure by asking: Is there additional information that you would like to add? Have I missed anything that you can think of?

Secondary questions play a significant role in the continuity of the interview. In addition to seeking essential information, they help to make the interview more conversational. Interviewers and interviewees need to be aware of their importance in various types of interviews.

QUESTION SEQUENCES

In addition to the above types of questions, sequences of questions also might be used. That is, a series of questions are interconnected to form a sequence within a topic area or subtopic area. A series of questions helps to develop more closure on a topic area. The basic types of sequences are *funnel, inverted funnel, quintamensional,* and *tunnel sequence.*

Funnel Sequence

The funnel sequence moves from a general question to questions of greater and greater specificity. This deductive approach is used when interviewees know the topic well and feel comfortable talking. This sequence is used in various types of interviews. Technical writers might use the funnel sequence to gather information from technical experts. It can be used by employment recruiters to pursue a specific topic such as the employment history of the interviewee, and it can be used by a psychologist in a counseling interview where the interviewee wants to disclose information about himself/herself, and in a persuasive interview to lead a customer to the desired conclusion.

The funnel sequence helps the interviewer to avoid biased questions by beginning with an open-ended question which provides the interviewee with an opportunity to respond with statements of information, feelings, and attitudes about the topic. The following is a funnel sequence:

What are your reactions to the new computer software package for your writers?

How will the system enhance the writing?

How will the graphics enhance the quality of the manuals?

Which part of the software package is most important?

Do you think this is a good software package?

Inverted Funnel

Inverted funnel sequence is an inductive approach to questioning, moving from the specific to the general. The interviewer begins with a specific question or several specific questions and then uses more general questions. This type of sequence can be used in various types of interviews. For example, in a problem-solving interview the interviewer might begin by asking closed-ended questions which hopefully will motivate the interviewee to respond to open questions. An employment interviewer might feel that an interviewee needs to relax so several closed-ended questions would be asked before asking open-ended questions. Using the example above, the questions would be asked in reverse order.

Do you think this is a good software package?

Which part of the software package is most important?

How will the graphics enhance the quality of the manuals?

How will the system enhance the writing?

What are your reactions to the new computer software package for your writers?

Quintamensional Design Sequence

The quintamensional design consist of five questions that probe for the intensity of an attitude or opinion. It was first described by George Gallup in 1947, and its primary use was to determine attitudes and was used extensively in opinion research. It, however, can be adapted to any topic area. For example, the Good Writers Company might be interested in interviewing users of a new software package and use the following set of questions:

1. *Awareness.* What do you think of the new software package?
2. *Uninfluenced attitude.* What contribution has it made to your production?
3. *Specific attitude.* Do you approve of the money you spend on the program?

4. *Reason why.* Why do you feel this way?
5. *Intensity of attitude.* How strongly do you feel about this—strongly, very strongly, not something you will ever change your mind on?

Tunnel Sequence

The tunnel sequence is sometimes referred to as a "string of beads." It consists of a series of closed-ended questions which means that the interviewee must select the most appropriate responses and might consist of classification questions and two alternative questions. This sequence can be used to obtain a quick index of someone's attitude toward a topic. It is less rigorous than the quintamensional design sequence. The following is a tunnel sequence:

1. Do you approve or disapprove of the new software package for your writers?
2. Do you think the new software is more or less effective than the previous one?
3. Are you more or less satisfied with the new software?
4. Do you prefer more or fewer software options?
5. Do other writers approve or disapprove of the software?

CLOSINGS

We began this chapter by discussing various types of openings and will end by discussing types of closings. Openings provide both parties with an opportunity to create a favorable first impression, while closings enable both parties to create a favorable lasting impression. Obviously, both are very important. Below is a list of several ways to close an interview.

Type of Closings

1. *Clearinghouse question* — We have already mentioned the importance of using a clearinghouse question to gain more complete information on specific parts of the body of the interview. Likewise, a clearinghouse question might be used to show that the interview is ending. For example, in Mary's interview, the interviewer might ask:

> Is there anything that we have not discussed that you would like to bring up at this time?

Mary might ask:

> I think I understand the job description, but is there anything else I need to know about the job?

2. *Statement of completion* — The interviewer declares that the interview is complete.

> Okay, the graphics provide me with all the necessary information that I need to design the brochure.

3. *Personal inquiries* — This might be used as a way to build trust and rapport. This closing can create a favorable lasting impression. When using this closing technique, the interviewer should be sincere and relaxed.

> How is your family enjoying the lake home? How do you feel about living in the midwest?

4. *Signal that time is up* — This technique would be used in on-going informational interviews. That is, writers and engineers might participate in several interviews when working on a project and request a certain amount of time. When the time is up, the interview is over.

> Okay, we have covered all we can for today. The amount of time I requested is up.

5. *Statement of appreciation* — This type of close can be used with others or by itself. Here is how it might be used in a persuasive interview:

> Thanks for giving me the opportunity to explain the advantages of our laser printer.

6. *Plan for the next meeting* — This type of closing would be used by group leaders and interviewers for on-going projects. Future planning might include time, place, topic, content, and purpose.

> Let's schedule our next interview on next Tuesday at 11:00 a.m. in the graphic lab. At that time we will discuss the graphics we plan to use in Chapter 1.

7. *Summary* — A summary is an excellent way to close an interview. The interviewer repeats important information which might include steps or processes and areas of agreement and disagreement.

> We agree that the first three chapters need to be improved by including more visuals and decreasing the number of words in the A, B, and C sections and developing tutorials for each of the lessons. You will contact the graphic designer to help assess the ways to improve these chapters.

8. *Nonverbal cues* — Standing up, placing hands on legs, offering to shake hands, breaking eye contact, and looking at the clock are nonverbal signals that the interview is over. We need to be aware of the nonverbal cues so that the other party does not misinterpret them and assume the interview is over.

Generally, the interviewer will use a combination of the above types of closings. The type of interview, the purpose, the contents, level of communication between parties, and other timely factors will determine the types of closings that are most appropriate.

SUMMARY

In this chapter we have discussed the fundamentals of interviewing. A knowledge of the various openings and closings, question types and sequences, and structured and nonstructured interview guides should help you to participate as an interviewer and interviewee. Now, answer the questions at the end of the chapter.

EXERCISES

This chapter provides you with the key contents of interviewing. The following sets of items focus on interview openings and closings, on sequences of questions and on types of questions. Please complete each of the exercises.

Interview Openings and Closings

Please write openings and closings for the five situations stated below. Then list the types of openings and closings you used for each situation.

1. Write an opening and closing for an employment interview for a position as a technical writer.
2. Write an opening and closing for an appraisal interview in which the interviewee performed poorly.
3. Write an opening and closing in which a technical writer is interviewing a subject matter expert for the first time.
4. Write an opening and closing to persuade your superior that you should purchase new word processors.
5. Write an opening and closing for an exit interview.

Question Sequences

Please identify the question sequence you would employ for each of the situations described below.

1. You are interviewing applicants for positions in writing and editing.
2. You are conducting a survey to determine users' options on the XYZ desktop publishing system.
3. You are conducting an exit interview with a writer who has decided to leave your company.
4. You are trying to obtain information on the lead writing for a project.
5. You are conducting a counseling interview; and the interviewee enjoys talking about his/her accomplishments.

Identifying Question Types

Please identify each of the following questions. Place a letter in the space to the left of the item indicating what type of question it is. Use the following abbreviations:

O—Open   HP—Hypothetical Probe
CC—Closed Classification   RP—Reactive Probe
CYN—Closed Yes-No   NP—Nudging Probe
REP—Reflective Probe   CP—Clearinghouse Probe
C—Closed-Ended   MP—Mirror Probe

1. _____ How do you feel about the new requirement in the technical communication program?
2. _____ Do you mean professional or technical writing?
3. _____ What if you had to work with technical people?
4. _____ Go on.
5. _____ Are you willing to work late to complete projects?
6. _____ As I understand it we need to complete these seven tasks . . . Is this correct?
7. _____ Are you satisfied or dissatisfied with your advisor?
8. _____ Have I missed anything?
9. _____ When is your favorite time to write?
10. _____ Some writers enjoy working with others, while other writers do not enjoy working with others. Which do you prefer?

REFERENCES

1. C. Stewart and W. Cash, *Interviewing: Principles and Practices*, Wm. C. Brown Publishers, Dubuque, Iowa, 1988.
2. R. Gordon, *Interviewing: Strategy, Techniques and Tactics*, Dorsey Press, Homewood, Illinois, 1975.

Part 2
INFORMATIONAL INTERVIEWS

CHAPTER 3

Information-Gathering Interviews

OBJECTIVES

On completion of this chapter you should be able to:
Understand types of informational interviews
Develop types of probing questions
Develop types of survey questions
Develop interview guides for probing interviews
Develop interview guides for survey interviews
Analyze specific interviewing situations

Information-gathering interviews are conducted by technical writers to obtain information from subject matter experts, other technical writers, graphics designers, as well as other team members to help complete a writing or research project. In this chapter we will discuss types of informational interviews, preparing for informational interviews, structuring the informational interviews, conducting the informational interviews, and recording information during the interviews.

As we begin this chapter think about your recent informational interviews as an interviewer and interviewee and think about these questions:

When interviewing a subject matter expert about an involved technical project, how do you lead the person to give you first a general overview and then specifics at a level you can understand?

How do you keep the subject matter expert from getting so deep into technical descriptions that the content is over your head?

How do you avoid having the interviewee lead you up to a highly technical area that you have no background in and then give you two specialized texts that supposedly will provide you with all the background information that you need to accurately process the information?

RESEARCH ON INFORMATIONAL INTERVIEWS

Limited research has been completed on the role of informational interviewing in the technical writer's "world of work." Leslie Levine reported in "Interviewing for Information" in the *Journal of Technical Writing and Communication* that interviewing often plays a larger role in documentation processing than does the writing and the editing, that some writers spend approximately 75 percent of their time gathering information, and that a significant amount of this time is spent interviewing [1, pp. 55-56]. After reading this statement, as well as the article, you should be aware of the importance of information-gathering interviews. In addition, an informational interviewing study by McDowell, Mrozla, and Reppe reports the results of a comprehensive survey interview study in which 176 writers responded to questions on demographics, involvement with information gathering interviewing, methods of preparing for and structuring interviews, and the dynamics of the interviewing process [2]. After reading this chapter go to Part 5 and read the article, "An Investigation of the Interviewing Practices of Technical Writers in Their World of Work."

Overall, the results of the study indicate that interviewing is an essential part of the technical writer's "world of work" and that the technical writer needs to develop effective interviewing skills to perform job tasks.

TYPES OF INFORMATIONAL INTERVIEWS

Informational interviews can be classified into two basic types: *probing and survey interviews*. Both types of information-gathering interviews are used frequently in the technical writer's "world of work." *Probing interviews* are conducted by journalists, lawyers, health care professionals, technical writers, teachers, graphics experts, scientists, engineers, parents, as well as anyone seeking information. Probing interviews are generally conducted face-to-face, but telephone and questionnaire methods are sometimes used to conduct the probing interview. *Survey interviews* also are completed by members of these professions but have a different purpose. In contrast, surveys are conducted by telephone or through the questionnaire method. However, greater differences exist between the two types of interviews.

Probing Interviews

The primary purpose of the probing interview is to gather as much information from the other party as possible. The research findings indicate that technical writers use this type of interview for almost all of their interviews.

Preparing for the interview — Interviewers must adapt to interviewees. For example, a technical writer who is interviewing a subject matter expert for the first time will complete research to gain background information on the interviewee. During this process the interviewer will try to answer the following questions:

1. Does the interviewee have the information that I need?
2. Is the interviewee available?
3. Is the interviewee willing to provide the needed information?
4. What are the personality characteristics of the interviewee?
5. How does the interviewee feel about the technical writer?

Structuring the informational interview — The structure of the interview will depend on your level of knowledge on the topic, your assessment of the interviewee's level of knowledge, and personality variables of the interviewee and yourself. Now let's assume you are meeting with a subject matter expert for the first time. You probably will use a nonscheduled or moderately scheduled interview guide because your primary purpose is to learn as much as possible about the subject area and the interviewee. In other words, you will adapt to the interviewee. Although you might use a variety of openings, a combination of requesting advice or assistance, asking questions, and an informal greeting might get you off to a good start.

The interview guide probably will use various types of order. Topical order might be used in the initial interview so that the interviewer gains knowledge of the subject area. The interviewer undoubtedly will use an unstructured approach which will allow for greater freedom to probe and explore the responses of the interviewee. The success of this method is contingent upon the skill and sensitivity of the interviewer who must be able to ask the right question at the right time. According to Schwartz and Jacobs, the unstructured interview [3, p. 137]:

> . . . assumed that the interviewer does not know in advance what questions are appropriate to ask, how they should be worded so as to be non-threatening or unambiguous, which questions to include or exclude to best learn about the topic under study or what constitutes an answer. The answers to these questions are seen to emerge from the interviews themselves, the social context in which they occurred, and the degree of rapport the interviewer was able to establish during the interview. In short, appropriate questions are seen to emerge from the process of interaction that occurs between the interviewer and interviewee.

An unstructured interview can be a conversational interview. During normal conversation, information is gathered from the interviewee. In addition, an unstructured interview can be nondirective in that the types of questions and topics for discussion are largely governed by the respondent. The interviewer encourages the interviewee to express true feelings and issues about a project.

In contrast, the focused interview is a type of structured interview. It is concerned with a specific situation and focuses on topics that have been predetermined. This type of interview will occur when both parties have had a common experience. For example, after several writers and graphic designers have met with the subject matter expert, they schedule a meeting to determine the writing and graphic changes. The lead writer prepares a brief interview guide and schedule to help focus the discussion and to add coherence to the session between the writers and graphic designers.

The interviewer will attempt to create a favorable first impression. Remember that expressions of interest and concern help to build trust. Excellent nonverbal communication and attentiveness are essential in the opening phases of the interview. Open-ended questions will be used by the interviewer to gain knowledge of the subject as a broad spectrum of responses is wanted. The interviewer will use informational probes, nudging probes, clearinghouse probes and reflective probes to increase understanding of the material.

Below is an example of each of these types of probes:

Open: What do you know about this project?

Closed: Must this step always be first?

Primary: How does this part of the program work?

Informational probe: Tell me more about desktop publishing.

Nudging probe: Go on.

Clearinghouse probe: Is there anything else I should know about the DTP system?

Reflective probe: Okay. The primary advantages of this laser printer are the clarity of the visuals and various print designs.

Mirror: So you're saying that all of this section of the program is just a contingency loop. Is that right?

The interviewer needs to avoid bipolar traps such as "Do you know what happened next?" Instead the interviewer should ask an open-ended question such as "What do you need to do to prepare the printer for output?" The interviewer also should avoid using double-barrelled questions such as "Tell me about A and B." All questions should be unidimensional.

The first interview with a subject matter expert might be concluded in several ways. The clearinghouse probe, declaring the completion of purpose or task, expressing appreciation or satisfaction, planning for the next meeting, and summarizing the interview are all appropriate ways to conclude the initial interview.

Probing interviews will continue to be conducted with a subject matter expert until the completion of a project. The interviews, however, will vary in time and degree of openness. As time passes, less time will be spent on the openings and closings, interviews will be more structured, and more closed-ended questions will be developed.

Conducting the probing interview — During the opening the interviewer will attempt to create an atmosphere of mutual trust. If it is a first meeting between two parties, the interviewer will spend more time on small talk and rapport building. Obviously, the interviewer will need to assess the relationship variables—

inclusion, control, and affection—before developing the interview guide. The relationship between the interviewer and interviewee is affected by the status of the interviewer and interviewee. That is, the interviewer (R) is superior to the interviewee (E), the interviewer is equal to the interviewee, or the interviewer is subordinate to the interviewee.

Stewart and Cash develop a list of advantages and disadvantages of the status relationships [4, pp. 84-85]:

(R) Superior to (E)

1. (R) can easily control the interview.
2. (E) may feel motivated to please (R).
3. (R) can observe (E) under pressure.
4. (R) can arrange the interview easily.
5. (E) might feel honored.
6. (R) can reward (E).

(R) Equal to (E)

1. Rapport is easily established.
2. Fewer communication barriers.
3. Fewer social pressures.
4. High degree of empathy possible.
5. (R) and (E) are at ease.

(R) Subordinate to (E)

1. (E) will not feel threatened.
2. (E) may feel freer to speak.
3. (R) does not have to be an expert on the subject.
4. (E) might feel sorry for (R) and want to help.

Obviously these three types of relationships might exist in the technical writer's "world of work." Conflicts can occur between a writer and subject matter expert concerning how content should be stated or how visuals should be used to reinforce verbal messages. How the interviewer will handle the situation will depend on perceptions of the relationship variables, as well as the perceived status between the two parties, and personality variables of the two parties. At the end of this chapter is an exercise where you can decide the status between the two parties.

Note taking and tape recording — The primary responsibility of the interviewer is to gather information. The two primary ways to record the information are by note taking and by tape recording the information. Obviously, a technical writer will need to record much information on technical subjects during the initial interviews. The writer can reduce interviewee curiosity or concern by asking permission to take notes, to maintain eye contact while taking notes, and to write down only important information. Interviewers generally take some notes throughout the interview rather than waiting until the end of topic areas and then writing down the main ideas. By writing down information throughout the interview, the interviewer is able to determine the accuracy of information by using clearinghouse and reflective probing questions.

Tape-recording information given by the interviewee enables the interviewer to relax more and concentrate on answers and develop follow-up questions. The interviewer needs to test the recorder in advance of the interview session to make sure it functions properly. For example, a graduate student recently interviewed me on the purpose and scope of my information-gathering interviewing study with technical writers. The student developed an interview guide and schedule. Here are some of the questions she asked me:

1. Why was the study done?
2. Who was involved in this study?
3. How was the questionnaire developed?
4. What were the results of this survey?
5. How do technical writers prepare for information-gathering interviews?
6. For what audience are these people writing?
7. How do these technical writers structure their technical writing?
8. How are information-gathering interviews conducted?
9. How do technical writers feel about the people they are interviewing?
10. What factors can have an effect on the interview?
11. How do technical writers feel about their own interpersonal skills?
12. Overall, what can you conclude from the study?

These open-ended questions provided the interviewee with the freedom to respond with a short or long response to the question. The interviewer used a tape recorder so that she could focus on the interviewee's responses and ask probing questions.

Survey Interview

Unlike the probing interview, survey research might ask respondents to complete a questionnaire, be a telephone interview, or a face-to-face interview. Cochrane and Barasch claim that each method has certain advantages and disadvantages [5, pp. 16-17]. The survey is meticulously planned and executed (see Figure 4).

Preparing for the survey interview — The purpose of the survey is to gather a wide range of quantifiable information from specific target groups. For example, if Apple Computer Company wanted to find out how users of Macintosh feel about its DTP capabilities as well as a variety of other factors, a research team might plan a comprehensive study. The researcher might begin by developing a few open-ended questions and ask a small sample of Macintosh users how they feel about the mouse, MacWrite, MacPaint, MacDraw, Hypercard, ImageWriter, and numerous other aspects. Likewise, in the study we discussed earlier on the interviewing practices of technical writers, we wanted to record background information, to determine how writers prepare for work, structure and conduct interviews, and to determine the interviewing dynamics of the interviewer.

During the planning phase the research project team will need to define the population and sample. For example, in the study on the information interviewing practices of technical writers, we used the list of members of the local chapter of the Society for Technical Communication and an alumni list of our graduates. Since we knew we wanted to complete a telephone survey, we limited our sample to the Minneapolis/St. Paul area. Many types of sampling techniques are available and used, but the three most common are *random, stratified,* and *systematic.*

Sampling Techniques

Random sample — In a *random sample* each person or sampling unit has an equal opportunity to be selected. A table of random numbers might be used to select a random sample. For example, let us assume that the local chapter of the Society for Technical Communication has 1000 members and the goal is to interview 100 members. To begin, we would number the members from 1 to 1000. Next, we need to determine the number of digits in a random number. Thus, we need to randomly select 100 numbers between 0001 and 1000. Randomization assures that all members will have an equal opportunity to be selected to participate in the survey interview.

Stratified sample — If we want to find out if differences exist between biological sex groups in their perceptions of interviewing, *stratification* might be used as a sampling method. That is, we would select the same percentage of male and female writers and interview each person who was selected. The *stratified sample* is a way to obtain a greater degree of representation of the target populations by organizing the population into homogeneous subsets and then selecting appropriate numbers of each subset. For example, if there are 500 male and 500 female technical writers, and we want to interview 50 from each group, we would use the same procedures for both the male and female writer groups as we did for the *simple random sample*. Thus, we would select fifty random numbers in a range from 001 to 500 for each group.

Systematic sample — In a *systematic sample* initially each person has an equal opportunity to be selected. For example, if we know that 150 are in the population and we are going to sample 50, we would randomly select a number between 1 and 3 and then select every third person to obtain the composite sample for our study.

$$\text{Sampling Interval} = \frac{\text{Population Size}}{\text{Sample Size}}$$

Type	Description	Advantages	Disadvantages
Personal Interviews	Personal interviews are well-suited for complex concepts requiring excessive explanations Information is sought in face-to-face sessions. The interviewer usually has a questionnaire to guide him, although this form is not necessarily shown to the respondent. The interviewer can use a formal questionnaire with a pre-arranged ordering, or have a list of general discussion subjects and make up questions as the interview progresses.	1. Allows more detailed information to be gathered. 2. Usually gets a higher percentage of completed answers, since interviewer is there to explain exactly what is wanted. 3. Can use visual aids (e.g., tables, schematics, samples, prototypes) to demonstrate concepts. 4. Is flexible to allow interviewer to adjust questions to respondent's greatest interests.	1. Can be costly when compared to other methods, especially when wide geographic areas must be covered. 2. Interviewer bias can seriously cause misleading responses and misrecording of answers. 3. Requires detailed supervision of data-collection process. 4. Time-consuming to train interviewers and to obtain data. 5. Different approaches by different interviewers made it difficult to standardize surveys.
Telephone Survey	Telephone interviews are best suited for well-defined concepts. Information sought is usually well-defined, nonconfidential in nature, and limited in amount. Telephone surveys should be used to supplement other research techniques. It is often best to employ a professional telephone interview service, rather than attempt the interviewing yourself.	1. Fast (e.g., quicker than personal interview or mail). 2. Inexpensive (e.g., cost of an equal number of personal interviews would be substantially greater). 3. Easier to call back again if respondent is busy at the time (personal is more difficult). 4. Usually has only a small response bias because of closed-end questions. 5. Has wide geographical reach.	1. Limited to telephone subscriber locations (e.g., cannot interview a man in the field; and many businessmen are out of the office most of the day). 2. Can usually obtain only a relatively small amount of information. 3. Difficult for highly technical issues. 4. Can become expensive if long distance calls are involved, unless Wide Area Telephone Service (WATS) is available.

| Mail Survey | They are most effective when well-defined concepts are involved and specific limited answers are called for.

The questionnaire is usually accompanied by a letter explaining the survey's purpose and requesting the respondent answer and return the questionnaire in an enclosed postage-paid envelope. Sometimes the questionnaire can be printed on the back of a post card to avoid the cost of envelopes and the chance of respondents misplacing envelopes and not being able to mail the completed questionnaire back. | 1. Can get wide distribution at relatively low cost per completed interview.
2. Helps avoid possible interviewer bias, absence of interviewer may lead to a more candid reply.
3. Can reach remote places (e.g., drilling engineer on site in Saudi Arabia).
4. Unless his name is requested, the respondent remains anonymous and, therefore, may give confidential information that otherwise would be withheld.
5. Respondent may be more inclined to answer since he can do so at his leisure. | 1. Accurate, up-to-date mailing lists are not always available to ensure successful distribution.
2. Returns may not be representative, since respondents may differ from those not replying. As many as 80-90% may not return questionnaires. Respondents generally have stronger feelings about the subject than nonrespondents.
3. Questionnaire length is limited.
4. Inability to ensure that questions are understood fully and answers are properly recorded.
5. Time consuming.
6. Troublesome with certain highly technical products. |

Chase Couchrane and Kenneth Barach, *Marketing Problem-Solver*, Chilton Book Co., Radner, Pennsylvania, 1977. Reprint by permission of Chilton Book Company.

Figure 4. Types of Survey Methods.

Each of the sampling methods can be used in informational interviewing studies. We would determine the sampling technique we will use early in the development of a survey.

Prior to developing the structure for the interview, a research team should create a flow plan and appropriate strategies for completing the research project. The interviewer or research team should answer the following questions:

1. Is my purpose clearly stated?
2. Is my sampling plan reliable?
3. Is my sampling plan valid?
4. Is the interview guide appropriately arranged?
5. Are the interviewers adequately trained?
6. Can the data be easily coded?
7. Can the data be easily tabulated?
8. Will the results of the analysis be understandable?

Structuring the Survey Interview

After appropriate pilot testing in which several probing interviews using non-scheduled and moderately scheduled interview guides have been completed with members of the target population, a highly standardized scheduled interview guide will be developed for a survey interview. Structured interviews follow a predetermined schedule of questions that seek to delve into the interviewee's attitudes and beliefs. The interview can supply details about the past and present that no other method can collect. In short, all interviewees will hear the same opening and closing and answer the same questions. For example, in the information-gathering interview study we discussed earlier in the chapter, we began with the following introduction:

Hello Mr./Mrs. _____. My name is _____. I am a research assistant in the Laboratory for Research in Scientific Communication at the University of _____. We are conducting a telephone survey of technical writers on information-gathering interviews and, since I understand you are technical writer, I would like to interview you. The interview should take about thirty minutes to complete, and I am willing to schedule it at a time convenient for you. Your responses will be treated confidentially. The information will be used to revise the content of the interviewing course in the Technical Communication program. Initially, I have three questions for you.

1. Do you conduct information-gathering interviews in your work?
   _____ Yes _____ No (terminate interview)

2. Would you be willing to participate in this survey?
   _____ Yes _____ No (terminate interview)

3. When would be a convenient time to call you for the survey? _____
   Phone Number _____.

In addition to the types of questions listed and discussed in Chapter 2, other types of closed-ended questions are important in the survey interview. For example, the first two questions in the above introduction would be classified as contingency questions. That is, if a respondent indicated that he/she did not conduct information-gathering interviews, the interview would be terminated at that point. If the respondent indicated that he/she did conduct interviews, the second question would be asked.

A *leaning* question strategy might be used to reduce the number of undecided respondents. In comparing different types of word processing equipment, the researcher might ask respondents:

1. If you had your choice, would you use word processing program A or B? (if undecided ask question 2)
   A _____
   B _____
   Undecided _____
2. Well do you lean more toward A or B?
   A _____
   B _____

The interviewer also might be interested in the level of knowledge of the interviewee. To determine the level of knowledge, the interviewer might use the *filter approach*. For example, the lead writer might ask the following questions:

Interviewer: Are you familiar with the extra software of the MacX?
Interviewee: Yes, I am.
Interviewer: What is the MacX?

A *shuffle strategy which varies the order of questions or answer options within questions* from one interview to the next is done to eliminate ordering effects as a confounding variable. That is, the same number of participants responded to items in different order. For example, if we had a list of three items, we would divide the composite group into three small groups so members of Group 1 would respond to the items in A, B, C order; members of Group 2 would respond to items in B, C, A order, and members of Group 3 would respond to items in C, A, B, order. Table 5 shows how this technique might be used to assess how respondents feel about graphic possibilities with Macintosh.

Two types of interval scales might be used to assess software. *Likert scales are used to rate the level of agreement (strongly agree, agree, undecided, disagree, and strongly disagree) such as the following example*:

MacDraw is easy for me to use.
MacPaint is difficult for me to use.

Table 5. Rating Graphic Software Packages

	Software Types		
Groups	Time 1	Time 2	Time 3
G1	MacPaint	MacDraw	Hypercard
G2	MacDraw	Hypercard	MacPaint
G3	Hypercard	MacPaint	MacDraw

Another example might deal with *the level of frequency (very frequently, frequently, uncertain, infrequently, very infrequently).*

How frequently do you use MacDraw?
How frequently do you use Hypercard?

Nominal scales which provide mutually exclusive variables and ask the respondent to pick the most relevant category are used frequently in interviewing.

Are you a freelance, contracted or employed writer?
_____ Freelance
_____ Contracted
_____ Employed

Ordinal scales also are used by interviewers to rank various types of information. Below is a list of ways to obtain training in interviewing techniques and an example of how ranking was used to determine technical writers' perceptions of training in interviewing techniques. Participants were asked to rank order the ways to obtain training from 1 to 7 with 1 being most important.

_____ academic coursework
_____ in-house staff development
_____ seminars
_____ workshops
_____ reading interviewing books
_____ talking with interviewers
_____ observing interviews

THE INTERVIEWER IN INFORMATIONAL INTERVIEWS

We have already discussed how to prepare, how to structure, and how to conduct the probing and survey interviews. Now let's discuss the role of the interviewer in each of these interviews.

In the probing interview, the interviewer will review related literature, talk with other writers, talk with technical experts, and complete an overall assessment of the objectives of the project. The interviewer needs to prepare as much as possible by developing open-ended questions. During the interview, the interviewer will use various types of probes to obtain the desired information. Critical listening skills are essential to obtain accurate information.

A technical writer generally uses probing interviews to discover the information needed to complete a project, write the project, and revise the project. In the final stages the interviewer might use a variety of different types of closed-ended questions to determine the accuracy of information. Sometimes a writing organization might want to test users on various aspects of a document. In this case the project director might need to train interviewers to conduct face-to-face or telephone interviews. For example, companies that develop software documentation will complete survey research to discover the program's strengths and weaknesses.

Training Interviews

Let's assume that the project director's responsibility is to train individuals to conduct interviews. Stewart and Cash suggest that interviewers do the following [3, p. 117]:

1. Study the question schedule and "ask" rather than "read" questions.
2. Dress appropriately.
3. Be on time for all appointments.
4. Be friendly, businesslike, and sincere.
5. Speak clearly and loudly enough to be heard easily, maintain good eye contact, and do not rush through the interview.
6. If the respondent does not answer the question as asked, repeat the question but do not rephrase it.
7. Record answers as prescribed on a schedule.
8. Ask every question on the interview guide, in the order that each appears.
9. Interview respondents in a private place.
10. Always conclude the interview in a positive fashion so that interviewees will think well of you, your organization, and the entire experience.

In addition, the interviewer needs to use the same vocal inflection and pronunciation so that voice is not a confounding factor in how the interviewee responds to questions. Overall, interviewers need to be carefully trained to be familiar with the interview schedule, to follow the question wording and question ordering exactly, and record the information exactly. Ideally, members of the interview team will practice with each other so that the interviewer is not a factor in how participants respond to items on the questionnaire.

Question Sequences in Informational Interviews

Various types of question sequences might be used in informational interviews. For example, in a probing interview the *funnel sequence* would be used to obtain as much information as possible. If the interviewer is somewhat introverted, the *inverted funnel* might be used to obtain information. In a survey research such as assessing current software, tutorials, visuals, as well as the quality of manuals, the *quintamensional design sequence* might be used. Here is an example:

Awareness: Tell me what you know about Hypercard.
Uninfluenced attitudes: How, if at all, would this software help desktop publishing?
Specific attitude: Do you approve or disapprove of it to replace XYZ?
Reason why: Why do you feel this way?
Intensity of attitude: How strongly do you feel about this—strongly, very strongly, not something you will ever change your mind on?

The *tunnel sequence* also might be used to gather information on the attitudes an audience has about a specific topic. Hypercard, for example, has been used to develop software for a variety of educational programs. Here is an example of how the tunnel sequence can be used to determine the reaction and attitudes of users about Hypercard:

Do you approve or disapprove of Hypercard?
Do you think it will facilitate desktop publishing?
Are you personally involved with the decision-making aspects of the software?
Do you prefer something else?
Do most of the writers in your group approve or disapprove of the software?

The closing is generally very brief in a survey. For example, in the survey on the informational interviewing practices of technical writers, we concluded with the following:

> Thank you. That completes our survey. Once again I'd like to express our appreciation for your cooperation and insights. If you would like a copy of the survey results we'd be glad to send them to you. Thank you.

SUMMARY

This chapter has focused on two types of informational interviews: probing and survey. In a probing interview the interviewer uses a nonscheduled or moderately scheduled interview guide, open-ended questions, and can use a variety of openings and closings. The interviewer needs to be highly skilled to conduct probing interviews. The interviewer's primary responsibility is to record a large amount of information.

In contrast, in a survey interview, the interviewer uses a highly standardized schedule, closed-ended questions, and a standard opening and closing. Interviewers need to have excellent communication skills, but do not need to have knowledge on the topic. The interviewer's basic responsibility is to record information that is quantifiable.

AN INTERVIEW FOR REVIEW AND ANALYSIS

Now let's suppose that you are a student in an interviewing class and you want to interview a technical writer to discover information about the writer so you decide to conduct an information-gathering interview. Below is a dialogue that occurred between a technical communication student and a professional technical writer. Please assess the opening, closing, types of questions, and structure. How effectively does the interviewer use probing questions? Write an introduction and conclusion to the interview. Identify where you would use probing questions. What types of nonverbal cues would be most appropriate? Add the nonverbal cues where necessary.

Q. How long have you worked at Medtronic?
A. Two years.

Q. How long have you been a technical writer?
A. Three years. I started at Honeywell writing technical reports.

Q. Why did you come to work for Medtronic?
A. I came as a part-time temporary technical writer. I was a contractor at Honeywell, which means that they could hire me out to other companies.

Q. Do you mean that Medtronic didn't have a technical writer before you came?
A. In the Neuro division, a secretary was doing all the writing. Within six months I had been hired as a technical writer, given a considerable raise and quite a lot of responsibility.

Q. What are your duties at Medtronic?
A. I write patient and clinician manuals. Occasionally, I need to write manuals for hospital staff members to help them interface with the patient and clinician.

Q. What types of devices do you write manuals for?
A. I write about implantation devices for the spinal cord and the brain.

Q. What do you tell the patients and clinicians in the manuals?
A. I tell the patient what to expect from the device and give the clinician information to get the patient to use the device, to help keep them calm, and to help them learn how to use the device.

Q. Is there a great deal of research involved before you begin writing?
A. I do very little research. I learn how the device works by picking it up at the prototype stage. I don't very often meet the other people—clinicians, patients, or hospital staff. I have seen a couple of implants.

Q. Does it make it easier to write about a device by observing it being implanted?

A. It was an experience for me, going to the OR. It made me more sensitive to the patient.

Q. How do you convey in your manuals or instructions that the device will cause pain without being emotional or uncaring?

A. I have tried the muscle stimulation devices. I tell the truth when I write. I say that the stimulation may be uncomfortable at first, but you can get used to it, and that is the key.

Q. What do you mean?

A. Most of the patients are highly motivated when it comes to our devices. It is usually their last chance to receive some relief from their pain. Just making the patient aware of what to expect is usually all I have to do.

Q. Are you in on your projects from their conception?

A. Yes, because I am the only technical writer in Neuro.

Q. What is the first thing you do when you get assigned to a project?

A. I usually attend a team meeting. They tell you what the product is going to be and what they hope it is going to have, so you can get an idea of what to expect. I usually take notes on things I may want to question later. I will ask if it's like another device, so that I can go back to the manual to get help in starting the new one.

Q. What procedure do you use if it is a new device?

A. If it is a brand new product and we have never done anything like it before, then it is a chore to get the information from the engineers. It becomes a question of my stopping their work to interview them to find out what the product will do and how it works. They usually don't know how to tell me and don't want to take the time. They don't understand that what I do is just as important as the rest of the project.

Q. What type of time frame do you work under when on a project?

A. Time frames are a big problem. I've got a deadline that I must work within. They want to get the product out of the door and my manuals get packaged with the product, so it has to be ready. There have been times when someone doesn't review my work on time, and I have to assume that it is right and get it printed—and take my chances. In Neuro our devices have between a four to six month turnaround time.

Q. What do you mean?

A. From the conception to the time the company wants the device ready to sell. That's very quick when you are working on five or six manuals at a time.

Q. How do you determine how much information is needed for the patient to understand the device?

A. In some cases I have to determine how much technical information is too much for the patient to understand. Sometimes all the patient needs to know is that if the magnet is placed over the implantation device it will turn on, and touch it again and it will turn off. I try to give them enough information so that they will feel comfortable with the device.

Q. Is this decision yours to make?

A. No, I get help.

Q. Whom do you get help from?

A. I go to marketing because they have studied what the market is like. Sometimes I go to other device manufacturers, who have similar types of systems, to see what they have done.

Q. Do you ever get any feedback from the patient?

A. Yes, to one system we added a question and answer survey.

Q. Besides marketing, what other departments do you work with?

A. I interface with marketing, engineers, and the product planning department.

Q. What is the product planning department?

A. Product planning tells the company what kind of devices they could be getting into, what device will help us, and where the money is.

Q. Do you have any difficulty if you want to include or omit certain material from the manuals?

A. Sometimes it is very hard to get the engineers to understand the patient's viewpoint. I have experienced conflict with them on occasion. I have to tell them that an instruction cannot be written a certain way because the patient either is not going to understand it, or it is really going to upset them to read that kind of information.

Q. What changes will they allow you to make?

A. Usually they will accept my changing the language. But they will insist on the instruction remaining in the manual.

Q. Is this job a very stressful one?

A. For some it could be, but I love it.

Q. Does your tight time frame interfere with the quality of the manuals?

A. No, certainly not.

Q. What do your co-workers think of your work?

A. The engineers here have been very respectful of me. Most of them feel that if I think something should be written a certain way, that's the right way to do it, and it is OK with them.

Q. Who has final approval over your work?
A. Outside of my boss, everything I write has to be approved by the FDA. A lot of what I write is controlled by them also. When I make up my schedule I always include time for my work to be approved by them and to get back to me in time for packaging with the product.

Q. I guess my last job related question is what is the most innovating project you have ever worked on?
A. All of them are great.

Q. Doesn't one stand out over the others?
A. I have to think about what is confidential and what is not. There are several things going on now, but I don't feel comfortable discussing them. The products are not at the stage where we are ready to release information.

Q. OK, what about something you have finished?
A. One that we have just completed is a totally implantable system. There were eight manuals for that product. That was a job just to decide what information had to go into which manual to be packaged with what device. The device was used for several different applications.

Q. What makes you good at your job?
A. I try to be serious about what I write. I know that it is a major step for the patient to receive one of our devices. They have to be comfortable with it and hopefully by the time they have the device implanted they will have read my manual and know what to expect.

Q. You mentioned in a previous conversation that you are getting your masters at the university. Are you satisfied with the program?
A. It was a real disappointment to me, as a graduate student, to find out that I could not get a degree in technical communication. I will get a Masters of Agriculture degree.

Q. Does that matter much?
A. Yes. I will go through the rest of my life justifying why I have a Masters of Agriculture and explaining what that degree has to do with technical writing.

Q. How long have you been in the program?
A. Four years.

Q. When will you finish?
A. Hopefully in the fall.

Q. What are you writing your thesis on?
A. Audience analysis; it's a boring topic, and one I didn't choose.

Q. With all your work here and working on your thesis, I know that you must be pretty busy. I want to thank you for taking the time to answer my questions. You've been very helpful. Are there any questions that you would like to ask me?

A. Yes, when do you expect to graduate?

QUESTIONS

Below is an interviewing situation which you might encounter as a technical writer. How would you prepare for this situation? Please read the case and answer the questions.

Now let's assume you are the product manager. You are responsible for testing the software. One of your subordinates developed a short questionnaire which trained interviewers will use to ask users about the latest software. Because you are familiar with questionnaire development, you are responsible for correcting any pitfalls in the questionnaire. Please list any problems that you find with the questionnaire.

Hello Mr./Mrs. _____. My name is _____. I am an interviewer for the Good Writers Company. We are calling to ask you some questions on the software package, *Better Letter Writing*, designed to help to organize various letter types. Would you be willing to answer a few questions? It only will take about 5 minutes. Do you have the time right now? If yes, begin the questions. If no, set up a time.

Please answer the following question with a "yes" or "no" or "it depends." (If the interviewee says "no" or "it depends," ask why). Yes=1; No=2; Depends=3.

_____ The tutorials are easy to follow.
_____ The directions are clear.
_____ I have learned to write more interesting and clearer appreciation letters as a result of reading the examples in the tutorial.
_____ I would buy this software again.
_____ The tutorials are difficult to follow.
_____ I would recommend to a friend to purchase the product.

Please identify the status relationship between the following interviewers (R) and interviewees (E): (R) equal to (E), R superior to E, and R subordinate to E.

1. A technical writer consults with a subject matter expert on content to appear in the opening of a computer manual.

2. A technical writer consults with an expert on how to arrange verbal and visual content in a computer manual.

3. A technical specialist consults with an instructional designer to determine how to develop a tutorial.
4. A technical communication specialist wants to know how users feel about new desktop publishing equipment.
5. A project manager for the Cutting Edge Writing Company wants to interview each of the writers working on the latest project.

Evaluate each of the following situations.

1. A technical writer is working on a manual for a complex piece of equipment and finds that he must consult with one of the engineers who designed it. The writer has heard from others that although the engineer is a technical wizard, he is very apprehensive about speaking to other people—he avoids eye contact, stares into the video display terminal, and says very little.
   How would you prepare to interview this technical expert?
   What type of opening would you use?
   What types of questions would you develop prior to the interview?
   How would you close the interview?
   Would you approach the interview differently if the engineer were extroverted and used excellent nonverbal communication? If yes, explain how you would approach the interview.
2. A recently hired technical writer needs to interview an older computer scientist who is known for having a low regard for technical writers in general and has a reputation for being very argumentative.
   How would you prepare to interview this technical expert?
   What type of opening would you use?
   What types of questions would you develop prior to the interview?
   How would you close the interview?
   Would you approach the interview differently if the subject matter expert had a high regard for technical writers? If yes, explain how you would approach the interview.
3. Create your own scenario for your discipline and technical elective. Next answer the five questions listed in the examples above.
4. How would you approach a hostile interviewee? (for a probing and a survey interview)
5. How would you approach an emotional interviewee? (for a probing and a survey interview)

REFERENCES

1. L. Levine, Interviewing for Information, *Journal of Technical Writing and Communication*, 14, pp. 55-56, 1984.

2. E. McDowell, B. Mrolza, and E. Reppe, An Investigation of the Interviewing Practices of Technical Writers in Their World of Work, *Technical Writers' Institute*, R.P.I., pp. 1-18, 1987.
3. H. Schwartz and J. Jacobs, *Qualitative Sociology: A Method to the Madness*, Free Press, New York, 1979.
4. C. Stewart and W. Cash, *Interviewing: Principles and Practices*, Wm. C. Brown Publishers, Dubuque, Iowa, 1988.
5. C. Cochrane and K. Barasch, *Marketing Problem Solver*, Clinton Book Company, Radnor, Pennsylvania, 1977.

CHAPTER 4

Information-Giving
Interviews

OBJECTIVES

On completion of this chapter you should be able to:

Understand the importance of information-giving interviews

Understand the roles of the interviewer in information-giving interviews

Understand the roles of the interviewee in information-giving interviews

List guidelines for conducting the information-giving interview

Discuss positive and negative factors of the information-giving interview

Describe how you would handle different types of information-giving
interviews

In Chapter 3 we focused on the information-gathering interview. In this chapter we will focus on the information-giving interview. This interview is a method of instruction, a way of introducing a writer to a new project. Unlike the information-gathering interview where the primary task of the interviewer is to gather information from the interviewee, the primary purpose of the interviewer in the information-giving interview is to give information. The interviewer is primarily a receiver in the information-gathering interview and primarily a sender in the information-giving interview. Thus, the interviewer in the information-giving interview provides information to the interviewee. Remember that the interview is directive as the interviewer will develop an interview guide and schedule to conduct the interview which will consist of two parties, but, in some cases, several interviewees make up one party.

In this chapter we will discuss background information about the information-giving/orientation interview, guidelines for conducting the information-giving interview, the role of the interviewer and interviewee in the information giving interview, and an evaluation of the information-giving interview. We will focus on information-giving in the orientation interview of technical communicators.

BACKGROUND INFORMATION

The new employee might be oriented to the job and the company by the Personnel and/or Human Resource Departments. Likewise, the specific department in which the person is working will probably conduct part of the information-giving interview. The responsibility for orientation within the department rests with the manager, the project director, mentor, and co-workers. The information might range from highly specific procedures to general notions about the department to corporate culture. Information also might be presented in formal classes (usually by human resources) and written materials handed out by the mentor (informational material, the company style guidebook, maps, a company telephone directory, and company mission statement). Remember that the first objective of an orientation program is to provide a new employee with a comfortable environment in which to adjust to the new environment.

The following factors will determine how to conduct the information-giving interview [1, pp. 187-190]:

1. Determine the specific information the new employee needs to know. For example, the interviewer might provide information on such things as hours of work, location of washrooms and lunch rooms, passes and badges, dress code, primary supplies, essential safety rules, and primary job duties and responsibilities. This might include much routine information which might be part of a handout given to all new employees. Remember to create a positive first impression.
2. Organize the interview into appropriate categories. You should develop an interview guide to make sure that you cover all the main points. Encourage the interviewee to ask questions. Remember that some redundancy is essential.
3. Follow a good questioning pattern. You should develop an interview schedule. Remember to have the new employee talk as soon as possible by asking open questions and encourage the interviewee to ask questions. Make sure that the interviewee understands the information you are giving by asking clearinghouse questions such as: Have I covered everything you need to know on policies and procedures?

Remember a new employee will be dependent on others during the first few days and weeks of a new job.

GUIDELINES FOR CONDUCTING THE INFORMATION-GIVING INTERVIEW

Several articles have been written about ways to orient new employees. The following list of guidelines developed by McGarrell [2, pp. 82-84] could be used to orient new employees or could be used as a guide concerning any new project:

1. Try to create a positive first impression. For example, when you orient a subject matter expert or other writer about your project, you will want to create a favorable first impression as you might be working with these individuals for several months.
2. The prearrival period should be a part of the orientation. Arriving early will provide you with an opportunity to organize your thoughts prior to the interview.
3. Day one is crucial as the new employee will need to obtain much information. In addition, new hires tend to remember the first day of employment for years.
4. New hires are interested in the entire organization. You should provide as much information as necessary.
5. Primary information should be given first. The interviewer needs to be organized in order to provide the information so that the interviewee will be able to process it.
6. Encourage new employees to assume major responsibility for their own orientation. For example, prior to the interview a lead writer might provide written information on a new manual to be written.
7. Provide information to fit the employee's need.
8. Don't give too much information at one time—especially technical information. You need to plan so that you have a dialogue with the other party.
9. The supervisor should provide the key information. For example, the long-term effects on writers depend to a great extent on how superiors carry out their responsibilities.
10. Emphasize solid orientation. A vital part of the total management system is a solid orientation on all important aspects of the position and company.

Obviously, different people will handle different parts of the orientation. Thus, the above guidelines need to be evaluated in terms of each individual who is part of the orientation process. For example, managers will present to new employees what they need to know to perform their jobs as well as expectations of quality of work by the company and department, and the daily tasks and responsibilities of the jobs.

Ideally, according to Lopez, there are four phases to a proper introduction of an employee to a new job in a new company [3, p. 85].

1. During phase one the new employee meets a company representative. During this phase the new employee receives information about the job, the company, and its benefits.
2. During the second phase the new employee reports to his or her supervisor. The supervisor will introduce the new employee to other employees and learn details about the work environment. Informal orientation is an important part of this phase of the orientation. For example, a writer will be introduced to other writers of the unit.

3. The third phase might consist of a formal classroom environment. For example, if a group of writers is working with new software, the manager might teach writers the new software. A new writer also might be instructed on policies and procedures and employee benefits.

4. During the last phase of the orientation, the employee is presented with the final details of the various job responsibilities.

To help managers become proficient at orientation, they should attend a formalized orientation program. The orientation program should be taken during the first twelve months on the job as a manager. During this program trainers will cover materials such as general management guidelines, performance reviews, coaching and motivating, and handling performance problems. Through this orientation procedure the manager will learn to conduct appraisal, counseling, problem-solving, and disciplinary interviews.

For example, a lead writer might sit down with a new writer on the first day of the job and review requirements of the job with the new employee. The information-gathering and information-giving interviews will be done throughout the project period. Through the process of giving and receiving information the new employee will perform the various tasks to complete the project. Below is a sample dialogue between a lead writer, project writer, and subject matter expert:

Lead Writer: Thanks, Jim and Tom, for coming in to talk about our new project. Before discussing with you about our specific role in the project, I would like to outline what I think are the essentials of the project. First, the software must be user friendly. Second, page design is important. We will need to check with the graphic experts on page design and visuals. (The lead writer provides background information and a purpose statement of the project.)

Jim: (project writer) I understand the purpose, but would you provide a summary of the material you have gone over? (Jim asks a closed-ended questions but wants the lead writer to create the summary.)

Tom: (technical expert) I have listened carefully to your orientation and understand that my role is entirely as an information source. I have collected most of the sources you mentioned, and I will organize them before our next meeting.

This interview has been a very successful one because the lead writer prepared well for the interview. Remember that a well organized and executed orientation program can increase the rate of development and degree of quality within a team. The following team-building characteristics, reported in *The Training and Development Journal*, will improve the interpersonal relationships between interviewers and interviewees and among employees working on a project [4, p. 23]:

Purpose: In information-giving interviews the interviewer and interviewee understand the purpose. For example, writers and subject matter experts share the purpose.

Attitude: The interviewer and interviewee develop a cooperative and a unified purpose. Through self-disclosure and open communication both parties interact at level 3.

Development: The two parties deal with different questions of content and with the various roles that each will play during the orientation session.

Strength: The two parties gain strength from each other. A sense of interdependence and mutuality develops between the two parties.

Results: Together, the two parties are capable of achieving results that individual members could not complete alone.

THE ROLES OF THE INTERVIEWER AND INTERVIEWEE

The Interviewer

The interviewer plays a dominant role in the information-giving interview. The interviewer needs to create a favorable first impression by establishing rapport. As indicated in Chapter 2, a variety of ways is available to complete this task. Obviously a firm handshake, direct eye contact, smiling, overall attentiveness, and a friendly voice are important factors to consider in establishing rapport. In many cases the interviewer will be orienting several new employees at the same time, or a lead writer might be orienting several writers and technical experts at the same time. Thus, the interviewer needs to plan in advance the introduction and to establish rapport so that everyone will feel comfortable and be part of the interviewing process. Overall, the interviewer attempts to create the feeling that each individual is part of a work group.

The various types of introductions, discussed in Chapter 2, might be used as part of the orientation process. Next, the interviewer will provide key information on the company and the specific tasks of the employee.

The orientation should not be a monologue although the interviewer might talk 80 percent of the time. Much preparation should have been completed by both parties prior to the interview. The interviewer needs to be well organized, to develop an interview guide, and to develop questions. Basically, the interviewer will ask closed-ended questions to determine if the interviewee understands the information. The interviewer also might ask clearinghouse probes and open-ended questions. Both parties should feel comfortable with their level of interaction during the interview. In addition, the interview does not just end, as the interviewer needs to develop a conclusion. Such closings as *planning for the next meeting, statement of appreciation, statement of completion, and personal inquiries are ways to close the interview.* Overall, the interviewer wants to establish a positive, lasting impression.

The Interviewee

The interviewee also wants to create a favorable first impression. Prior to the interview the interviewee will review all materials concerning the company and job description. The interviewee should appear as knowledgeable as possible about the company. As indicated in the introduction of the chapter, the primary role of the interviewee is to listen, but the interviewee also will ask questions and respond to the questions of the interviewer. It is essential that the interviewee be as attentive as possible throughout the period. For example, if you are a technical writer and want to be oriented about a new project, you will develop open-ended questions and reflective probe questions to make sure you understand the project. By being an active listener you will be able to develop appropriate and timely questions during the interview.

Open-Ended Question: What are some ways we can test the readability of the document?

Mirror Probe: Let me see if I understand what you have been saying. First, we want the document to be user friendly. Second, we need to discuss with the graphic designer the page design and other visuals, and we are most concerned about marketing our manual. It is essential that we do some usability testing. Have I covered everything?

EVALUATION OF THE ORIENTATION INTERVIEW

The orientation interview will determine the impression new employees will have of a company as well as the impression a writer will have of a lead writer as they begin working on a new project. Obviously, it is important to create a favorable first impression. The human relations department might gather information from new employees concerning the effectiveness of the orientation program. Perhaps, a survey would be done after the employees have had an opportunity to adjust to their new environment—perhaps one or two months after the new employee has been with the company. Likewise, the lead writer or publication manager might seek feedback from new employees concerning a project they have worked on together. An evaluation form might be completed by each of the members working on a project. It could be a written questionnaire or an information-gathering interview. Both open-ended and closed-ended questions might be used to gather information about the orientation process.

Closed-Ended Questions

Zima suggested that the interviewer should ask several closed-ended questions. Here are some examples [1, p. 194]:

1. Was the orientation program a good idea?
2. Did you receive adequate information about the company?

3. Did you receive adequate information about the project?
4. Were co-workers friendly?
5. Were co-workers helpful?
6. Were you provided with all the necessary information to perform your job?
7. Were you given full information about rules and regulations, opportunities and benefits?
8. Has the training program been adequate?
9. Do you feel free to question your supervisor about job problems or other matters?
10. Should the orientation program be continued?

Open-Ended Questions

1. What features of your orientation were useful and helpful?
2. In what ways do you think it could be improved?

SUMMARY

This chapter has focused on the information-giving interview. The interviewer is primarily a sender and the interviewee is primarily a receiver for this type of interview. Guidelines for conducting and evaluating information-giving interviews are the key parts of the chapter.

INFORMATION-GIVING INTERVIEW FOR REVIEW AND ANALYSIS

Below is an example of an information-giving interview. The publication manager knows the academic background and work experience of Frank and Sally. Thus, it is not essential to provide an elaborate rapport building phase for the meeting. What type of opening does the publication manager use? What type of closing does the publication manager use? What types of questions would you ask Frank and Sally? As you read this dialogue you will notice that Frank and Sally will be conducting information-giving interviews.

How would you approach this task? What type of preparation would you do? What type of opening would you use? What type of closing would you use? What types of questions would you ask?

Character Description

Narration: Frank and Sally, two young technical communication graduates and recent hires at the Good Writers Company, have been asked to come to the publication manager's office to discuss conducting a survey on the company newsletter. No orientation had been done prior to this meeting. They arrived on time and were curious why they had been selected for this project.

Publication Manager: Thanks for coming (motioning to them to have a seat). I would like to talk to you about a survey interview that I would like you to conduct on your Good Writers Newsletter. As you know, we have been publishing our newsletter for over five years but have not elicited any feedback from our readers. We have several parts to the newsletter including new software, desktop publishing, Society of Technical Communications meetings. . . . Specifically, I want to find out if our readers are pleased with the newsletter and how important they feel each of the sections are. I have completed a draft of a questionnaire. I know both of you took Dr. McDowell's research course in communication strategies, so you have a good background in designing surveys.

Frank: Do you think we should ask any questions about readability? (looking at Sally and the publication manager).

Sally: Perhaps, we should ask some questions on graphics. (Sally is wondering whether this should be done.)

Publication Manager: I hadn't thought about these areas. I will gather some information and summarize my findings. After you have had an opportunity to read the summary, I will call for another meeting. We also will need to train other writers to help conduct the survey interview. Would you develop a lesson plan on how we will teach (orient) this information to the interviewers?

Narration: This was the first information-giving interview. The publication manager will conduct another information-giving interview after researching the possibility of completing a readability study and the use of graphics. After this interview Frank and Sally will orient the survey interview team and teach them how to conduct face-to-face and phone interviews. Interviewers will need to rehearse and be evaluated by Frank and Sally.

QUESTIONS

1. Think about your present or last job.
   A. What were your overall feelings about the job?
   B. Please list as many pleasant experiences as you can concerning the orientation of the job.
   C. Please list as many unpleasant experiences as you can concerning the orientation of the job.

REFERENCES

1. J. Zima, *Interviewing: Keys to Effective Management*, Science Research Associates, Inc., Chicago, Illinois, 1983.
2. E. McGarrell, An Orientation System that Builds Productivity, *Personnel Administrator*, pp. 75-85, 1984.
3. F. Lopez, *Personnel Interviewing: Theory and Practice*, McGraw-Hill Book Company, New York, 1965.
4. D. Day, Training 101: A New Look at Orientation, *Training and Development Journal*, pp. 18-23, 1988.

Part 3
EMPLOYMENT CYCLE INTERVIEWS

CHAPTER 5

Employment Interviews

OBJECTIVES

On completion of this chapter you should be able to:
Define employment interviewing
Understand the interviewer role
Understand the interviewee role
Develop a cover letter
Develop a resume
Develop an interview guide
Develop an interview schedule
Develop a post-interview evaluation form
Analyze the employment interview
Participate in role playing interviews

The employment interview is the most common type of interview. Practically everyone has played the role of the interviewee in the employment interview, and many also have played the role of the interviewer. During the employment interview the interviewer and interviewee give and receive information. A thorough knowledge of Chapters 3 and 4 should help you to perform both roles.

Generally, the employment interview is a face-to-face dyadic communication event. It is moderately or highly structured, and the interviewer prepares a standard set of questions to ask all interviewees. Through the process of interviewing, the interviewer and interviewee exchange information to determine whether the potential employee should be hired for the position. During the interview both will inform and attempt to persuade each other and both will play the roles of sender and receiver. Situational variables such as type of interview setting, interviewer approach, time of day, seating arrangement, status and gender are just a few variables that can affect the willingness of both parties to exchange information.

Remember that the purpose of the employment interview is to select candidates for employment. We will begin this chapter by discussing how the interviewer and interviewee should prepare for the interview. Then we will focus on pre-interview factors and interviewing factors of both the interviewer and the interviewee.

PREPARING FOR THE EMPLOYMENT INTERVIEW

The Interviewer Role

Before preparing to conduct an interview, the interviewer or another person in the organization must determine the job requirements. A job analysis will probably be completed to determine the key job elements which include areas of responsibilities and primary duties to be performed on the job. Next qualification standards will be determined for the position such as education, training, work experience, and any special skills. For example, the Good Writers Company prepared the following list of key job requirements, applicant qualifications, and selection techniques for the technical writing position. Mary, as indicated in Chapter 1, applied and was hired for this job. She used the list of key job requirements and applicant qualifications to gather and prepare the materials for the selection interview. Below is what the director of personnel listed under key job requirements, applicant qualifications, and selection techniques:

Key job requirements
1. Interviewing subject matter experts
2. Operate desktop publishing system
3. Write software documentation
4. Make presentations to other writers
5. Administer writing projects
6. Conduct meetings with writers and subject matter experts

Application qualifications
1. Experience in interviewing technical experts
2. Knowledge and experience in using Basic, Cobol, Fortran, and Pascal
3. Proficient with word processors
4. Experience in making technical presentations
5. Experience in writing computer manuals
6. Experience in conducting meetings
7. Extroverted personality

Selection techniques
1. Cover letter
2. Application form
3. Resume
4. Transcript
5. References
6. Interviews with director of personnel and publication manager
7. Drug test

Next, the interviewer will develop an interview guide and interview schedule. The interviewer should be knowledgeable about Equal Employment Opportunity guidelines. The Civil Rights Act of 1964 and its amendments should be reviewed. It is against the law to discriminate because of race and color, sex, national origin or ancestry, religion, age, physical handicaps, citizenship, pregnancy, marital status, credit record, spouse's background, arrest record, and garnished record. Below is a list of some illegal questions:

1. What is your age?
2. Do you have children?
3. Do you practice birth control?
4. What is your race?
5. What church do you attend?
6. What clubs or organizations do you belong to?
7. Where did your parents come from?
8. Have you ever been arrested for a crime?
9. Have your wages ever been attached or garnished?
10. Are you married?
11. What are your parents' professions?
12. How does your spouse feel about you having a career?

The Interviewee Role

Prior to developing a cover letter or resume you should conduct a thorough search of yourself and what you want from a job. Crystal and Bolles suggest you have to know what you want or someone is going to sell you a bill of goods somewhere along the line that can do irreparable damage to your self-esteem, and your sense of worth [1, p. 246]. In short, you should complete a self-assessment of your strengths and weaknesses.

1. *Self-assessment variables* — You might begin by asking yourself a series of open-ended questions for various types of positions in technical communication:

1. What are my communication strengths as a writer?
2. What are my communication weaknesses as a writer?
3. What are my intellectual strengths in technical communication?
4. What are my intellectual weaknesses in technical communication?
5. What kind of technical communication work do I enjoy doing?
6. What have been my greatest successes as a technical communicator?
7. What have been my greatest failures as a technical communicator?
8. What have been my professional strengths?
9. What have been my professional weaknesses?
10. What type of job would give me the greatest satisfaction?
11. What do I want for myself in the future?

By brainstorming for each of these questions you will develop greater insight into your self-concept. As you reflect, you should determine what are the must objectives. For example, in assessing your career goals how important are the following: advancement, benefits, company, co-workers, hours, pay, security, supervisor, and type of work conditions. You might use these items to determine whether to apply for a position or to assess after an interview whether you are interested in the position. You also might ask yourself several closed-ended questions:

1. Do I prefer to work alone or as part of a team?
2. Do I want a great deal of responsibility?
3. Do I need to make a certain amount of money?

By answering these questions you should understand yourself and your must objectives.

Through the process of self-assessment you also will analyze your educational and employment background, and assess your personality to determine what is important to you in selecting a specific job. In addition, you should be able to develop cover letters and resumes that target on your past and present work experiences and education and provide insight into your future career plans. Now go to the end of the chapter and complete the Self-Assessment Personality Inventory and Employment Needs Inventory.

2. *Knowledge of company* — Employers expect applicants to be knowledgeable about the company. You should do research for two reasons: 1) to demonstrate your knowledge during the interview and 2) to determine if the company is right for you. By researching the company Einhorn, Bradley and Baird suggest that you should be able to answer the following questions [2, p. 37]:

1. What is the company history?
2. What are its products and services?
3. What is its growth record?
4. How is the company financially?
5. What are its new software packages?
6. Who are the companies major competitors?
7. What are the most serious organizational problems?
8. What type of training does the company provide?
9. What is the rate of attrition in the company?
10. What are the company's prospects for growth?
11. What are the duties and responsibilities for the job?
12. Does the company pay competitive salaries?
13. Do I know anyone working for the company?
14. Why is this position available?
15. How does the company rank in the industry?

By finding answers to these open-ended and closed-ended questions, you will be able to prepare a better cover letter and resume for the position.

3. *Cover letter* — The cover letter is a vital part of the pre-interview. You should focus on the employer's needs, identify specific abilities related to the position, and stress your accomplishments. The cover letter should capture the reader's attention. The body of the letter should be well written, should contain no spelling or typing errors, and should tell how you are qualified for the position. It should conclude with a statement such as "I am available for an interview at your convenience." Research indicates that cover letters are quickly evaluated and should be only one page. After reading this chapter, you should go to Part 5 and read McDowell's article, "Perceptions of the Ideal Cover Letter and Ideal Resume" [3]. This article provides detailed information on recruiters', teachers' and students' perceptions of the cover letter and resume (see Figure 5).

Other results, reported by Janes, indicate that cover letters should do the following [4, pp. 372-373]:

1. Be addressed to a specific person in the organization.
2. Be an original copy.
3. Reveal specific reasons why the applicant is interested in the position.
4. Indicate when the applicant will be available for an interview.
5. Indicate how the applicant learned about the position.
6. Amplify and not merely repeat the resume.
7. Be original and somewhat creative.
8. Be an introduction and need not tell the comprehensive, "life" story.
9. Be signed.

4. *Resume* — The resume is an organized summary of an applicant's professional, educational and work background, abilities, and professional objectives. It is your agent and will determine if you will be offered an interview. Lathrop concluded that the resume should focus upon an employer's needs and identify an interviewee's abilities [5, p. 31].

According to Einhorn and associates [2, p. 69], the resume should:

1. Contain an objective that is narrow and employer-oriented.
2. Describe clearly and concisely all significant facts about your educational and work experience.
3. Cover your abilities.
4. Prove that your experiences and assets qualify you for your job objective.
5. Indicate how well you have performed.
6. Stress accomplishments.
7. Focus on the needs and interests of the employer.
8. Reflect your character and personality as a human being.
9. Use headings and underlinings to arouse interest and to highlight important information.
10. Be visually attractive.
11. Use an interesting choice of words.

Mr. John Smith
Director of Personnel
Good Writing Company
St. Paul, MN 55108

Dear Mr. Smith:

Dr. Write, Head of the Department of Rhetoric at the University of Minnesota, has informed me that you have an opening for a technical communicator with a background in computer science. I have read the job description and feel qualified for this position.

In addition to the information contained in the resume, I have completed courses in conducting meetings, group discussion, and interpersonal communication and have conducted information-gathering interviews with subject matter experts and technical writers. Because of the balance between my oral and written communication courses and my strong technical background, I am well qualified for this position.

My resume also points out that I have had internships at two of the top computer companies in the Twin Cities. These experiences have helped me to mature as a technical communicator. I am excited about the possibility of working for your company and am available for an interview at your convenience. Thank you.

Sincerely,

Mary K. Winters

Figure 5. Cover letter.

12. Contain correct spelling.
13. Be typed neatly.
14. Be limited to one or two pages.

We obviously could generate additional factors that might be included in the resume. Specifically, my article, "Perceptions of the Ideal Cover Letter and Ideal Resume," reveals that over 60 percent of recruiters feel that over twenty-five types of information should be reported in the resume [3, p. 187]. In addition, other research suggests that interviewers prefer a specific resume targeted for a specific job in a specific company. Your self-assessment should assist you in making the right decisions. For example, if you use a straight arrow approach in your job search, you would write a specific resume for each position as you would only apply for a limited number of positions. If, on the other hand, you use a shotgun approach, you might use a generic resume as you would be applying for a large number of positions.

Your approach to the job search will help you to decide whether to develop a traditional or contemporary resume. The traditional resume is used by applicants who apply for a number of jobs, generally using a shotgun approach. The contemporary approach can be used for both the straight arrow and shotgun approaches. If you were to use it for a specific job, you might include a list of work related abilities (see Figures 6 and 7).

Mary K. Winters
1910 York Lane
Bloomington, Minnesota 55438
Home Phone: (612) 831-4879
Office: (612) 373-0817

Professing Goal: To become a lead writer and editor for a computer company.

Education: 1984-88 — Graduated from the University of Minnesota with a B.S. degree in Technical Communication and a technical elective in computer science.

Technical Communication Courses: Writing in Your Profession, Newsletter Writing, Proposal Writing, Documentation Design, Electronic Publishing, Desktop Publishing, Technical Editing, Interviewing, Scientific and Technical Presentation, Managerial Communication, Transfer of Technology, Organizational Communication.

Computer Courses: Software Documentation, Pascal, Fortran, Programming and Problem Solving, Perspectives of Computers and Society.

Work History: 1988-present — Employed as an intern for IBM. Duties include interviewing subject matter experts and preparing reports to share with the Publication Manager.

1986-87 — Internship with Cray Research. Duties included writing software documentation and field testing documents.

References and additional information furnished upon request.

Figure 6. Traditional resume.

Mary K. Winters
1910 York Lane
Bloomington, Minnesota 55438
Home Phone: (612) 831-4879
Office: (612) 373-0817

Career Objective: Technical writer for a computer company. My goal is to to combine my writing skills and technical skills to become a lead writer and editor.

Work History: 1988-present — Employed as an intern for IBM. Duties include interviewing subject matter experts and preparing reports to share with the Publication Manager.

1986-87 — Internship with Cray Research. Duties included writing software documentation and field testing documents.

Education: 1984-88 — Graduated from University of Minnesota with a B.S. degree in Technical Communication and a technical elective in computer science.

Technical Communication Courses: Writing in Your Profession, Newsletter Writing, Proposal Writing, Documentation Design, Electronic Publishing, Desktop Publishing, Technical Editing, Interviewing, Scientific and Technical Presentation, Managerial Communication, Transfer of Technology, Organizational Communication.

Computer Courses: Software Documentation, Pascal, Fortran, Programming and Problem Solving, Perspectives of Computers and Society.

References and additional information furnished upon request.

Figure 7. Contemporary resume.

THE INTERVIEW PLAN

Prior to the employment interview both the interviewer and interviewee have certain responsibilities. As already indicated, the interviewer will develop a job description, and the interviewee will complete a self-assessment and research the company. Next both parties will develop questions. Initially, the interviewer will develop an interview guide and then develop an interview schedule. The interviewee also should generate a list of questions that the interviewer might ask and should rehearse answering them. The interviewee also should develop questions

Table 6. Types of Questions

Type	Definition	Example
Open	A question that opens the range of responses	Why do you want to be a technical writer?
Closed	A question that closes the range of response	Do you like working with engineers?
Mirror	A question that mirrors back a response	Do you mean . . .
Leading	A question that attempts to lead the respondent in a particular direction	You feel you can make more money here than at other writing companies, don't you?

which might focus on the history on the company, the job description, and salary. Table 6 shows the four types of questions that both parties might use during the employment interview.

Interviews have four sequences: *establish rapport, information getting, information giving*, and *summarizing*. Lopez points out that the interviewer needs to establish rapport with the applicant [6, pp. 48-50]. The interviewer can establish rapport by creating a friendly climate and showing a personal interest. During the information-gathering phase the interviewer asks questions about previous work experiences, life history, education, and personal qualifications. During the information-giving phase the interviewer discusses the job and company. Finally, the interviewer summarizes the interview and tells the procedures that will be followed in selecting an applicant for a position. The information-gathering phase should last 55 percent of the total interview time, while the three other phases each last about 15 percent of the time.

PERFORMING THE INTERVIEWER ROLE

As mentioned earlier the interviewer will use the job requirements and job qualifications to help develop an interview guide and list of questions. Four factors will determine if the interviewee will be offered a job: *educational training, work experience, personality characteristics*, and *motivational level*.

Frank concluded that a good interviewer asks few closed-ended questions or embarrassing questions [7, pp. 202-204]. That is, leading questions or questions that compel the applicant to defend a statement or admit an error in an earlier statement should be avoided. Likewise, leading questions, or questions that invariably elicit the same answers from all applicants should be avoided. The proper use of the question techniques can create rapport, stimulate thinking, determine if the applicant is knowledgeable, alter the direction of a dialogue, and reach a conclusion.

Open-ended questions help the interviewer to achieve a cordial environment by using low impact and high acceptance. This provides the interviewee with an opportunity to verbalize ideas, even if extra time is required, rather than having extra words supplied for the applicant. The mirror question is particularly effective if it not only can reflect on what is actually said but can express what an applicant means but cannot articulate. The interviewer, however, should not read in messages that are not meant. Rather the interviewer should build on what the candidate has already said and repeat certain selected words that will amplify those selected areas.

According to Gootnick, fifteen *key questions* are asked in an interview [8, pp. 41-42]:

1. Tell me about your job experiences.
2. Why do you want to leave your job?
3. Why have you chosen this particular field?
4. Why should we hire you?
5. What are your long range goals?
6. What is your greatest strength?
7. What is your greatest weakness?
8. What is your current salary?
9. What is important to you in a job?
10. Why are you interested in working for this company?
11. What do you do in your spare time?
12. What features of the job interest you most?
13. How do others describe you?
14. What are your plans for continued study?
15. Tell me about your schooling.

The employment interviewer probably will ask questions on job-related areas. For example, Mary K. Winters had two internships. The skilled interviewer will want to know what she has gained from these internships that will help the Good Writers Company. The interviewer also will explore how her education will help her to perform her job. In addition, the interviewer will want to know about the applicant's career plans and goals.

Interviewers also will use *closed-ended* questions such as:

1. What was your salary on your last job?
2. Who is your present employer?
3. How long did your internship last?
4. Which of the following best describes your personality?
   a) cooperative
   b) competitive
5. Are you willing to work with engineers?

As indicated in Chapter 2 interviewers might use question sequences. The *funnel sequence* is a deductive strategy. It begins with a broad open-ended question and proceeds with even more restricted questions. It is ideal for the employment interview as it provides the interviewee with an opportunity to disclose in-depth information about a topic. The interviewer leads the candidate to respond to general questions and then to specific questions. Below is an example of how an employment interviewer might use the funnel sequence:

Why did you choose technical writing as a career?

Tell me about your technical writing
experiences.

What have you found to be
most satisfying about
your major?

What skills have you
developed through
your studies that
might be helpful
for this job?

When did you make
the decision to
become a technical
writer?

In contrast, the *inverted funnel sequence* is an inductive strategy. It forces the interviewee to respond to specific questions and then general questions. This sequence might be effective toward the middle or end of the interview if the interviewer has established rapport and trust with the interviewee. It also provides the interviewer with an opportunity to ask a clearinghouse probe question. Below is an example of how an interviewer would use the inverted funnel sequence:

Where have you
been employed
as a technical
writer?

What type of
responsibilities did you have?

What type of responsibilities
do you hope to have with this job?

How do you feel about being a lead
writer on the Emmie Ingram project?

Tell me about your career goals as a technical
writer.

Interview Guide

As indicated in Chapter 2, the interview guide is an outline or checklist of topics to be covered in an interview. Generally, in an employment interview a topical sequence is used. Topic areas include work experience, educational background, and personality variables. The interviewer will use the job requirements, list of qualifications, as well as the cover letter and resume of the applicant as sources to help to develop the interview guide.

An interview contains an introduction, body, and conclusion. During the introduction the interviewer will establish rapport, gain trust and confidence, create a favorable first impression, and orient and motivate the interviewee. To establish credibility, the interviewer should be spontaneous by showing interest in the applicant's background. After engaging in some small talk, the interviewer might discuss the structure of the interview, indicating that educational background, work experience, and career interest will be discussed.

The body of the interview must be carefully planned so that it is germane to the job requirements. Generally, a directive method is used to obtain information from the applicant. By using a directive method the interviewee should do most of the talking, and, as a result, the interviewer will be able to evaluate the qualifications of each applicant. Remember that the interviewer should provide transitions between topic areas and interact freely with the applicant. The interviewer also should provide the applicant with an opportunity to ask questions. The interviewer should assess the qualifications of the applicant to perform each of the tasks listed in the job requirements.

An effective conclusion summarizes the contents of the interview and provides the applicant with an opportunity to ask a clearinghouse question. The closing also can be initiated by nonverbal cues. Generally, the interviewer will indicate when the applicant will be informed about the position. See Figure 8 for an interview guide for the position of technical writer.

Based on the interview guide the interviewer will develop an interview schedule. This is a standard set of questions that the interviewer will ask all applicants. See Figure 9 for an interview schedule for the position of technical writer.

Immediately after an interview, the interviewer should complete a post-interview evaluation, which might consist of writing responses to several open-ended questions. Zima suggests recruiters respond to the following questions [9, p. 152]:

1. Is the applicant's education job-related?
2. Is the applicant's training job related?
3. Do they match the qualifications for the position?
4. What is the applicant's history of effective work performance?

5. Are the applicant's goals and aspirations consistent with the opportunity in this position?
6. Are the applicant's salary and benefit expectations consistent with what the organization can offer?
7. Is the applicant's self-assessment compatible with the position?

The post-interview evaluation might include a set of standardized closed questions in which all candidates are rated on a scale from poor to excellent (see Figure 10). All applicants might be rated in terms of their interest in the position, attitude, maturity, motivation, self-confidence, ability to get along with co-workers, ability to communicate, appearance suitable for this job, knowledge of the company, and related work experience.

Finally, the interviewer should evaluate his/her own performance, assessing the effectiveness of the introduction, body, and conclusion. The interviewer should assess ability to answer interviewee's questions, to follow EEO guidelines, to listen carefully to the interviewee, and to encourage the applicant to speak freely and openly.

I. Introduction
   A. Greeting
   B. Introduction of self
   C. Welcome applicant to company
   D. Explain interview procedure

II. Body
   A. Writing experiences
      1. Courses in writing
      2. Internship computer experiences
   B. Computer experience
      1. Courses in computers
      2. Internship computer experiences
   C. Oral communication experiences
      1. Courses in oral communication
      2. Internship oral communication experiences
   D. General questions
      1. Personality characteristics
      2. Level of motivation
      3. Goals

III. Conclusion
   A. Brief summary of interview
   B. Answer any final questions

Figure 8. Interviewing guide technical writing position.

I. Introduction
   A. Did you have any trouble finding our office?
   B. Do you have any questions concerning how we will proceed?
   C. We will talk about the job later in the interview, but before I begin to
      question you, do you have anything you would like to ask?
II. Body
   A. Writing Experiences
      1. I see you have completed several writing courses. Please tell
         about your software documentation course.
      2. What writing classes did you enjoy most of all?
      3. How did these writing classes help you to perform your writing
         tasks during your two internships?
      4. Based on your knowledge of this position, what do you consider
         your writing strengths?
      5. What type of writing do you want to do in the future?
   B. Computer Experiences
      1. In what computer language are you most competent?
      2. What do you like best about writing computer programs?
      3. What do you like least about writing computer programs?
      4. What would your supervisors for the internships say about your
         computer skills?
      5. Do you enjoy working with hardware specialists?
   C. Oral Communication Experiences
      1. I see that you've taken several courses in oral communication.
         Which ones have been the most interesting?
      2. How did your interview course help you to prepare to conduct
         information-gathering interviews with technical specialists?
      3. How do you prepare to interview subject matter experts?
      4. Do you prepare differently when you interview writers than when
         you interview subject matter experts?
      5. How do you prepare for an oral presentation?
      6. How do you analyze an audience?
      7. Describe some of your leadership characteristics?
      8. As you know any business has many meetings, how do you feel
         about conducting meetings with subject matter experts and
         writers?
   D. General Questions
      1. What are your long range goals?
      2. What are your major strengths?
      3. What are your major weaknesses?
      4. What do you like to do when you're not at work?
      5. How well do you deal with pressure?
      6. What are some adjectives your supervisor would use to
         describe you?
III. Conclusion
   A. Are there any additional questions that you would like to ask me?
   B. Thank applicant for interest in the job.

Figure 9. Interviewing schedule technical writing position.

Rate the interviewee from poor to excellent on the following qualifica-
tions/factors. Place a number between 1 and 5 in the space to the left
of each item for each qualification/factor: 1=poor, 2=below average,
3=average, 4=above average, and 5=excellent.

_____ 1. Ability to communicate
_____ 2. Level of motivation
_____ 3. Appropriate work experience
_____ 4. Appropriate education
_____ 5. General intelligence
_____ 6. Knowledge of technical communication field
_____ 7. Knowledge of company
_____ 8. Maturity
_____ 9. Ability to get along with co-workers
_____ 10. Interest in the job

Figure 10. Post-interview evaluation form.

PERFORMING THE INTERVIEWEE ROLE

The interviewee should complete a self-assessment, research the company, and develop a cover letter and a resume. With the knowledge of self and the company, the applicant should prepare for the interview by developing a list of questions that the interviewer might ask each candidate for the position. Moreover, the applicant should rehearse and role-play with someone familiar with the job description. In fact, to prepare for the role of the interviewee, the applicant might develop a list of questions that the interviewer might ask and practice answering the questions. The interviewee also should prepare a list of questions to ask the interviewer. Some typical questions are:

1. What would be my initial duties and responsibilities?
2. What methods do you use to evaluate employees?
3. What type of training program does the company provide?
4. What are my chances for advancement?
5. What have you liked most about your position in this organization?
6. As a new employee, how much supervision would I receive?

The applicant needs to create a positive first impression to obtain a job. As indicated in Chapter 1 nonverbal, paraverbal, and verbal communication play significant roles in face-to-face oral communication situations and are essential in the employment interview. Watson and Smeltzer, in summarizing much of the nonverbal literature, concluded that eye contact, facial expressions, appearance, clothes, gestures and smiling are important nonverbal cues during an interview

[10, pp. 72-37]. Research that we have completed indicated that the applicant's handshake, overall appearance, vocal variety, clean smell, body shape, and clean nails are important nonverbal cues in evaluating applicants. Other findings by Washburn and Smeltzer were that the use of the eyes is probably the most important nonverbal cue in establishing rapport, and that a firm handshake from both male and female candidates has been demonstrated to have a positive impact on the selection procedures, while a "sweaty" hand or a soft grip from a male has a negative impact [11, pp. 140-141]. Tschirgi revealed that more attention should be focused on perceptual rather than substantive data; recruiters are more impressed with how well candidates communicate with them in the interview than with evidence of academic achievement and work experience in employment dossiers, unless such information is unusually impressive [12, p. 78].

Dress to create a favorable first impression in the interview. Molloy asserts that you should dress for success, but also consider your craft [13, pp. 35-36]. For example, a female should wear a gray or medium range suit. Other acceptable colors are navy, beige, camel, dark brown, deep rust, and black. Females should also wear solid color business blouses made of cotton or silk. Likewise, a male's wardrobe for success includes a navy, gray, or tweed suit, a soft, light colored shirt, black shoes, and black belt and a formal tie.

In addition to effective nonverbal communication, the interviewee should have an excellent command of the English language. The candidate should use personal experiences, explanations, comparisons, and transitions in responding to interviewers' questions. A combination of effective nonverbal, vocal, and verbal communication is necessary to be a successful candidate for employment.

A few days after the interview, the interviewee should write a letter of appreciation to the interviewer. The letter should help to create a positive lasting impression (see Figure 11).

SUMMARY

This chapter has focused on the employment interview—the most common type of interview. The chapter discusses how to prepare for the interviewer role, how to prepare for the interviewee role, how to develop the interview plan, how to perform the interviewer role, and how to perform the interviewee role. Now complete the exercises: Appendix A—the Self-Assessment Personality Inventory and Appendix B—Employment Needs Inventory. Next, go to the end of the book and complete the Employment Interviewing Digest.

EXERCISES

1. Develop a job description, cover letter, and resume for a job of your choice. You can use this chapter, the article on the cover letter and resume, as well as Appendix A to develop your resume and cover letter and to prepare to play both

Mr. John Smith
Director of Personnel
Good Writing Company
St. Paul, Minnesota 55431

Dear Mr. Smith:

Thank you for the opportunity to interview for the position of technical writer. I was quite impressed with the writers and like the supportive climate of the company.

Thank you for a good interview. Your questions enabled me to share myself with you and the other writers. I liked the way Mr. Green manages the writers and editors. I also appreciate the opportunity to ask questions.

I look forward to hearing from you concerning the position.

Sincerely,

Mary K. Winters

Figure 11. Letter of appreciation.

the role of the interviewer and interviewee. After completing the job description, cover letter, and resume, exchange this information with someone in your class. Each individual should take the materials and develop an interview guide and schedule to interview the other party. The instructor can arrange for you to videotape these interviews.

APPENDIX A

Self-Assessment Personality Inventory

Please rate yourself on the following personality characteristics. Place an "X" in the box that best represents your feelings.

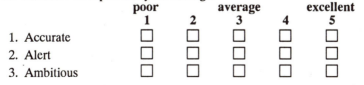

	poor 1	2	average 3	4	excellent 5
1. Accurate	☐	☐	☐	☐	☐
2. Alert	☐	☐	☐	☐	☐
3. Ambitious	☐	☐	☐	☐	☐

	poor 1	2	average 3	4	excellent 5
4. Analytical	☐	☐	☐	☐	☐
5. Artistic	☐	☐	☐	☐	☐
6. Assertive	☐	☐	☐	☐	☐
7. Attractive	☐	☐	☐	☐	☐
8. Broad-minded	☐	☐	☐	☐	☐
9. Capable	☐	☐	☐	☐	☐
10. Competent	☐	☐	☐	☐	☐
11. Competitive	☐	☐	☐	☐	☐
12. Confident	☐	☐	☐	☐	☐
13. Conscientious	☐	☐	☐	☐	☐
14. Consistent	☐	☐	☐	☐	☐
15. Constructive	☐	☐	☐	☐	☐
16. Cooperative	☐	☐	☐	☐	☐
17. Creative	☐	☐	☐	☐	☐
18. Decisive	☐	☐	☐	☐	☐
19. Dependable	☐	☐	☐	☐	☐
20. Determined	☐	☐	☐	☐	☐
21. Disciplined	☐	☐	☐	☐	☐
22. Efficient	☐	☐	☐	☐	☐
23. Energetic	☐	☐	☐	☐	☐
24. Enthusiastic	☐	☐	☐	☐	☐
25. Fair	☐	☐	☐	☐	☐
26. Flexible	☐	☐	☐	☐	☐
27. Forceful	☐	☐	☐	☐	☐
28. Friendly	☐	☐	☐	☐	☐
29. Honest	☐	☐	☐	☐	☐
30. Independent	☐	☐	☐	☐	☐
31. Innovative	☐	☐	☐	☐	☐
32. Inspiring	☐	☐	☐	☐	☐
33. Intelligent	☐	☐	☐	☐	☐
34. Logical	☐	☐	☐	☐	☐
35. Loyal	☐	☐	☐	☐	☐
36. Mature	☐	☐	☐	☐	☐
37. Mechanical	☐	☐	☐	☐	☐
38. Moral	☐	☐	☐	☐	☐
39. Motivated	☐	☐	☐	☐	☐
40. Objective	☐	☐	☐	☐	☐

	poor 1	2	average 3	4	excellent 5
41. Optimistic	☐	☐	☐	☐	☐
42. Organized	☐	☐	☐	☐	☐
43. Outgoing	☐	☐	☐	☐	☐
44. Patient	☐	☐	☐	☐	☐
45. Perceptive	☐	☐	☐	☐	☐
46. Persevering	☐	☐	☐	☐	☐
47. Pioneering	☐	☐	☐	☐	☐
48. Pleasant	☐	☐	☐	☐	☐
49. Poised	☐	☐	☐	☐	☐
50. Practical	☐	☐	☐	☐	☐
51. Professional	☐	☐	☐	☐	☐
52. Punctual	☐	☐	☐	☐	☐
53. Realistic	☐	☐	☐	☐	☐
54. Respectful	☐	☐	☐	☐	☐
55. Responsible	☐	☐	☐	☐	☐
56. Sensitive	☐	☐	☐	☐	☐
57. Serious	☐	☐	☐	☐	☐
58. Sincere	☐	☐	☐	☐	☐
59. Stable	☐	☐	☐	☐	☐
60. Tactful	☐	☐	☐	☐	☐
61. Thorough	☐	☐	☐	☐	☐
62. Tolerant	☐	☐	☐	☐	☐
63. Unique	☐	☐	☐	☐	☐
64. Versatile	☐	☐	☐	☐	☐
65. Other	☐	☐	☐	☐	☐

What are your five most outstanding personality characteristics?

What are your five weakest personality characteristics?

L. Einhorn, P. Bradley, and J. Baird, Jr., *Effective Employment Interviewing: Unlocking Human Potential*, Scott Foresman and Company, Glenview, Illinois, pp. 24-25, 1982. Reprint by permission of authors.

APPENDIX B

Employment Needs Inventory

Please indicate the level of importance for each of the following employment needs. Place an "X" in the box that best represents your feelings.

	not important				extremely important
	1	2	3	4	5
1. Challenge	☐	☐	☐	☐	☐
2. Responsibility	☐	☐	☐	☐	☐
3. Stable company	☐	☐	☐	☐	☐
4. Secure job within company	☐	☐	☐	☐	☐
5. Good training program	☐	☐	☐	☐	☐
6. Interesting initial job duties	☐	☐	☐	☐	☐
7. Lots of opportunities for advancement	☐	☐	☐	☐	☐
8. Lots of contact with coworkers	☐	☐	☐	☐	☐
9. Lots of contact with the public	☐	☐	☐	☐	☐
10. High starting salary	☐	☐	☐	☐	☐
11. Lots of financial rewards "down the road"	☐	☐	☐	☐	☐
12. Allowed to work independently	☐	☐	☐	☐	☐
13. Lots of involvement in decision making	☐	☐	☐	☐	☐
14. Interesting type of industry	☐	☐	☐	☐	☐
15. Reputable organization	☐	☐	☐	☐	☐
16. Prestigious job	☐	☐	☐	☐	☐
17. Immediate results seen from job	☐	☐	☐	☐	☐
18. Varied duties	☐	☐	☐	☐	☐

	not important 1	2	3	4	extremely important 5
19. Pleasant relationship with boss	☐	☐	☐	☐	☐
20. Reasonable hours	☐	☐	☐	☐	☐
21. Good fringe benefits	☐	☐	☐	☐	☐
22. Short commuting distance	☐	☐	☐	☐	☐
23. Lots of overnight travel to interesting places	☐	☐	☐	☐	☐
24. Little or no travel	☐	☐	☐	☐	☐
25. Little or no relocation required in the future	☐	☐	☐	☐	☐
26. Lots of work with data	☐	☐	☐	☐	☐
27. Lots of work with machines	☐	☐	☐	☐	☐
28. Lots of work with ideas	☐	☐	☐	☐	☐
29. Lots of involvement in the job	☐	☐	☐	☐	☐
30. Limited involvement in the job (can forget about it when leaving for the day)	☐	☐	☐	☐	☐
31. Spend a lot of time indoors	☐	☐	☐	☐	☐
32. Spend a lot of time outdoors	☐	☐	☐	☐	☐
33. Job located in metropolitan area	☐	☐	☐	☐	☐
34. Job located in suburban area	☐	☐	☐	☐	☐
35. Large organization	☐	☐	☐	☐	☐
36. Small organization	☐	☐	☐	☐	☐
37. Exciting work	☐	☐	☐	☐	☐
38. Learn a great deal from the job	☐	☐	☐	☐	☐

	not important				extremely important
	1	**2**	**3**	**4**	**5**
39. Possess power	☐	☐	☐	☐	☐
40. Possess freedom in scheduling work hours	☐	☐	☐	☐	☐
41. Lack of bureaucracy	☐	☐	☐	☐	☐
42. Nice physical surroundings	☐	☐	☐	☐	☐
43. Adequate physical equipment (if needed for job)	☐	☐	☐	☐	☐
44. Recognized for good work	☐	☐	☐	☐	☐
45. Lots of feedback from supervisors	☐	☐	☐	☐	☐
46. Lots of autonomy	☐	☐	☐	☐	☐
47. Opportunity to make the world a better place in which to live	☐	☐	☐	☐	☐
48. Able to set own work pace	☐	☐	☐	☐	☐
49. Opportunity to try out own ideas	☐	☐	☐	☐	☐
50. Other	☐	☐	☐	☐	☐

L. Einhorn, P. Bradley, and J. Baird, Jr., *Effective Employment Interviewing: Unlocking Human Potential*, Scott Foresman and Company, Glenview, Illinois, pp. 28-31, 1982. Reprint by permission of authors.

REFERENCES

1. J. Crystal and R. Bolles, *Where Do I Go from Here with My Life?*, Ten Speed Press, Berkeley, California, 1974.
2. L. Einhorn, P. Bradley, and J. Baird, *Effective Employment Interviewing: Unlocking Human Potential*, Scott, Foresman and Company, Glenview, Illinois, 1982.
3. E. McDowell, Perceptions of the Ideal Cover Letter and Ideal Resume, *Journal of Technical Writing and Communication, 17*, pp. 177-189, 1987.
4. S. Janes, The Cover Letter and Resume, *Personnel Journal, 48*, pp. 732-733, 1969.
5. R. Lathrop, *Who's Hiring Who?*, Ten Speed Press, Berkeley, California, 1977.

6. F. Lopez, *Personnel Interviewing: Theory and Practice*, McGraw-Hill Book Company, New York, 1965.
7. F. Frank, *Communicating on the Job*, Scott, Foresman and Company, Glenview, Illinois, 1982.
8. D. Gootnick, Selling Yourself in Interviews, *MBA*, pp. 37-42, 1978.
9. J. Zima, *Interviewing: Keys to Effective Management*, Science Research Associates, Inc., Chicago, 1983.
10. K. Watson and L. Smeltzer, Perceptions of Nonverbal Communication During the Selection Interview, *ABCA Bulletin*, pp. 30-34, 1982.
11. P. Washburn and M. Hakel, Visual Cues and Verbal Content as Influences of Impressions after Simulated Employment Interviews, *Journal of Applied Psychology, 58*, pp. 137-141, 1973.
12. H. Tschirgi, What Do Recruiters Really Look for in a Candidate? *Journal of College Placement*, p . 78, 1973.
13. J. Molloy, *The Woman Dress for Success Book*, Warner Books, New York, 1977.

CHAPTER 6

Appraisal Interviewing

OBJECTIVES

On completion of this chapter you should be able to:
Define appraisal interviewing
Explain theories and types of appraisal interviews
Understand the roles of the appraiser and appraisee
Define disciplinary interview
Explain how to conduct the disciplinary interview
Understand the roles of the interviewer and interviewee in the disciplinary interview

After Mary was hired to be a technical writer for the Good Writers Company, she has performed both the roles of the writer and editor in working on a software program. Time has passed quickly, and it is time for her first performance appraisal interview. During the appraisal period she has received several informal appraisals as she works closely with her supervisor. She also has talked to Brian who has been with the company for over a year, and he also will be evaluated. She was surprised that she would complete a self-appraisal before the scheduled interview with her supervisor.

In this chapter 1) a definition of purposes of appraisal interviews, 2) a summary of research, 3) theories of appraisal interviews, 4) types of appraisal interviews, and 5) conducting the appraisal interview are discussed. In addition, disciplinary interviewing is defined, and techniques to plan and conduct a disciplinary interview are presented.

DEFINITION AND PURPOSE OF APPRAISAL INTERVIEWS

The performance appraisal interview is a face-to-face interpersonal communication event between an interviewer and interviewee, a manager and a subordinate, designed to review the subordinate's job performance over a period of time by asking and answering questions. As in other types of interviews, inclusion, control, and affection, as well as the other interviewing variables discussed in the first two chapters, will determine how the interviewer and interviewee will plan for the interview.

Informal evaluation about job performance should occur frequently between managers and subordinates. In contrast, formal appraisal interviews occur between supervisors and subordinates once or twice a year. The appraisal interview enables the interviewer to conduct systematic assessments of an employee's work performance in a comfortable and open environment. Through the interviewing process both parties can clarify their perceptions about job responsibilities and future expectations. An open discussion between the interviewer and interviewee can provide information to evaluate the interviewee's training and development needs, future promotion potential, and salary increases. In short, Maier indicated that the performance appraisal interview has three basic functions [1, pp. 2-3]:

1. To provide adequate feedback to each employee on performance.
2. To serve as a basis for modifying or changing behavior toward more effective working habits.
3. To provide data to managers with which they may judge future job assignments and composition.

RESEARCH ON APPRAISAL INTERVIEWING

Past research by Heneman indicated that appraisal interviews are anticipated with about as much enthusiasm as death and taxes; they cause discomfort and stress, and appear to be the "Achilles heel of most professions" [2, p. 62]. Researchers have concluded that merit raises are hollow, that only 25 percent of interviewers have had training in interviewing, and that the interview is stressful because it is full of uncertainty [3, p. 11]. Conant concluded that a lack of adequate training has led supervisors to some major sources of measurement distortion [4, pp. 76-78]:

1. The halo-effect is a tendency to appraise some employees higher in all performance activities because they are nice people.
2. The devil-effect is a tendency to rate negatively people whom you don't like.
3. The recency-effect is when the supervisor uses the last few weeks or months of an employee's performance period to determine how to rate the subordinate.
4. The exceptional performance effect is when the supervisor focuses too narrowly on a few peaks and valleys which might distort the overall evaluation.
5. Lenient grading is when the supervisor rates all subordinates toward the high end of the scale no matter what the actual performance.

6. Tough grading is when the supervisor rates the employees toward the low end of the scale.
7. Central grading occurs when the supervisors avoid rating their employees either very high or very low. Most employees are rated as average.

In contrast, increased participation on the part of the interviewee leads to increased job satisfaction and a higher level of performance. Specifically, Burke and Wilcox suggested that successful appraisal interviews have at least four characteristics [5, pp. 294-296]:

1. A high level of subordinate participation in the appraisal and development process.
2. A helpful and constructive attitude on the part of the supervisor.
3. The solution of job problems that may be hampering the subordinate's current job performance.
4. The mutual setting of specific goals to be achieved by subordinates in the future.

THEORIES RELATED TO APPRAISAL INTERVIEWS

Successful appraisal interviews depend upon how the two parties feel about each other prior to the interview. McGregor used Theory X and Theory Y to characterize two types of managers [6, pp. 33-34; 47-48]. As you read this section think about your present supervisor. Does your manager use a Theory X approach or a Theory Y approach? Does your manager use a Theory X approach for some employees and a Theory Y approach for other employees?

Theory X

The Theory X manager assumes:

1. Human beings have an inherent dislike of work and will avoid it when they can.
2. Because human beings dislike work, they must be coerced, controlled, directed, or threatened with punishment to get them to put forth adequate effort toward the achievement of organization objectives.
3. Human beings prefer to be directed, wish to avoid responsibility, have relatively little ambition, and want security above all.

Theory Y

In contrast, a Theory Y manager assumes:

1. The expenditure of physical and mental effort in work is as natural as play and rest.

2. Human beings will exercise self-direction and self-control in the service of objectives to which they are committed.

3. Commitment to objectives is a function of the awards associated with their objectives.

4. Human beings, under proper conditions, not only accept but seek responsibility.

5. The capacity to exercise a relatively high degree of imagination, ingenuity, and creativity in the solution of organizational problems is widely, not narrowly, distributed in the population.

6. Under the conditions of modern industrial life, the intellectual potentialities of average human beings are only partially utilized.

The differences between the Theory X and Theory Y manager are obvious. The Theory X manager creates a defensive climate by constantly evaluating, controlling, showing superiority and certainty. The Theory Y manager, on the other hand, creates a supportive climate and acts as a helper and problem-solver. In addition, the manager encourages upward communication and stimulates creative and constructive thinking, maintains a neutral position, and appraises the job and not the individual.

TYPES OF APPRAISAL INTERVIEWS

Interviewers can use a variety of methods to evaluate the performance of subordinates. The most common methods are tell-and-sell, tell-and-listen, problem-solving, and management-by-objectives. Since the primary purposes of the appraisal interview are to let employees know how they are doing in the workplace and to help develop and motivate the employees to higher standards, the interviewer needs to decide which method or methods are best for each employee. The personality of the interviewer and company policy will determine the method or methods that the interviewer will use to conduct the interview.

Now let's look at each of the methods. Which method or methods does your supervisor use? Which method do you prefer? If you are a supervisor which method or methods do you use to evaluate employees?

Tell-and-Sell

The tell-and-sell method is characterized by the supervisor preparing an appraisal, giving it to the employee, and trying to convince the employee it is valid. The interviewer uses no discussion, and, thus, the word interview is probably a poor label as the supervisor actually gives a speech to the employee. The interviewer simply informs the interviewee about his or her performance rating, and no opportunity is offered for input from the employee. The interviewer attempts to solve complex issues in a dictatorial, over simplistic manner which suggests "do it my way or else."

Maier indicated that the interviewer assumes the role of judge, communicates evaluation, and persuades employees to improve [1, pp. 4-5]. The interviewer assumes that the employee desires to correct weaknesses and profits from criticism and appreciates help. As Maier indicated [1, p. 8]:

> From the viewpoint of the company, it is an efficient method, providing it works. It takes less time to present an evaluation than to discuss one, and if the person accepts the presentation, a fairly complete interview can be covered in a matter of fifteen minutes.

The tell-and-sell method might work well with young or new employees, those who are inexperienced and insecure. It, however, might create passive resistance and verbal acceptance which might conceal the employee's anger. Remember that this is downward, one-way communication that creates "yes persons."

Tell-and-Listen

The tell-and-listen method is similar to the tell-and-sell method as the interviewer still plays the role of judge and communicates evaluation. In contrast, the supervisor encourages disagreement to discover the true feelings of the employee. The interviewee has an opportunity to release defensive feelings, and thus some upward communication does occur between the interviewer and interviewee. The method also rests on the theory of catharsis, that the verbal expression or release of frustration tends to reduce the feelings. Basically, the interviewer becomes a nondirective counselor during the second part of the interview. Remember that the interviewer still plays the role of judge, but provides an opportunity for the interviewee to express feelings.

Problem-Solving

The problem-solving method takes the interviewer out of the role of judge and makes him or her a helper. The interviewer might be described as a coach and mentor. By using the problem-solving method, the interviewer stimulates growth and development. Erhart, who has written exclusively about the problem-solving appraisal method, indicated change is essential to healthy growth [7, p. 239]. When using this method, the employee discusses job problems which can lead to improved performance. In addition, both parties listen carefully to each other, reflect on each other's responses, establish level 3 communication, and develop new ideas and mutual interests. Both parties talk about the same amount of time.

The problem-solving method stimulates both the interviewer and interviewee to communicate with each other. A dialogue occurs between the two parties. Through this dialogue the interviewee knows where strengths and weaknesses lie, and this awareness will help to improve understanding between the supervisor and subordinate. Both parties talk about the same amount of time.

Management-by-Objectives

When using the management-by-objective methods (MBO), the employee is evaluated by a predetermined set of objectives. This method helps to clarify written and oral appraisal duties. It is designed to measure and judge performance, to relate individual performance to organizational goals, to foster the increasing competence and growth of subordinates, and to enhance communication between superiors and subordinates. McGregor suggested that the manager and employee should jointly identify common goals and define each individual's major areas of responsibilities in terms of the results expected of the interviewee [6, pp. 47-48]. Overall, this method lets an employee know where he/she stands, makes clear what is expected, and encourages the employee to develop a plan for self-improvement.

Wexley and Klimoski indicated several advantages of behaviorally-based measures [8, p. 40]:

1. Can account for far more job complexity.
2. Relate more directly to what the employee actually does.
3. Minimize irrelevant factors not under the employee's control.
4. Facilitate explicit performance feedback and goal setting by encouraging meaningful employer-employee discussions regarding the employee's strengths and weaknesses.

As indicated in the introduction of this section, interviewers need to decide what method or methods they will use to control the appraisal interview. It might be that the manager will use different methods based on the type of job that is performed by the interviewee. For example, if the primary responsibilities of an employee are quantifiable, the interviewer might use the MBO method along with one of the other types of evaluation methods.

In contrast, suppose a writer is working on a specific type of manual in which there is a need to interact with a graphic designer, a page designer, a subject matter expert, and many other people. The supervisor might be more interested in the quality of manuals, and although a target date is important, it is not as important as in production work. Thus, the supervisor might use a problem-solving method to conduct the appraisal interview.

PREPARING FOR THE APPRAISAL INTERVIEW

Careful preparation is the key to a successful appraisal interview. Ideally, the interviewer will arrange a pre-interview meeting with the subordinate to request a prepared written evaluation of his/her performance. Specifically, both parties should be completely familiar with the interviewee's job description. The interviewer and interviewee will review records including memos, letters, directives, and written notes on various conversations concerning the subordinate's job performance. As both prepare for the interview by reviewing various types of documentation, they will be psychologically preparing for the interview. As a result, they should enter the interview prepared to review openly and honestly the job description, job objectives, and human relation factors. Now let's examine some specifics of the interviewee and interviewer roles.

Interviewee

Limited attention has been given to the role of the interviewee in a performance appraisal interview. The interviewee needs to develop a positive attitude about the interview. If the interviewee has had much contact with the interviewer throughout the appraisal period, then it should not be difficult to enter the appraisal interview with the idea that much benefit can occur from the critical review of the supervisor. Specifically, Stano suggested the following [9, pp. 13-14]:

1. Request help in handling problems.
2. Ask questions when something is not understood.
3. Freely take responsibility for failing to meet objectives.
4. Have materials well organized.
5. Express an interest in the welfare of the company.
6. Receive criticism without being defensive.
7. Speak openly and candidly.
8. Plan an active role in the interview and do a good share of the talking.
9. Willingly discuss problems and solutions to problems.
10. Self-analyze problems and try to determine ways in which objectives can be achieved.

Remember that communication skills are critical to successful interviews. In an interview be aware of your nonverbal, vocal, and verbal messages. If you have kept records, communicated frequently with your supervisor, and evaluated how you have met the objectives, you should enter the interview situation with a positive attitude about yourself. This positive attitude should help you to discuss your present job description and, perhaps, revise it based on the tasks you have or will be performing during the next appraisal period. Likewise, you will be able to play a more active role in developing your objectives for the next appraisal period.

Interviewer

Prior to conducting the interview the supervisor will assess the objectives, analyze their importance, and determine how effectively the subordinate has met them. A variety of forms can be used to assess the performance levels of the interviewees. For example, the Performance Appraisal Summary Form [10, p. 186], Figure 12, might be used to assess each objective.

Figure 13 and Figure 14 can be used to find out how subordinates feel about supervisors and supervisors feel about subordinates. Next the interviewer could

Objectives	Review key results	Rating (A-F)
1.		
2.		
3.		
4.		
5.		

Figure 12. Performance appraisal summary form (completed by both interviewer and interviewee). C. Stewart and W. Cash, *Interviewing: Principles and Practices,* Wm. C. Brown Publishers, Dubuque, Iowa, p. 186, 1988. Adaption of original materials by permission of Wm. C. Brown Publishers.

assess variables such as cooperation, ability to get tasks done, willingness to accept responsibility, and supervision. The interviewer could use an open-ended approach to the evaluation or a series of closed-ended questions. Here is how the interviewer might use open-ended and closed-ended questions to assess technical writers:

1. How effectively is the writer performing on the job?
2. What accounts for this performance?
3. What, if anything, should be done to increase this performance?
4. What is the writer's greatest strength?
5. What is the writer's greatest weakness?
6. Has the writer responded well to supervision?
7. Did the writer make a contribution to the productivity of his or her work unit?
8. Is the writer innovative?
9. Did the writer show leadership?
10. Does the writer get along well with his or her peers?

Please indicate your level of agreement with the following statement about your supervisor: 5=strongly agree, 4=agree, 3=uncertain, 2=disagree, and 1=strongly disagree.

_____ My relationship with my immediate supervisor is satisfying.
_____ I trust my immediate supervisor.
_____ My immediate supervisor listens to me.
_____ My immediate supervisor praises me for a good job.
_____ I trust my co-workers.
_____ My co-workers get along with each other.
_____ My relationship with my co-workers is satisfying.
_____ I have a say in decisions that affect my job.
_____ I influence operations in my unit and department.
_____ I have a part in accomplishing my organizational goals.

Figure 13. Writer's assessment of supervisor, co-workers and workplace. B. Spikes and T. Daniels, Information Adequacy and Communication Relationships: An Empirical Examination of 18 Organizations, *The Western Journal of Speech Communication, 45*, p. 351, 1981. Reprint by permission of the Western Speech Communication Association.

Please indicate your level of agreement with the following statements about your subordinates: 5=strongly agree, 4=agree, 3=uncertain, 2=disagree and 1=strongly disagree.

_____ My relationship with my subordinates is satisfying.
_____ I trust my subordinates.
_____ My subordinates understand the job.
_____ My relationship with other supervisors is satisfying.
_____ Subordinates have a say in decisions that affect their job.
_____ Subordinates have a part in accomplishing organization goals.

Figure 14. Supervisor's assessment of subordinates. B. Spikes and T. Daniels, Information Adequacy and Communication Relationships: An Empirical Examination of 18 Organizations, *The Western Journal of Speech Communication, 45*, p. 351, 1981. Reprint by permission of the Western Speech Communication Association.

In summary, before the scheduled interview, both the interviewer and interviewee will independently evaluate the interviewee's job performance, attitudes toward his or her job, supervisory skills and future potential.

CONDUCTING THE APPRAISAL INTERVIEW

Based on the evaluation of the subordinate, the supervisor will decide the appraisal method or methods to use in conducting the interview, will structure the interview guide, and will develop questions. Because both parties have completed an extensive pre-interview evaluation, they should be prepared to listen carefully to each other, provide feedback to each other, and reflect the feelings of each other. Now let's look more critically at the opening, body and conclusion of the actual interview.

Opening

The purposes of the opening are to gain rapport and to provide an orientation for the interview. The interviewer will assume a leadership role and schedule the time and place for the interview. Naturally, the interviewer should establish a supportive climate. Assuming appropriate coaching has occurred throughout the review period and appropriate planning has been completed for the interview, limited rapport building should be needed. Both parties may communicate at level 3. Next the interviewer should explain how the interview will be conducted. For example, the interviewer might indicate that they will discuss major accomplishments, areas that need to be improved, performance areas in which the writer generally receives praise, and performance areas in which the writer receives criticism. Obviously, the opening will depend upon the relationship between the interviewer and interviewee, the personalities of the two parties, and the purpose of the interview.

Body

During the body of the interview the two parties will review the results and plan for the next appraisal period. Since both parties have completed independent evaluations of the interviewee, they can check on areas of agreement and disagreement. Let's assume that the interviewer is using problem-solving and management-by-objective methods to conduct the interview. In the beginning the interviewer will ask open-ended questions such as "What are some reasons you were unable to meet the time schedule on the manual?" and "How can we make sure that the time scheduling problem won't happen again?" Throughout the interview the interviewer will use reflective, mirror, and clearinghouse probes, as well as additional open-ended questions.

In contrast, if the interviewer decided to use the tell-and-sell method, he/she would do all the talking. As indicated earlier the interviewee plays a passive role. Assuming that this is the first appraisal interview, the supervisor might use the tell-and-listen method. The interviewer will provide an overview of the interviewee's performance and give the interviewee an opportunity to share information. Remember that this method can be used successfully if the interviewer has been providing informal feedback on the subordinate's performance throughout the appraisal period.

Closing

In closing, the interviewer should provide a review of the appraisal session. It is important to end the session on a positive note. The interviewer should create a final impression that tells the interviewee to "come and see me once a week or when necessary." The interviewer also should review the up-dated job description and job objectives.

DISCIPLINARY INTERVIEWS

Disciplinary interviews are conducted when employees fail to meet performance standards, fail to adhere to company policies or regulations, or fail to maintain a proper attitude.

The interviewer should assess several factors prior to deciding to conduct a disciplinary interview. For example, to discipline because of race, color, sex, national origin, ancestry, religion, and physical handicap is unlawful. The interviewer also needs to be certain of the facts of the case.

Research indicates that formal disciplinary interviews are not conducted very often. In fact, only one technical writer that was surveyed indicated that he had participated in a disciplinary interview. Generally, the supervisor will conduct a problem-solving interview to tell the interviewee the responsibilities for the job. If this meeting is unsuccessful, an oral warning should be given to the employee. Next, a written warning should be given. Finally, the interviewer should tell the interviewee that a disciplinary interview will be conducted.

PLANNING AND CONDUCTING THE DISCIPLINARY INTERVIEW

According to Zima, the person who conducts disciplinary interviews should 1) establish objectives, 2) prepare documentation, 3) prepare the opening, 4) develop an effective body, 5) prepare the closing, and 6) conduct a post-interview evaluation [11, p. 283].

Establish Objectives

A great deal of critical thinking should go into establishing the objectives for the disciplinary interview. If steps and procedures have been established by company policy or union contract, the interviewer should follow them. If not, the interviewer should attempt to show a relationship between the offense and the penalty. The interviewee should be given answers to the following questions:

1. What did I do wrong?
2. Why was it wrong?
3. What is the penalty?
4. Why is it fair?
5. What will happen if I do it again?
6. What can I do to improve my performance of behavior?

Documentation

Managers will prepare for the disciplinary interview by gathering information. That is, the manager will review the interviewee's previous job records, appraisal statements, and policies and procedures that relate to the offense. For example, let's say Mary was being disciplined for arguing with other writers about how the final draft of a manual should look in terms of layout, page design, white space, and graphics. A review of Mary's records indicates that several co-workers had talked to their supervisor about her behaviors, and the supervisor had recorded this information and discussed the specific complaints with her at her last appraisal interview.

Documentation is important as a discipline action is based on fact. Thus, documentation should help the supervisor plan the interview and help the interviewer be more objective when conducting the interview.

Opening

Prior to the interview the interviewee must know why the interview is being conducted. As in all face-to-face interviews, verbal, nonverbal, and vocal messages are extremely important. As the interviewer you need to prepare each of these messages so that a frank and candid discussion will occur. Remember that in a disciplinary interview, not an exit interview, you are trying to solve a specific problem, and your ultimate goal might be to reach level 3 communication. You, however, will begin the interview in a formal manner. For example, "Mary, I've called you in to discuss your communication style when interacting with co-workers in your work group." You might suggest that you are aware of tensions that members of writing groups experience, state your desire to be objective by discussing interpersonal problems between other writers and her, and stress your willingness to listen to all viewpoints on all aspects of the case.

Body

The disciplinary interview is highly directive as the interviewer needs to maintain control of the interview. In some cases, when rapport can be established, a problem-solving approach can be used to discuss specific problems.

Zima suggests the following steps when conducting the disciplinary interview [11, pp. 286-287]:

1. Tell the employee the behavior is not acceptable and why it is not acceptable.
2. Let the employee state the case.
3. Explain the penalty you are imposing and why.
4. Explain precisely what will happen if the behavior continues.
5. Advise the employee of what can be done to improve or change his/her performance or behavior.

Closing

The supervisor or personnel director should attempt to end the disciplinary interview in a positive manner. Convey to the employee that you will evaluate future behavior, not past performance.

Post-Interview Evaluation

After participating in a disciplinary interview, both parties should complete a self-assessment. Zima suggests that the interviewer should answer the following questions [11, p. 288]:

1. Was the interview conducted in private?
2. Did I listen to the interviewee state the case?
3. Did I criticize the behavior, not the person?
4. Was I certain of my facts?
5. Did I remain calm?

The interviewee should ask the following questions:

1. Did I have a chance to state my case?
2. Did the interviewer listen to me?
3. Did the interviewer focus on the problem?
4. Do I feel better as a result of this experience?
5. Will I be judged by my future behavior?

SUMMARY

This chapter has focused on appraisal and disciplinary interviews. Most employees, no matter what their position in an organization, participate as interviewees in appraisal interviews at least once a year. In contrast, only a small percentage of employees participate in disciplinary interviews. Both the appraisal and disciplinary interviews are important, but only a small percentage of managers have been trained to conduct these types of interviews. In addition, few employees have had training to participate as interviewees in appraisal and disciplinary interviews.

QUESTIONS

Appraisal Cases

For each of the following cases complete the following questions:

1. How would you prepare to interview the technical writer?
2. Would you use Theory X or Theory Y? Why?
3. What appraisal method or methods would you use? Why?
4. How would you prepare if you were the interviewee?

Case 1—John Techwrite has worked on one project during this appraisal period. He has had some difficulty in completing his work on time. John is somewhat introverted, and other writers tend to take advantage of him so that he sometimes does not only his work, but also the work of other writers.

Case 2—Georgia Toogood, another writer, working on the same team as John, has performed well during this appraisal period, but has a tendency to dominate the work discussion meeting. She writes well and has met all of her objectives.

Case 3—According to Bill's co-workers, he has a good background in graphics and has developed excellent graphics for this same project. Unfortunately, the engineers don't like graphics.

Disciplinary Cases

For each of the disciplinary cases, please answer the following questions:

1. How would you prepare to interview the technical writer?
2. Would you use a Theory X or Theory Y approach?
3. Would you allow the employee to explain his or her case?
4. What penalty would you impose? Why?

Case 1—Terry is the editor for the writing project. She has been with the company for two years and overall has done an excellent job of editing several manuals. Unfortunately, she has not done well on this project and has refused to make editorial changes recommended by her supervisor. You have informally discussed with her the insubordination and her abrasive personality. You also have warned her both in oral and written form about these problems.

Case 2—Bob is an excellent writer, but he has a tendency to report to work an hour late every morning. You have talked to him about this problem, and he informed you that he is not a morning person, but that he will try to make it to work on time. Unfortunately, he has not done so, and as a result, other writers have had to wait for him to complete his part of the job.

Case 3—Marie is a perfectionist. She tends to be very picky about everyone's work. Her perfectionism has caused some human relation problems with her co-workers. You have discussed this problem with her, but other writers are still complaining about her.

AN APPRAISAL INTERVIEW FOR REVIEW AND ANALYSIS

Below is a description of an appraisal interview for review and analysis. Identify the appraisal methods used by the interviewer. What type of opening did he use? What type of opening would you use to begin the interview? What type of closing did he use? What type of closing would you use to end the interview? What types of questions does the interviewer use? What type of questions would you use? How would you change the way the interview was conducted? Given this situation, would you use a tell-and-sell, tell-and-listen, problem-solving or management-by-objective appraisal method? Rewrite the dialogue of the interview if you feel the method used by the interviewer is inappropriate.

Character Description

Harry Brown (manager) is a middle-aged publication manager for the Good Writers Company. Harry started as an editor in the company and after three years was promoted to a writer where he worked as part of a writing team and as lead writer for 10 years. For the past four years he has been the publication manager.

Joann Dunne (employee) has been a writer in the company for four years. She has a bachelor's degree in Technical Communication. She completed an internship at this company and was hired because of her excellent writing skills.

Manager: (To the Phone) Okay Jones, Yeah, I hear ya. . . . Sit down, Joann. Now listen, Jones, get that summary to me by five, and I don't want to hear any more excuses!

(Mumbles to himself) The help these days . . . where do they find them . . . (turns to Joann). Okay, Joann, let's see what we have here (Shuffles paper on desk and then shows her a copy of her performance appraisal). Did you get a copy of this?

Employee: Ahhh, no, Mr. Brown, I don't think so.

Manager: Incompetent secretaries . . . Well let's get on with it anyway. You're here for your annual appraisal. You've been here for two years now, so you know the ropes.

Employee: Well, I think I do, yes.

Manager: Fine. It says here on your appraisal that you completed fewer manuals than the previous year. Sounds like you're slowing down, Dunne. There also is a note from the lead writer of your present project saying your work is substandard.

The little mistakes you have made on some of the manuals this year have cost us a pretty penny. (stares at Joann) Not so good is it, Dunne?

Employee: Well, Mr. Brown, you know with the cutbacks in staff that you've made . . .

Manager: (interrupts) Not when the burden of proof is on you, Dunne. (points at Dunne). Maybe you should have told me about the problems with the other writers before now. You should have dealt with any possible problems before you began feeling your oats. Now what are you going to do to resolve your problems with co-workers?

Employee: Mr. Brown I must say that I am really surprised at this appraisal. I've been a loyal, faithful employee at this company for the past four years, and I turned down a job at the XYZ Writing Company because of the friendly and professional climate here. I'm sorry you are disappointed with my performance.

Manager: Now don't get me wrong, Joann. You're not a bad employee. But there are some things you've got to do. You've got to make some attitude changes. Either you start completing your part of the writing project on time, or you will be replaced on the project. Stop inventing trouble. Work harder at getting along with co-workers. Take more initiative, especially with the new writers. Assume a leadership role on the present project. Do these things and everything will work out fine. If you don't, I guarantee you, there will be trouble.

Employee: Well, all right, Mr. Brown. I'll try.

REFERENCES

1. N. Maier, *The Appraisal Interview: Objectives, Methods, and Skills*, John Wiley and Son, Inc., New York, 1966.
2. H. Heneman, Research Roundup, *Personnel Administrator, 20*, pp. 61-64, 1981.
3. R. Schuler, Taking the Pain out of the Performance Appraisal Interview, *Supervisory Management, 26*, pp. 8-13, 1981.
4. J. Conant, The Performance Appraisal: A Critique and Alternative, *Business Horizons*, pp. 73-78, 1973.
5. R. Burke and D. Wilcox, Characteristics of Effective Performance Appraisal Reviews and Development Interviews, *Personnel Psychology, 22*, pp. 291-305, 1969.
6. D. McGregor, *The Human Side of Enterprise*, McGraw-Hill Book Company, New York, 1960.
7. J. Erhart, The Performance Appraisal Interview and Evaluation of Student Performances in Speech Communication Courses, *Communication Education, 25*, pp. 237-245, 1976.
8. K. Wexley and R. Klimoski, Performance Appraisal: An Up-Date, *Research in Personnel and Human Resource Management, 2*, pp. 35-79, 1984.

9. M. Stano, Guidelines for the Interviewee in Performance Appraisal Interview, Paper presented at the International Communication Association Convention, San Francisco, California, 1984.

10. C. Stewart and W. Cash, *Interviewing: Principles and Practices*, Wm. C. Brown Publishers, Dubuque, Iowa, 1988.

11. J. Zima, *Interviewing: Key to Effective Management*, Science Research Associates, Chicago, 1983.

CHAPTER 7

Exit Interviews

OBJECTIVES

On completion of this chapter you should be able to:
- Understand the importance of voluntary and involuntary exit interviews
- Understand the importance of the role of the interviewer and interviewee in the exit interview
- Explain how to prepare for the voluntary and involuntary exit interviews
- Develop openings and closings for voluntary and involuntary interviews
- Develop interview guides for the voluntary and involuntary exit interviews
- Analyze exit interviews
- Conduct information-gathering interviews on the uses of exit interviews

The exit interview provides employees with an opportunity to express their reasons for leaving an organization. The interviewer will gather information from the exiting interviewees to finalize housekeeping chores, to determine why the employees are leaving, to try to create goodwill for the company, and, in some cases, try to persuade an employee to stay. Sherwood indicated that the formal exit interview is one of the best ways to find out where personnel, operating, and employee relation problems exist, as well as what attitudes employees hold about their jobs, management, and the company itself [1, p. 744]. For example, in Chapter 1, Bill was having an exit interview with the Director of Personnel when Mary was being interviewed for the new position. The interviewer's objective was to gather information from Bill because he was a good writer and the company wanted to determine the real reasons he was leaving. This chapter focuses on types of exit interviews, preparing the exit interview, and conducting the exit interview.

TYPES OF EXIT INTERVIEWS

Voluntary

There are positive and negative reasons for leaving a position. Common positive reasons include finding a better job with better working conditions and, perhaps, more money. For example, suppose that one of your goals is to become a

117

manager, and you discover that an opening exists at another company where you would be offered more leadership responsibility, better desktop publishing facilities, and more money. These might be viewed as positive reasons for leaving a company. Other positive reasons might be the transfer of a spouse, desire for further education, desire for other responsibilities not included as part of your present position and retirement. (See Figure 15.)

In contrast, some employees might resign from their positions and not state the real reasons for leaving. Thus, it is important to establish rapport with the interviewees before focusing on the real reasons they have decided to resign from their positions. Sherwood's research supported the idea that interviewees feel that they

---

29 July 1990

Mr. L. David Schuelke
Personnel Director
Good Writers Company
7009 W. 83rd St.
Minneapolis, Minnesota 55348

Dear Mr. Schuelke:

I have been a writer and an editor for the past three years at the Good Writers Company. I have enjoyed working here. I have increased my writing and editing skills by working with quality people.

I have spent the last three months thinking about and writing down my long term goals. Basically they include being a director of publication for a large company. Approximately one month ago I applied to the XYZ Writers Company for a job as a lead writer for Project Sunrise. I interviewed for, and have been offered the position. This is to inform you that I am resigning my position here at Good Writers Company effective September 30, 1990.

Thank you for hiring me as a writer. I have increased my writing skills and my self-esteem.

Sincerely,

William E. Smith
:ms

Figure 15. Letter of resignation.

have nothing to hide when they resign from a position, and, thus, will tell the truth [1, pp. 744-746], whereas Dessler's research revealed that exiting employees are not honest [2, p. 9]. Dessler's study reported that salary and benefits were listed as the two reasons most employees leave a job. However, in a follow-up study eighteen months later, supervision was listed as the primary reason. To increase the probability that the exiting employees tell the truth, interviews should be conducted by people trained and experienced in personnel training. Exit interviews should be set up independently from the employees' work unit as well as from any other department except those concerned with personnel administration.

Involuntary

Generally, technical communicators would not be terminated on the spur of the moment. Rather they would be counseled, receive written reprimands, have an opportunity to appeal, and be given final warnings before being terminated. In addition, prior to final termination the fired employee probably would have taken part in counseling and disciplinary interviews.

There are several types of involuntary exits. First, unsatisfactory performance might be a reason for termination. For example, a writer might have difficulty in understanding technical material and, thus, cannot write it in a lucid matter. Another example is that the writer might find it difficult to work as a member of a team and, thus, causes interpersonal problems among members of the writing group. After appropriate warnings the employee might be fired.

A second reason for dismissal is that the writer is guilty of insubordination. For example, a writer might continually challenge the credibility of the lead writer or publication manager. If the supervisor has provided appropriate warning, the employee might be terminated.

Other reasons for termination might be reorganization of the company, layoffs, mergers, and forced retirement. For the past ten years many companies have provided outplacement assistance to employees who have been terminated due to layoffs, mergers, and reorganization.

PREPARING FOR THE EXIT INTERVIEW

Administrative and fact-finding are the two phases of the exit interview—Michal-Johnson indicates that both are important to prepare to conduct a voluntary or involuntary exit interview [3, p. 76]. The administrative phase covers details of housekeeping chores, such as severance pay, vested pension rights, insurance, other entitlements, and documents that must be signed. The interviewer will use the directive approach or information-giving method to conduct this phase of the interview. During the information-giving phase of the interview, the interviewee might ask questions such as:

1. What benefits will I receive?
2. When do I get my last paycheck?
3. When do I turn in all of my keys, library card, etc.?
4. When do I turn in my company car?
5. How will the information that I give you be used?

The fact-finding phase is very important for the voluntary exit interview. The interviewer should prepare for the interview by reviewing a current job description, personal history, work performance, performance evaluations, list of previous projects, and any other information. For example, let's examine Bill's current job description:

> Interview subject matter experts and write technical manuals using the desktop publishing system. Edit other manuals and conduct usability studies on manuals.

After reviewing all of the information available on the employee, the interviewer will need to develop the exit scheduling procedures and design an interview format that corresponds to the needs of the company. Remember that the interview guide should be standardized so that the company can group various types of data. The interviewer wants to create a favorable lasting impression of the company. To accomplish this, Dorst, Obrien and Marsh point out seven steps to better exit interviews [4, pp. 107-109]:

1. Start with the assumption that open and honest responses will not be easily obtained.
2. Conduct the interview a day or two before the interviewee leaves.
3. Use skilled interviewers, preferably from the personnel department.
4. Conduct the interview at the work site in a comfortable environment free of interruptions.
5. Assure the employee that individual names will not be associated with information shared during the interview.
6. Use a structured interview format.
7. Use questions on the interview questionnaire that are open-ended and allow for deeper probing.

Basically, the interviewer should be attentive, pleasant, and neutral in order to find out the real reasons the employee is leaving and to determine the perceptions the employee has about the company and work environment.

Areas of Concern

The interviewer also should be concerned about seven general areas: establishing rapport, stating the purpose of the interview, discussing characteristics of the old job, explaining reasons for leaving, comparing the old and the new, recommending revisions in the old job, and conducting the interview.

Establishing rapport — The type of exit interview might determine the rapport level between the interviewer and interviewee. For example, if it is a voluntary exit interview where the interviewee has positive perceptions of the company, the interviewer should be able to establish rapport without much difficulty. If it is an involuntary exit interview, it could be difficult to establish rapport. Remember that rapport building begins when the appointment is made and continues until the end of the interview.

Purpose of the interview — The interviewer will need to orient the interviewee about the purpose and procedures to be followed during the interview. The interviewer will develop a moderately scheduled interview guide and use both open-ended and closed-ended questions to maximize the results of the interview. In an involuntary exit interview where the interviewer might have been fired, the interviewer will ask primarily closed-ended questions and focus on administrative details. Remember that the interviewer needs to be skilled at taking notes as most interviewees would not operate at level 3 if they were being tape-recorded.

Discuss characteristics of the old job — The interviewer is interested in Bill's perceptions of his old job. For example, the interviewer wants to know what Bill likes and dislikes about his job. Based on a review of Bill's file and communication with Bill's supervisor and co-workers, the interviewer will prepare an interview schedule to find out Bill's perceptions of the old job and how it might be improved. During an involuntary exit interview in which the interviewee is hostile, the interviewer might not discuss this part.

Explore reasons for leaving — The interviewer has read Bill's letter of resignation which spelled out his reasons for leaving the company. Using this information, the interviewer will explore if there is any way that he would stay with the Good Writers Company. Identifying the reasons that Bill is leaving is an essential part of the interview. By discovering what conditions, incompatibility with supervisors, and salary motivated the decision, the company might make changes to avoid losing good writers in the future. In addition, as the interviewee self-discloses, the interviewer might feel that the interviewee really does not want to leave or at least has doubts about leaving, and, thus, will try to persuade the exiting employee to stay. For example, his verbal communication might indicate that Bill is excited about his new position, but his nonverbal and paraverbal messages suggest that he still has reservations about the decision to leave. If this were the case, the interviewer might try to persuade the interviewee to stay.

Comparing the old and the new — The interviewer wants to determine the positives and negatives of the old and new job. If Bill gives primarily factual data, it means that he thought carefully before making the decision to change positions. This area would not be discussed in an involuntary exit interview.

Recommending revisions in the old job — This area obviously is related to reasons for leaving. In this area the interviewer treats Bill as an authority on his job and seeks information that will improve the position. Recommending revisions in the old job would be optional in an involuntary exit interview. If the interviewee is somewhat hostile during this phase of the interview, the interviewer might not discuss this part with the interviewee.

Concluding the interview — The objective is to create a favorable lasting impression. The interviewer might select several closing techniques. A statement of appreciation and making personal inquiries are two of the best ways to close a voluntary exit interview. If it is an involuntary exit interview, using a clearinghouse question and declaring the completion of the purpose or task are two effective ways to conclude the interview.

After reviewing the exiting employee's materials and general ideas for conducting the interview, the interviewer will develop an interview guide. Below is an example of a voluntary exit interview guide. Zima indicated that the guide covers both administrative and fact-finding phases of the interview [5, pp. 354-358]. The interviewer will use both the directive and nondirective methods to conduct the interview. The interviewer will use the directive method at the beginning, but the nondirective method in gathering information on the company, salary, reasons for leaving, and work environment. The interviewer is hopeful that appropriate rapport building will lead to level 3 communication.

Interview Guide (voluntary)

  I. Administrative Chores
     A. Benefits
     B. Policies and Procedures
     C. Company Property
 II. Company
     A. Impressions of Company
     B. Type of Writing
     C. Recommended Changes
III. Salary
     A. Appraisal System
     B. Salary
     C. Benefits
 IV. Reasons for Leaving
     A. Why
     B. Advantages of New Writing Position
  V. Work Environment
     A. Evaluate Supervisor
     B. Evaluate Co-workers

In contrast, if this is an involuntary exit interview, the interviewer might just discuss the administrative chores if the interviewee is somewhat hostile. If, on the other hand, the interviewee is willing to provide information on the company and work environment, the interviewer should listen to the interviewee's information. The interviewer will use primarily the directive method. Michal-Johnson stressed in her book, *Saying Goodbye: A Manager's Guide to Employee Dismissal* [3, pp. 30-31], that exit interviews are sometimes conducted by managers and suggested the following checklist to help prepare for the exit interviews:

1. Termination interviews must be conducted in a private setting.
2. Termination interviews should be avoided on holidays.
3. Termination interviews should be avoided on Friday afternoons as the employee has the entire weekend to become upset.
4. Double check the frequency with which you counseled, warned, and evaluated the employee. Include dates and time.
5. Plan the interview, including the opening, the middle, and the closing.
6. Treat the person who is losing the job with dignity, even though they might not be willing to reciprocate.
7. Anticipate as many reactions to termination as possible, remembering who the terminee is. Prepare yourself for loud outbursts, arguments, silence, tears, and disbelief.
8. Do not offer the exiting employee advise on how to handle the firing.
9. Keep the interview short. Long drawn-out termination interviews prolong the agony and pain for both parties involved.
10. Carefully evaluate the advisability of terminating.

CONDUCTING THE EXIT INTERVIEW

Conducting the Voluntary Exit Interview

How you conduct the exit interview will depend on whether the termination is voluntary or involuntary. As indicated in the interview guide, the interviewer will generally use a directive method at the beginning of the interview and will tell the interviewee the reasons for the interview and how it will be conducted. Remember that the primary objective of the exit interview is to obtain perceptions of the company from employees who have nothing to lose. The interviewer should begin with "I" or "me" or "we" statements. Now let's examine how the director of personnel might open the interview if it is a voluntary exit.

> **Interviewer:** Bill, thanks for coming in today. Our records show that you have been a writer here for three years and have always received positive appraisal reviews. I enjoyed reviewing your materials. Now, I would like to ask you some questions about our company. The information that you share with me will be held in

confidence. (The overall objective is to allow Bill to tell his story. You are interested in the feelings of the exiting employee as well as the content.)

INTERVIEW SCHEDULE

Housekeeping Duties (a checklist)

_____ Earned Vacation Pay
_____ Identification Cards
_____ Passes and Badges
_____ Keys
_____ Manuals
_____ Word Processing Equipment
_____ Credit Cards
_____ Name and Address of New Employer
_____ Other

The Work

1. What were your first impressions of our company?
2. What was your favorite aspect of the job?
3. What else did you like about this job?
4. What did you like least about the job?
5. How satisfied were you with the word processors?
6. Did you like the type of work you were doing?
7. What are some improvements we could make in this position?
8. Were your job responsibilities clearly communicated?
9. Were you properly trained to do your job?
10. Did you feel that our company was interested in you?

Salary

1. What are your views on our appraisal system?
2. Was the appraisal system fair?
3. How do you feel about our fringe benefit package?
4. Were you satisfied with your salary?

Reasons for Leaving

1. Why have you decided to leave our company?
2. Is there any way we could persuade you to stay?
3. What recommendations do you have for improving this position?
4. Do you think co-workers share your views?
5. Would you consider working for us again?

6. What do you consider as the advantages of your new position over your position with us?
7. Do you consider your new position a promotion?
8. What made you start to look for a job outside of our company?

Work Environment

1. How would you evaluate your supervisor?
2. How could supervision be improved?
3. What would you like to tell your supervisor?
4. How did you feel about your co-workers?

Persuade the Interviewee to Stay

1. What if we were to offer to transfer you to another writing department?
2. Would you consider additional training on the desktop publishing system?
3. Would a 10 percent raise persuade you to stay?
4. Would you stay if we made you the lead writer on a new project?

Perhaps you might ask if the interviewee has any final questions and finish on a positive note.

> **Interviewer:** Bill, do you have any final questions? I'd like to thank you for coming in. As I indicated at the beginning, we feel fortunate to have had you as part of our writing staff. I can understand your desire for more responsibility. We wish you well. We will have leadership positions available in a few months. If you decide to switch jobs again, keep us in mind.

(Both appeared relaxed as both were smiling, showed good eye contact and facial expressions, and were leaning forward as they shook hands.) This example appears to be an effective way to conclude the interview. The interviewer complemented Bill, and both should feel good about themselves as well as the company. Level 3 communication probably occurred during this interview.

Conducting the Involuntary Exit Interview

Now let's suppose that Bill was fired from the position. The Good Writers Company might still be interested in conducting an exit interview. The approach to this interview, however, would be quite different. One of the objectives is to try to create good will, but the primary objective is to complete processing of the employee.

The interviewer who conducts an involuntary exit interview uses the directive method. The interview is generally short and concise—perhaps a total of 15 to 20 minutes. Typically the interviewee experienced counseling and disciplinary interviews prior to the exit interview. Appropriate record keeping should supply the interviewer with enough documentation so that the interview summarizes the reasons for the firing and explains that the decision is irreversible. The termination might be a result of absenteeism, tardiness, dishonesty, rules violation, insubordination, incompetence, or alcoholism. The introduction might be short and contain limited information.

> **Interviewer**: Bill, thanks for coming in to see me. I know your last few months here have been unhappy, and I know you probably have negative feelings about your supervisor and, in general, about this company. As you know, the decision to terminate your employment with us is irreversible. I'd like to cover the administrative details of your exiting, and ask you some questions about our company and work environment.

(The interviewer looks at Bill as he states the introduction; he is sincere. Bill, in contrast, looks at the floor and desk—appears tense.)

Interview Schedule

_____ Earned Vacation Pay
_____ Identification Cards
_____ Passes and Badges
_____ Keys
_____ Manuals
_____ Word Processing Equipment
_____ Credit Cards
_____ Name and Address of the New Employer
_____ Other

Work

1. What is your impression of our company? (note that the interviewer is interested in the present)
2. What did you like most about your job?
3. What did you like least about your job?

The interviewer will probably ask closed-ended questions such as: Were your job responsibilities clearly communicated? Were you properly trained to do your job? Did you feel that our company was interested in you? The interviewer is interested in closing the interview in a positive manner.

> **Interviewer**: Thanks, again, Bill. I realize this has been difficult for you, and I want to thank you for coming in today. I want you to stop to see Vicki concerning our outplacement counseling. We have hired Writing Dynamics to help exiting employees find new jobs. Vicki will explain the services available to you. I hope you find an excellent writing position.

(Both appear more relaxed at the end of the interview, and Bill seems interested in Writing Dynamics as it provides details on preparing cover letters and resumes and provides a search of various regional and national companies who are hiring writers.)

TECHNICAL COMMUNICATION STUDENTS' EXIT INTERVIEWS

Exit interviews can be used to obtain students perceptions of their internship experiences, as well as perceptions of their technical communication program. For example, graduating students in the undergraduate and graduate technical communication programs at the University of Minnesota were asked the following [6, pp.RET-62-53]:

1. How helpful was your advisor in assisting you in deciding on appropriate course work?
2. How knowledgeable was your advisor about current requirements for the technical communication program?
3. What three technical communication courses did you like best? Least?
4. How important was your technical elective?
5. How satisfied were you with your internship experience?
6. How satisfied were you with the quality of instruction?

This type of feedback is important for Technical Communication Departments. Because students conducted the interviews and students were told the information was confidential, the results appear to be reliable and valid. By using the exit interview method with students, the director of our program and faculty members can revise the major to meet the needs of students.

POST EXIT INTERVIEW EVALUATION

Immediately after conducting the exit interview, the interviewer should complete a post-interview evaluation. The interviewer might answer each of the following questions with a "yes" or "no":

1. Was the writer interested in his job?
2. Was the writer interested in the company?
3. Did the writer understand the job?
4. Did the writer show good judgement about the job?
5. Did the writer show initiative?
6. Was the writer industrious?
7. Was the writer reliable?
8. Did the writer work well with others?
9. Would the writer be interested in working for us again?
10. Did I create a favorable lasting impression?

SUMMARY

This chapter has focused on the exit interview. Exit interviews should be used to discover why employees have decided to leave an organization and to determine the real reasons why employees have been terminated. This chapter has discussed how to prepare and conduct voluntary and involuntary exit interviews. Now read the Exit Interview for Review and Analysis and answer the questions.

AN EXIT INTERVIEW FOR REVIEW AND ANALYSIS

The exit interview is an important source of information for writing companies. Now let's look at how the interviewer conducted parts of both the voluntary and involuntary exit interview. The introductions and closings have already been covered. Would you have done them differently? If yes, how? As you read the dialogue, think about how you would do them differently. How would you prepare to conduct a voluntary exit interview? an involuntary exit interview? How would you reach level 3 communication? Would you use more closed-ended questions when conducting the voluntary exit interview or the involuntary exit interview?

Voluntary Exit Interview

Interviewer: First, I'd like to ask you, what were your first impressions of our company? (looking directly at Bill).

Bill: As I told Tom (my supervisor) during my first review, this is a great place to work. I remember the friendliness of all of the other writers. This made me feel at home, and, quite frankly, this friendliness has made me a more confident writer.

Interviewer: That's great to hear! This has been our plan during the orientation to the company. I also understand that you have displayed this same friendliness to new writers. Thanks! I'd like to go on with the next question. What was your favorite aspect of this job? (both appear relaxed)

Bill: I liked working with the graphic designers. They are so competent and so eager to build visuals that will reinforce the writing. (Bill smiles throughout this period. Goodwill prevails throughout the discussion on the work and salary areas.)

Interviewer: Now I'd like to discuss your reasons for leaving. I know that this is more personal, but the company can use your input to help improve your current position with us. Bill, why have you decided to leave?

Bill: That's a good question and one which I have thought about for several weeks. As you know based on our earlier discussion, I like it here, but feel this is a good career move. I think that I have good leadership skills, and they have improved by being part of such a fine group of writers. Now, I feel that I am ready to assume a greater leadership role. (Bill is very sincere.)

Interviewer: Thank you for your candor. Now I want to ask you the most difficult question. Is there any way we could persuade you to stay? (The interviewer looks directly at Bill. Bill breaks eye contact momentarily.)

Bill: I have thought of this question. As I indicated before I think this is a good career move. I certainly would consider returning to this company, but now I think that this is the best possible career move I could make. (Bill is very serious using appropriate facial expressions and a sincere voice.)

The dialogue continues in a friendly manner throughout the interview. The closing, which was stated earlier, ends the interview in a positive manner.

Involuntary Exit Interview

Interviewer: Now that we have finished with the household chores, I'd like to ask you a few questions. I know you must be as mad as hell, but we still value your feedback. What are some of the things you like about your position? (The interviewer attempts to look at Bill, but looks primarily at the floor. Bill looks defensive; his arms are crossed and he is looking at the floor).

Bill: Well, I'm not sure what to say. As you know, I worked on a number of writing projects. I felt that I worked better with younger writers who had undergraduate degrees in technical communication. You also know that I was twice the employee of the month when I worked on projects with younger writers. (Bill seems more relaxed as though he is sharing a very special moment with the interviewer.)

Interviewer: Thanks! I recall when you were named the employee of the month. Unfortunately, the past two years have been difficult for you. Why was it so difficult to work with engineers?

Bill: Well as Rodney Dangerfield would say, "I don't get no respect." When I first went to the division, I felt I would be treated as a peer. Several of the engineers were defensive with me. As you know, I have a temper. I really didn't mean to tell Harold that he is incompetent. I didn't react very well to the stress of the situation. (Bill appears somewhat reluctant to elaborate on this answer and stops talking.)

Interviewer: Now I'd like to ask you some closed questions. Bill, when you first came did you feel our company was really interested in you?

Bill: Yes I did.

Interviewer: Did you feel that our company was interested in you this year?

Bill: Definitely not. None of my supervisors would listen to my concerns. (Bill speaks forcefully when making this statement.)

Interviewer: I'd like to ask a question about your position. Were your job responsibilities clearly communicated?

Bill: Definitely not. I was not given a new job description. I tried to meet with my supervisor four times during the first two weeks, but he was too busy. I was on my own—It was like the "blind leading the blind."

Interviewer: I have one more question. Were you properly trained to do your job?

Bill: Definitely not. I had no training. I was given a couple manuals and a brochure. I tried to use my interviewing skills by developing a lot of open-ended questions, but no one would talk to me. I was disappointed that I made the change to work with the engineer group. (Even though Bill did not need to elaborate on his responses to these closed-ended questions, he did as he felt comfortable with the interviewer.)

QUESTIONS

Below are three case studies. Please read the case studies and answer the questions.

1. How would you prepare to conduct each of these interviews?
2. Write an introduction and conclusion for each of the cases.
3. What are the primary questions you would ask for each case?
4. How would you conduct each interview?

Case 1—Joan

Joan has been a staff writer for the past eight years at the Good Writers Company. She has not progressed as rapidly as many of the other writers as she has a bad attitude about the work, co-workers and the company. Joan has been moved from one writing unit to another on four different occasions. She has received three different warnings and participated in a disciplinary interview. Her superiors decided to terminate her.

Case 2—Laurie

Laurie has been with the XYZ Writing Company for two years. She has done well. She is especially good at field testing and conducting usability tests. Laurie, while conducting a usability test with ABC Writing Company was offered a job that pays $10,000.00 more a year and has decided to leave the XYZ Writing Company. You have heard through the grapevine that Laurie has some reservations about leaving the XYZ Writing Company, but she feels that it is a good career move. She decides to leave.

Case 3—Lon

Lon is an ambitious young man. He likes to be involved in all phases of the development of manuals. Sometimes he creates problems as he advises others on how they can improve their products. He has had some problems with the lead writer, subject matter experts, and graphic designers. He has decided to leave. Lon is very talented, and you would like him to stay.

Contact a writing company in your area that conducts exit interviews. Try to interview an individual who conducts voluntary exit interviews and an individual who conducts involuntary exit interviews. To prepare for these interviews review Chapter 3 on information-gathering interviews.

1. Who conducts the interviews?
2. How do they prepare for the interview?
3. What types of questions do they ask?
4. Do they enjoy conducting exit interviews? Why? Why not?
5. Write a summary of the results of your interview.

REFERENCES

1. A. Sherwood, Exit Interviews: Don't Just Say Goodbye, *Personnel Journal*, pp. 744-750, 1980.
2. G. Dessler, *Exiting Employees Don't Show Candor*, Pioneer Press, St. Paul, p. 9, April 1, 1985.
3. P. Michal-Johnson, *Saying Goodbye: A Manager's Guide to Employee Dismissal*, Scott, Foresman and Co., Glenview, Illinois, 1985.
4. D. Drost, F. Obrien, and S. Marsh, Exit Interviews: Master the Possibilities, *Personnel Administrator*, pp. 104-110, 1987.
5. J. Zima, *Interviewing: Key to Effective Management*, Science Research Associates, Chicago, 1983.
6. E. McDowell, Exit Interviews: Don't Just Say Goodbye to Your Technical Communication Students, *International Technical Communication Proceedings, 33*, pp. RET 51-53, 1988.

Part 4

INTERNAL AND EXTERNAL INTERVIEWS

CHAPTER 8

Problem-Solving Interviews

OBJECTIVES

On completion of this chapter you should be able to:
Understand the differences between supportive and defensive communication
Understand the reflective thinking process
Understand the importance of task and maintenance roles in the problem-solving interview
Develop openings for different types of problem-solving interviews
Develop closings for different types of problem-solving interviews
Develop interview guides for different types of problem-solving interviews
Analyze problem-solving interviews

Problem-solving interviews are common in the workplace. Publication managers, lead writers, editors, graphic designers, subject matter experts, vendors, as well as others who are involved in the documentation process, face numerous tasks and people problems in their work. In Chapter 6 problem solving was discussed as an important method to handle appraisal interviews. Initially, this chapter focuses on types of climates in the workplace, types of questions, the reflective thinking process, and the roles played in the problem-solving interview. The chapter then focuses on preparing and conducting task problem-solving and counseling interviews on the job. Finally, the chapter focuses on reviewing and analyzing problem-solving interviews.

DEFENSIVE AND SUPPORTIVE CLIMATES

Interviewers and interviewees might become defensive when they feel threatened by the other party during a problem-solving interview. Problem-solving interviews occur frequently in the workplace. Managers, supervisors, and subordinates might be involved in a series of on-going, problem-solving activities. Thus, it is important that all parties understand the importance of creating a supportive climate in their world of work. Gibb's model [1, p. 32], presented in Figure 16, might be used as a guide to develop a supportive climate in the workplace.

Supportive Climates	Defensive Climates
1. Description	1. Evaluation
2. Problem Orientation	2. Control
3. Spontaneity	3. Strategy
4. Empathy	4. Neutrality
5. Equality	5. Superiority
6. Provisionalism	6. Certainty

Figure 16. Gibb's supportive and defensive climates. J. Gibb, Defensive Communication, *Journal of Communication,* p. 30, 1961. Reprint by permission of *Journal of Communication* and International Communication Association.

Evaluation Versus Description

Evaluation statements contain mostly negative judgment statements. Examples are:

The manual is sloppy. You will have to typeset it again.

This is the fifth time I have had to tell you to consult with the editors on terminology that you do not understand.

Be careful when you promise you can change visuals from the bottom to the top of the page.

In contrast, a descriptive statement will express the same message in a more supportive manner. Examples are:

We need to rethink the typeset for the manual.

Bill, you need to follow my directions and consult with the editors on terminology so that we don't face major problems when we do usability testing.

I'm excited also about the manual, but let's not brag too much about changing the location of visuals until we have consulted with the graphics department.

Control Versus Problem-Orientation

The interviewer or interviewee might use both control and problem-orientation statements during the interview. Control statements try to place demands on the other party and cause defensiveness. For example, the interviewer might tell the interviewee to do the following: "Complete the revisions by 7:00 pm on Tuesday, or I will replace you with another writer." On the other hand, the interviewer might use the problem-orientation method. The interviewer might say: "We have to complete revisions by 7:00 pm on Tuesday. That means we will both need to work tonight and tomorrow night." Obviously, the problem-orientation method will create a supportive climate.

Strategy Versus Spontaneity

Strategy attempts to manipulate people. Basically, the interviewer or interviewee who uses this type of communication is lying. For example, let's say that the publication manager at the Good Writers Company surveyed the writers about their preferences for the design of the new offices, but the writers discovered that the publication manager had already made the decision concerning the design of the office areas. The writers might feel angry if they found out the decisions were made before consulting with them. In contrast, writers might be less defensive if the publication manager had told the truth. The manager should tell subordinates that the office was designed for maximum use of space.

Neutrality Versus Empathy

Being neutral is the goal in a survey interview where the primary purpose is to gather information. In most interviews, however, neutrality contributes to a poor relationship between the interviewing parties. Both the interviewer and interviewee want to know that they are dealing with a human being. An example of neutrality is: You can correct that problem by looking in the original manual, and check the references to correct the problem.

Obviously, the interviewer might not have the answer to a specific problem. The interviewer, however, can show sincere empathy for the interviewee by using vocal and nonverbal messages that reinforce the verbal message.

> Tom, I don't know how to solve that problem. I know my computer had a virus last month. I did all the checking that I could. Finally, I called the help line. We discovered the virus had infected the entire system. I'll call Fred. Perhaps, he can come over and help us.

The interviewer's voice reinforces his verbal message, and he also puts his hand on Tom's shoulder.

Superiority Versus Equality

The interviewer takes on the role of superior or judge, using the directive method to solve problems. Taking the role of the superior or certainty can create a defensive environment. In a situation of this nature the interviewer would do all of the talking.

> Don't you think my solution is the best one? After all I have a degree in electrical engineering, and Janet doesn't. We will use my solution to solve this problem. Janet amazes me sometimes. Don't you think some of her ideas are ridiculous?

The interviewer, on the other hand, who is trying to show equality or provisionalism will use both the directive and nondirective methods so that both parties discuss the problem and solutions to the problem.

> **Rodney:** We seem to agree with my solution to the indexing problem, but you disagree with the glossary of terms section. Please talk to me about the glossary section. (Rodney is using the directive method.)

> **Leann:** OK! I think that if all the terms are defined, more users will benefit from the total software package. I agree with Janet that we need to provide these definitions so that users do not become lost in the technical aspects of the program and not complete the exercises in the manual.

> **Rodney:** I see! You think that the users will quit if they experience some anxiety in working with the first part of the manual. (Rodney is using the nondirective method to reinforce Leann's comments. This should cause her to provide more detailed information on this topic.)

TYPES OF QUESTIONS

In problem-solving interviews, questions can be categorized into questions of fact, questions of value, and questions of policy. A *question of fact* focuses on the truth or falsity of the statement. As the name implies the answer to the question is based on facts rather than inferences or judgment statements. Here are some examples:

What grade did you receive on your technical communication test?
How have costs increased since we developed the new desktop publishing system?
What are the results of the survey we did on the job satisfaction levels of technical writers in the medical writing group?

Questions of value are based on judgment statements. Generally, the interviewer and interviewee will make bipolar judgments such as good or bad, approve or disapprove, and accept or not accept. For example, here are some questions of value:

Are the new offices improving the morale of the office staff?
Are we making too little profit on our new software?
Are the tutorials good or bad?
Is the tutorial with graphics better than the tutorial without graphics?

Questions of policy call for a proposal and/or plan of action. Sample questions include:

Should technical communication students be required to take a course in informational interviewing?

Should the writing staff be allowed to smoke in the writing laboratory?
How can we require writers and subject matter experts to share information?
How can we control the number of graphics in our tutorials?

Obviously, all three types of questions might be used during a problem-solving interview. The use of these questions should help to keep the discussion focused on the specific topic. The questions also might suggest the need for additional information. In this case either the interviewer or interviewee might ask probing questions such as "Have we covered everything?" or "Have we covered all the available information?" Primary and secondary questions, as well as questions developed by Phillips, might be used to guide the interviewing participants through the problem-solving interviewing process [2, pp. 77-80].

Is the information factual, inferential, or evaluative?
Are the facts current?
Are the facts drawn from acceptable authorities?
Are the statistical statements biased?
Are eyewitness statements confirmed?

PROBLEM-SOLVING TECHNIQUES

Nominal Group Technique

The main purpose of many interviews is to solve problems. The problem-solving interview is task-oriented, on-going, and the goal involves anticipating action. Initially, the participants might brainstorm. This technique consists of a rapid, noncritical listing of ideas related to a specific topic. Participants might follow the *Nominal Group Technique* as it provides each person with an equal opportunity to generate ideas about a problem and solutions. This technique would be especially effective in the fact-finding and idea generation part of problem-solving. Delbecq, Van de Ven, and Gustafson suggest the following steps in completing the Nominal Group Technique [3, pp. 49-56]:

1. Once the problem is identified, either the interviewer (R) or interviewee (E) could suggest that each participant silently list ideas on a pad or paper.
2. After five or ten minutes, either R or E can act as a recorder. The recorder obtains one idea from each person in turn and writes that idea on the blackboard or flipchart. There is no discussion during this time.
3. The R and E take turns in giving their ideas until the ideas are listed.
4. Each idea in then discussed. Both R and E seek clarification and express support or nonsupport.
5. When all the ideas have been discussed, each participant then independently records a rank-ordering of ideas.

6. The decision is the idea that emerges in first place as a result of averaging the rankings of R and E.

Reflective Thinking Model

The Reflective Thinking Model, developed by Dewey, also can be applied to the problem-solving [4]. The pattern includes seven operational steps:

1. *Formulating the problem* — The interviewer and interviewee recognize that a problem exists. For example, let's say the problem is the cost of publishing the *Technical Writing and Communication Journal*. This can be developed into a more complete problem statement: Compared to 1986-87 academic year, the cost of producing 2,000 copies of the *Technical Writing and Communication Journal* has increased from $5,000.00 to $10,000.00.

2. *Defining the problem* — During this phase both parties define the problem and determine the exact nature of the problem. They define and clarify terms, recognize possible limitations, and establish the extent of the problem. The dyad will *focus on questions of fact* and to some extent *questions of value* and *questions of policy*. The following open-ended questions might be used to define the problem:

What is wrong?
What is the nature of the problem?
Whose problem is it?
When does the problem occur?
What is the extent of the problem?
How urgent is the problem?
How can the problem be broken down into a series of smaller problems?
What happens if the problem is left uncorrected?

Analyzing the problem — Participants isolate the particular facts concerning the problem. By brainstorming, the interviewer and interviewee can break down the problem into parts. In addition to brainstorming, the interviewer and interviewee might review written records and office records, and interview the staff responsible for producing the journal. By gathering factual information from staff members, their feelings about the cost of the journal will be discovered. The interviews also should help to determine answers to the following questions:

1. How serious is the problem?
2. Who is being affected?
3. Why is the problem occurring?

According to Zima the following questions might be used as a guide to conduct interviews with members of the journal staff [5, pp. 236-237]:

1. What kind of data is required to best achieve the desired goal?
2. Are the data already available that could be used?
3. When do the data have to be collected?
4. How are the data going to be analyzed?

Questions of facts are dealt with in this step.

1. How much does it cost to produce the journal?
2. How much does it cost to send the journal to each member?
3. How much does it cost to send an article out for review?

4. *Establish criteria for evaluating solutions* — The participants will establish standards for judging potential solutions. They will use these questions as guides to evaluate solutions:

What standards or criteria must be met before the solution can become acceptable to us?
Is the solution practical?
Will it cost too much?
Will the people who have the power to implement the solution do it?

5. *Suggesting solutions to problems* — During this stage the interviewer and interviewee suggest solutions to the problem. Brainstorming again will be used to generate a list of possible solutions. The criteria developed in the last step will be used to evaluate the solution to the problem. Some possible solutions to the journal problem include:

1. Increase the annual cost of the journal by $5.00.
2. Decrease the length of each issue of the journal by 10 pages.
3. Have a different firm produce the journal.
4. Require authors to pay $20.00 a page to have their articles published.

6. *Selecting the final solution* — Based on the criteria that have been generated, the dyad will evaluate each solution by listing the advantages and disadvantages of each and then select the best solution or solutions.

7. *Testing the solution* — Let's say that both the interviewer and interviewee agree that the best solutions to the problem are to decrease the length of each article by two pages and increase the annual cost of the journal by $5.00. Let's also assume that the *Technical Writing and Communication Journal* uses telephone interviews to evaluate the solutions to the problem. Both parties agree that a follow-up interview study will be conducted in one year.

Problem-solving groups and interviews are commonplace in organizations. Research indicates that Dewey's Reflective Thinking Model can be used as a model to define and solve problems in organizations [4]. The following outline might be used as an interview guide for the problem-solving interview:

I. Definition of the problem
   A. Definition of terms
   B. Definition of scope
II. Analysis of the problem
   A. History
   B. Causes
   C. Effects
   D. Extent
III. Criteria for solutions
   A. Generation of criteria
   B. Ordering of criteria according to priority
IV. Possible solutions
   A. Generation of possible solutions
   B. Evaluation according to criteria
V. Selection of optimum solution
VI. Plan of action

By following the reflective thinking process model, participants will be more organized as they discuss all phases and solutions to problems.

ROLES

In problem-solving situations participants will play task, maintenance, and self-centered functions. Benne and Sheets developed lists of these functions for group communication situations [6, pp. 43-47]. In problem-solving interviews participants also will play different types of roles. Interviewing participants might play several of these roles during different parts of the interview.

Task Functions

The interviewer will initiate communication with the other party. Likewise, both parties might seek and give opinions and information throughout the interview. Both might act as task leaders by giving and seeking information, by asking reflective, mirror, and clearinghouse probes, as well as open and closed primary questions. Below is a list of task roles that both might play throughout the interview:

1. **Initiating**: proposing new ideas, suggesting different procedures, identifying and defining unique problems.
2. **Information seeking**: requesting additional information.
3. **Information giving**: providing relevant facts for information when needed by the interviewer (R) or interviewee (E).

4. **Opinion seeking**: requesting expression of the opinions of the R or E.
5. **Opinion giving**: expressing belief or opinion rather than fact.
6. **Coordinating**: pulling various ideas together or showing the relationship among them.
7. **Energizing**: prodding the R or E to greater activity.
8. **Orienting**: clarifying the goals or purposes of the R or E.
9. **Recording**: keeping a written record of the ideas and suggestions that have been part of the interview.
10. **Evaluating**: appraising the value of ideas, suggestions, and proposals.

Maintenance Functions

The interviewing parties also will need to encourage, harmonize, and compromise in order to reach solutions to problems. Level 3 communication will occur if both parties are honest with each other. Through open communication tension will be relieved and both parties will focus on the problem.

1. **Encouraging**: acting supportively to invite, inspire, reassure, and comfort the other member of the interview.
2. **Harmonizing**: creating good will by disclosing feelings about self.
3. **Comprising**: reducing tension by modifying a position previously taken.
4. **Tension relieving**: lowering the level of stress within the dyad by changing the subject or using humor.
5. **Gatekeeping**: opening the channels of communication by asking the other party to contribute.

Self-Centered Function

Hopefully, communication between the interviewing parties will be so good that both parties will focus on the task and maintain a supportive climate. This, however, might not be the case. The more ego involved the parties are, the more likely they are to become self-centered and criticize each other rather than be problem-centered and depersonalized. If this occurs, the interviewer and interviewee might play these types of roles:

1. **Blocking**: preventing progress toward solutions by constantly raising objections.
2. **Attacking**: attacking the competence of the other party, name calling, impugning the motives of the other party instead of describing their own feelings; joking at the expense of the other party.
3. **Recognition seeking**: boasting, calling attention to one's own expertise or experience when it is not necessary to establish credibility with the other party.
4. **Horseplaying**: making tangential jokes, engaging in horseplay that takes the other party away from serious work or maintenance behavior.

5. **Dominating**: giving orders, interrupting and cutting off, flattering to get own way.

Task and maintenance roles are important for the success of a problem-solving interview.

PREPARING FOR THE PROBLEM-SOLVING INTERVIEW

Problem-solving interviews are both impromptu and planned. For example, some problems that surface can be handled without much preparation, while other problems demand much preparation. Planning will consist of brainstorming and utilizing the various steps of Dewey's Reflective Thinking Model. The interviewer needs to select an opening that will gain the interviewee's attention and orient the interviewee on possible solutions to the problem. The interviewer also needs to develop an interview guide and to develop a possible closing for the interview.

The interviewer also might use the directive and nondirective methods to conduct the interview. The directive method will be used when the supervisor knows exactly what needs to be done to solve the problem. This method might be viewed negatively by subordinates who want to voice their opinions in discussing problems and possible solutions to them. Here is an example of how the directive method might be used effectively:

Interviewee: I don't know if the readability of the tutorial is a problem.

Interviewer: We should complete information interviews with a sample of those who have used the abridged tutorial.

Interviewee: That makes sense. Let's develop the questions today.

In contrast, the nondirective method will help both parties to articulate their views on the problem. The nondirective method creates a neutral, non-evaluative atmosphere and a healthy climate in which both parties can share information about the problem.

Interviewee: We need to focus on computer anxiety. That is probably the problem with the abridged tutorial.

Interviewer: You feel our tutorial is too impersonal.

Interviewee: Yes! Students don't have any time to relax before they are asked to perform the tasks.

Interviewer: Students are anxious because they lack confidence in using the computer.

The directive and nondirective methods should be used at different times during the problem-solving interview. The level of knowledge and personalities of the interviewer and interviewee will determine when and for how long each method will be used.

CONDUCTING THE PROBLEM-SOLVING INTERVIEW

Opening

Summarizing the problem and explaining how the problem was discovered are two ways to begin a problem-solving interview. For example, suppose that a problem exists with the readability of the Good Writing Basic Manual in terms of its use for secondary students.

Summarizing the problem — Since secondary students are using the "Abridged Tutorials for the Basic Program," it takes them longer to complete the tutorial. In addition, they also make more mistakes and feel more apprehensive after the exercise. The problem is that the subject matter expert feels that the tutorials are appropriate and should not be changed, while students feel that there is a need to discuss this problem and ways to solve this problem.

Explaining how the problem was discovered — Yesterday when I was reviewing the scores of students who used the original tutorial and scores of those who used the revised tutorial, I noticed that those who used the original tutorial scored significantly higher on understanding the lesson. I would like to have your opinion on why this occurred.

Body

The body of the interview consists of the problem and solutions to the problem. Below is an example of an interview guide:

I. Too many mistakes on the tutorial exercise.
   A. Average four mistakes to complete the abridged tutorial.
   B. Average two mistakes to complete the original tutorial.
II. Assessment of time to complete the tutorials.
   A. Average four minutes to complete the original tutorial.
   B. Over 30 percent refused to complete the original tutorial.
   C. Average two minutes to complete the abridged tutorial.
III. Therefore, we should develop new solutions to the problem.
   A. Revise the manual to lower the readability level.
   B. Add three new visuals.
   C. Decrease the task complexity by creating more tutorials.

The problem-solving interview probably will not be as well organized as many of the others as both parties might digress at any point in the interview. The interview guide, however, provides a framework that will help both parties to return to the structure of the interview. The nominal technique, mentioned earlier in the chapter, also should provide both parties with an opportunity to communicate openly about the problem.

Closing

Several closing techniques might be used to complete the problem-solving interview. The three most appropriate ones for the problem-solving interview are a *clearinghouse question, declaring the completion,* and *expressing appreciation or satisfaction.*

Clearinghouse question — Is there anything else we should discuss before we revise the manual?

Declaring the completion of the interview — Okay! These solutions should solve the problem. The manual will be completed.

Expressing appreciation or satisfaction — I think we have accomplished our objectives. I appreciate your willingness to share your views with me. I'll have our writing team work on the solutions immediately.

TYPES OF PROBLEM-SOLVING INTERVIEWS

Preparing for the People Interview

The primary purpose of the people interview is to counsel the employee. For example, a writer might consult with a manager on domestic, legal and personal problems, while the manager might consult with the writer on job related developmental problems. The employee will generally initiate the discussion on people-related problems, while the manager will initiate the discussion on developmental problems. Basically, the motives, skills, and knowledge of the manager should be determined before offering advice to others. The interviewer will prepare for the developmental interview, while the interviewee will prepare for the personal problem interview. The interviewer will use the directive and nondirective methods in conducting the developmental interview, probably using the directive method more than the nondirective. In contrast, the interviewer will be a helper in the personal problem interview and will use primarily the nondirective method.

The manager generally initiates the developmental interview. The manager can prepare for this interview by developing a meaningful opening and an interview guide. Managers might prepare to conduct a developmental interview with the interviewee for some of the following reasons:

A problem in organizing time
A problem in meeting deadlines
Interpersonal problems

Lack of leadership skills
A problem in handling job stress
Inability to get along with others, to take criticism and to admit when wrong

Preparation should begin with a self-assessment. Personality variables such as the level of open-mindedness, optimism, and patience should be assessed. In addition, the manager should complete a personal assessment by answering these questions:

Am I a good listener?
Am I a skilled communicator?
How adequately have I been trained as a manager?
How do my subordinates view me?
Have I had training in counseling?

After completing a self-assessment, the manager will analyze the performance of the interviewee. For example, does the manager have knowledge of personal data on the interviewee such as the nickname, age, marital status, number of children, and goals and ambitions of the subordinate? Basically, the manager will review all available materials about the interviewee beginning with the work history, education, academic record, appraisal records and any information dealing with previous counseling.

The manager, according to Stewart and Cash, also needs to focus on how to respond to comments that the interviewee might state, such as the following [7, p. 201]:

I don't want your help.
I don't need your help.
I don't want my family contacted about this problem.
Why should I discuss my personal problems with you?
Why are you interested in helping me?
You're not my parent, so get lost.

The counseling interview can be divided into the affective and cognitive phases. The task and maintenance roles will determine how successfully these phases will be handled. Basically, the maintenance roles will help the interviewer to develop a helpful climate so that the interviewee wants to participate in the interview. Thus, both parties develop respect for each other, engaging in complete self-disclosure. During the cognitive phase the interviewer will encourage the interviewee to share information, to restate information, and to question for information. The interviewer will offer information, generate possible solutions to the problem and, in some cases, try to help the interviewee make decisions.

The manager also will assess the relational dimensions of inclusion, control and affection to determine at what level to communicate with the interviewee. By assessing the dimensions, the interviewer will be able to assess whether to conduct the interview or refer the interviewee to a counselor. After completing these assessments the manager is ready to develop an opening, interview guide, and conclusion.

Conducting the Developmental Interview

Developmental interviews are generally initiated by the manager. The manager should provide a quiet and private place, as well as a comfortable climate to increase the chances that the interviewee will operate at level 3 where maximum self-disclosure can occur. The interviewee might feel more relaxed and comfortable sitting at a round table as it has no authority location and both parties can sit beside each other.

Opening — The type of opening that the manager selects will depend upon the previous relationship with the interviewee. Most of the types of openings discussed in Chapter 2 would not be used to begin this type of interview. The opening of a counseling interview can consume much time as the interviewee might not feel comfortable in this environment. The amount of time is dependent upon the inclusion and affection variables. Simply stated: Do the manager and employee like each other? Does the interviewee want to be interviewed? With this in mind, the interviewer should prepare to begin with the most interesting topic, and rapport building should continue throughout the interview.

A question is a good way to begin the developmental interview. For example, suppose the problem has to do with interpersonal relationships with co-workers. The interviewer might begin with a variety of open-ended and closed-ended questions.

How are you getting along with the other writers on the Word Project?
Has playing softball with your co-workers improved your working relationships?
Do you think we should continue to have a group counseling session?
What do you think of being in an office by yourself?

Body — Below is an example of an interview guide.

INTERVIEW GUIDE

  I. Attitudes toward other writers in writing group
    A. Use of language in reviewing manuals.
    B. Comparison of self with others in writing manuals.
 II. Solutions to interpersonal problems
    A. Establishing rapport with other writers.
    B. Using appropriate language in reviewing manuals.
    C. Working on affection to build a positive relationship.
    D. Use of nondirective method in counseling.

During the developmental interview, the interviewer must be very attentive. Since the manager's goal is to build rapport with the other writers, he/she must be sensitive to their needs. The manager must thoroughly prepare for this interview, have the ability to digress from the planned guide, skip over parts of the guide, and maintain clear organization throughout the interview.

Based on the above interview guide, here is how the manager might handle the first main point:

> **Manager:** (an informal setting in the writing lounge) Well, Mike, I hear everything has been going smoothly on your project.
>
> **Mike:** That's right! Thanks for telling me about my attitude and how others were characterizing me. You know that I had no idea that I was causing problems. The course that I'm taking is helping me with my interpersonal problems both at home and here. (Mike looks directly at the manager as he is talking; he maintains excellent eye contact and is very sincere.)
>
> **Manager:** (leaning back in his chair and gesturing with open hands). You feel good about the progress you are making. (The manager decided to reflect on the remark rather than use the directive method.)
>
> **Mike:** That's right! I feel more relaxed in interacting with other writers and even the editors. In fact, I have begun to socialize with some of the writing staff. (Mike is smiling and looks directly at the manager.)
>
> **Manager:** It appears that you have begun to solve your problems with the writers and editors. How have you changed your language in interacting with other writers?
>
> **Mike:** I took your advice and have been keeping a log of my interpersonal communication with the writers and editors. I was surprised that I was so aggressive and that I used so much profanity, not to mention how mean I sounded sometimes. I didn't know that you recorded some of our meetings. It is really a telling experience when you hear yourself.

Closing

> **Manager:** I'm glad to see the improvement. Keep up the good work. Remember we are a family of writers. We want all members of the family to be happy and productive.

In this example the manager reflected on what Mike was saying. If Mike had not improved his relationship with the writers and editors, the manager would have offered additional advice to help solve the problem. If the problem had been severe, the company might have contacted a professional counselor to discuss the problem with Mike. If the manager felt it was an interpersonal problem that could not be resolved, disciplinary procedures which might lead to a disciplinary interview, and, possibly, an involuntary exit interview, could be initiated.

Conducting the Job-Related Personal Interview

In contrast to the developmental interview which is initiated by the manager, the job-related personal interview is initiated by the employee. In this case the manager does not have an opportunity to prepare as the interview will occur immediately. The interview might begin as the two are walking to a quiet area, or both parties might stand during the entire process. The manager's initial role is that of a listener and a reflector of information.

The employee has the responsibility to develop an opening and interview plan before approaching the manager. Requesting advice or assistance, summarizing a problem, and asking questions are appropriate openings to use for this type of interview. Below is an example of requesting advice:

Opening

Interviewee: I'm having some difficulty sleeping since I was passed over for the lead writer position on the Software Gift Package Program. I think that I am the best qualified for the position. My appraisals have been the highest of the writers. I also have a master's degree in Technical Communication. I feel that I should have been consulted about my interest in this position. Tom indicated that I am not the lead writer because I am the best writer, and the engineering group wanted the most talented writer to do most of the writing. They feel anyone can be a supervisor. I know I am a good writer. I, however, obtained my master's degree so that I could move into management, and now writers with less education are supervisors because they can't write well for the engineering group. (While the interviewee is talking, the manager will reflect on what the interviewee is saying to determine the hidden meaning. The manager must decide whether the directive or nondirective method should be used to handle this impromptu interview.)

Manager: I really feel sorry for you. This appears to be a "no win" situation. I hadn't heard why you were not given the lead writing position. I was just told to appoint Brian to this position. I will look into this situation immediately. I know you have worked hard and will make a good manager. (In this case the manager is using the directive method. The interviewer will investigate the situation and report back to the interviewee.)

Interviewee: I felt by obtaining my master's degree and showing my loyalty to the company that I would have an opportunity to advance more rapidly. I want to stay with this company, but I don't know if I will. (The interviewee is very upset and needs support from the manager.)

Manager: You feel disappointed that you were not selected for the writing position. (In this case the manager is using and will continue to use the nondirective method. The interview might take quite some time as the manager is providing the interviewee with an opportunity for psychological drainage, catharsis, or ventilation.)

In sum, during the job-related personal interview, the manager is very sensitive to the needs of the interviewee. The introduction might last several minutes. The problem might not be discovered until the interviewee feels comfortable. The interviewer might use the directive method occasionally, but most of the time will be spent listening to the interviewee's perceptions of the problem and possible solution to the problem. The interviewer will paraphrase information so that the interviewee will disclose his or her thoughts on the situation. It is difficult to tell where the opening ends and the body begins as the body is an extension of the opening.

Closing — The interview might end in a variety of ways. For example, the manager might indicate that time is up and that an investigation will be completed. Below is an example of using these two methods:

> **Manager**: I will look into the situation. As you know I have another meeting now, but I will try to get back to you by 2:00 p.m. In the meantime, try to relax.

SUMMARY

Problem-solving interviews are commonplace in an organization. Supervisors and subordinates will determine the climate, types of questions, problem-solving techniques, and roles each will play to prepare and to conduct the task and people interviews. This chapter has introduced you to several dimensions of the problem-solving interview. Now please read the Review and Analysis and case studies and answer the questions.

PROBLEM SOLVING INTERVIEW FOR REVIEW AND ANALYSIS

This is a problem-solving interview between a manager and a subordinate. The writer has had problems in writing for specialized audiences and has become somewhat belligerent when dealing with co-writers. The writer thinks that the others are distorting the facts and that he does a good job of product analysis, audience analysis, task analysis, and project analysis.

How effective does the manager handle the opening? How would you begin the interview? Does the manager use a directive, nondirective or combination approach? What types of roles do each play in the interview? At what level does each disclose information? If you were the interviewer, how would you prepare for the interview? How would you open the interview? How would you close the interview?

> **Manager**: Vince, you have a problem with the audience analysis phase of the project. You seem to think that you can do everything intuitively. You need to talk to the other writers. Let me explain to you the four types of audience analysis . . . (The manager talks for twenty minutes on audience analysis. Vince appears defensive, crosses his arms, and moves two steps backwards.)

Vince: Look! I have a background in audience analysis. I know what I am doing. (Vince is very forceful, but the manager interrupts.)

Manager: You will need to complete the four types of analysis; otherwise, you will be removed from the lead writer position; and that's final! (The manager is quite dogmatic, and Vince appears defensive again.)

Vince: OK! OK! Just exactly what do you want me to do? I can't be expected to do a product analysis. I don't have the background to figure out all the cost. Besides it is your responsibility to figure out the cost of the pages and the budget and schedule. (Vince is blushing and appears about ready to quit his job.)

Manager: Hold on, Vince! I thought you had the background to complete the analysis.

Vince: No I don't! I have studied previous reports on cost-per-page figures, days-per-page figures, technologies involved in the project, and how to determine the audience-analysis and task-analysis needs of the project. (Vince points out that he has limited experience in these various types of analysis.)

Manager: I've placed you in charge of this project; it is your responsibility to complete the analysis. If you can't do it, I'll appoint someone else. I'm too busy for this routine type of job.

Vince: I want to do the job. Is there anyone that you know who might help me with the task analysis and project analysis? (Vince is looking for guidance from the manager.)

Manager: I don't know. You check around, and if I have time I'll ask some other managers. In the meantime, if you can't do the job, let me know.

Vince: Okay. (Vince appears defeated; he was hoping for more direction from the manager.)

QUESTIONS

Please read each of the case studies and answer the questions.

Mary's Problem

Mary performed well during the first appraisal period and was rated highly for it. Unfortunately, during the second appraisal period she has experienced some difficulties. The new desktop publishing computers have decreased the overall cost; but all the writers have had to work five hours more each week. She has decided to take this problem to the publication manager. If you were the publication manager, how would you handle the problem?

Writing Team

The writing team wants to complete field tests on their new software. The researcher that they hired tends to be pompous and has a low regard for writers. The lead writer knows that the researcher is one of the best and wants his expertise on field tests and wants to avoid conflict between the writers and researcher. The lead writer hired the researcher. How would you handle the problem between the writers and researcher?

Sales Problem

You are the manager for the Buying and Selling Technical Publication Unit in your organization. Your responsibility is to conduct information giving interviews with a team of sales people. You discover that one of the salesmen has been more successful that the others in getting businesses to buy the new software. You discovered that the successful salesman lies about the product. You decide to discuss the problem with the salesman. How will you approach him?

REFERENCES

1. J. Gibb, Defensive Communication, *Journal of Communication, 11*, pp. 30-34, 1961.
2. G. Phillips, *Communication and the Small Group*, Bobbs-Merrill Company,, Inc., 1966.
3. A. Delbecq, A. Van de Ven, and D. Gustafson, Guidelines for Conducting Meetings, *Group Techniques for Program Planning*, Scott, Foresman and Company, Glenview, Illinois, pp. 40-46, 1975.
4. J. Dewey, *How We Think*, D. C. Heath Co., New York, 1910.
5. J. Zima, *Interviewing: Key to Effective Management*, Science Research Associates, Inc., Chicago, 1983.
6. K. Benne and P. Sheets, Functional Roles of Group Members, *Journal of Social Issues, 4*, pp. 41-49, 1948.
7. C. Stewart and W. Cash, *Interviewing: Principles and Practices*, Wm. C. Brown Publishers, Dubuque, Iowa, 1988.

CHAPTER 9

Persuasive Interviews

OBJECTIVES

On completion of this chapter you should be able to:
Understand the sales/selling interview
Understand the dimensions of the persuasive interview
Develop an interview guide and interview schedule for a persuasive interview
Develop openings and closings for persuasive interviews
Participate in persuasive interviews

Persuasive interviews also are common in the workplace. In fact, one of the purposes of most interviews is to persuade. For example, Mary, as indicated in Chapter 1, wanted to persuade the interviewer that she was the most qualified applicant for the position of technical writer, and the interviewer wanted to persuade Mary to become a writer for the Good Writers Company. Persuasion also might be a part of the tell-and-sell appraisal interview, voluntary exit interview and the problem-solving interview. This chapter will not focus on these types of persuasive interviews, but will focus on the selling interview.

In brief this chapter will focus on the dimensions of the persuasive interview, planning the interview and conducting the interview.

DIMENSIONS OF PERSUASIVE INTERVIEWS

Definition of Persuasive Interview

Persuasive interviewing can be defined as a process in which the interviewer attempts to induce a voluntary change of behavior in the interviewee (e.g., buying a certain type of word processor) by appealing to both feelings and intellect. Both parties are active participants in the persuasive interview. The interviewer has a preconceived goal regarding the expected change in the behavior of the interviewee.

Analyzing the Interviewee

Prior to planning for the interview, the interviewer needs to research the interviewee. The interviewer wants to know as much as possible about the interviewee and how the person will react to the proposal or certain topic. To answer this question the interviewer will gather information on the characteristics of the interviewee. Below is a list of some characteristics [1, pp. 89-105]:

1. **Biological** (age, sex, race, physical characteristics)
2. **Social** (education, occupation, status, organization, hobbies, group memberships, marital status, work experience)
3. **Political** (Republican, Democrat, Independent, conservative, liberal, etc.)
4. **Religious preference** (beliefs, ethics)
5. **Psychological** (personality characteristics—happy or sad, open-minded or closed-minded)

To obtain this information, the interviewer would search written records and engage in informal and formal communication with friends or acquaintances of the interviewee.

Motive Appeals

After gathering background information the interviewer might consider other factors germane to the persuasive situation. Rokeach and Parker indicate that the interviewer might use several motive appeals during an interview. For example, a vendor might want to sell a computer system with desktop publishing capabilities and the latest software. The vendor might use some of the following motive appeals [2, pp. 101-102]:

1. **Comfort and convenience** (e.g., a computer having desktop publishing capabilities)
2. **Health, safety and security** (e.g., a security system to protect your computers)
3. **Pride, prestige, and social recognition** (e.g., "state of the art" software, the quality of your graphics will be better, and you will have more self-esteem)
4. **Companionship** (e.g., gain a sense of belonging by networking with professionals in your field)
5. **Freedom from authority** (e.g., by being able to produce your own publication, you will develop a sense of independence)
6. **Competition** (e.g., the quality of the software will help improve the quality of the publication)
7. **Freedom from restraint** (e.g., with the new software the writer will be able to make more decisions concerning how the information is packaged)

8. **Education and knowledge** (e.g., the new software will update writers on the latest technology and enable them to produce quality work)
9. **Change and progress** (e.g., writers will be on the cutting edge of their professions)
10. **Sense of accomplishment** (e.g., the software will enable each writer to experience success)

Credibility

In addition to understanding the interviewee and possible appeals that might be used, the interviewer will need to assess the attitude that the interviewee has about the interviewer, as well as the attitude about the new computer. Obviously, if the interviewer perceives that the interviewee dislikes him or her based on past experiences, the interviewer needs to establish credibility with the interviewee. Basically, this refers to the interviewee's perceptions of the interviewer's trustworthiness and competence. Perhaps sending information about himself or herself, which portrays an accurate picture of him or her as well as the product he or she might be selling will increase the credibility of the interviewer. The interviewer also needs to be concerned with credibility at the end of the interview. Specifically the interviewer needs to be concerned about competence and character:

Competence—how the interviewee regards the interviewer's intelligence and knowledge on the subject.

Character—how the interviewee regards the interviewer's sincerity, trust-worthiness and concern for him or her.

In preparing for the interview, the interviewer should adhere to the following [3, p. 251]:

1. Lying is unethical. If the interviewee feels that the interviewer is lying, the interviewer will not be successful.
2. Name-calling is unethical. Try to avoid name-calling when referring to competitors. Focus on the good qualities of your idea or product.
3. Grossly exaggerating or distorting facts is unethical.
4. Suppression of key information is unethical. If an interviewer has the information, it should be disclosed to the interviewee.

After assessing the interviewee and topic, the interviewer should be able to assess the relationship variables. The interviewer should be able to answer such questions as:

1. Do I like the interviewee?
2. Does the interviewee like me?
3. Will I have control during the interview?
4. Will the interviewee want to participate in the interview?

For example, if the interviewer is introducing new software to a new client, he or she should be able to estimate whether the information will be well received and whether the interviewer will be well received or not. The interviewer should be able to answer these questions:

1. Does the interviewee want to participate in the interview?
2. Who will have control during this interview?
3. How well do both parties like each other?
4. Does the proposal/product satisfy an urgent need?
5. Does the proposal appear to be feasible? Does the proposal appear to be workable? Does the proposal appear to be practical? Does the proposal appear to be affordable?
6. Does the interviewee have beliefs similar to mine? Does the interviewee have values similar to mine?
7. Does the interviewee trust me?
8. Does the interviewee view me as a knowledgeable person?
9. Will it be difficult to establish common ground with the interviewee?

The interviewer would like to be able to respond "yes" to each of these questions. This, however, might be impossible to do. Thus, the interviewer needs to think through the entire interviewing process in a general sense before developing an interview guide, opening, closing, and interview schedule. The following guidelines by Rubin and Brown should help the persuader to be successful [4, pp. 5-18]:

1. Look for common ground and try to build agreement rather than conflict.
2. Try to maintain pressure, but try to avoid provocation.
3. Try to involve the persuadee by asking questions rather than making accusations or criticisms.
4. Frequently check understandings by reflecting back the response of the persuadee.
5. Know that a proposal is more acceptable if it is directly responsive to a need expressed by the persuadee.

Persuasive Tactics

The interviewer also needs to be aware of various persuasive tactics in order to stimulate, convince and actuate the persuadee to purchase a product. In addition to the materials discussed under Dewey's Reflective thinking Model in Chapter 8, the interviewer will attempt to persuade the interviewee by using various persuasive tactics. Stewart and Cash, as well as other communication scholars, list the following tactics [5, pp. 239-240]:

Identification
This device reveals how similar the interviewer's beliefs, attitudes and values are to the interviewee. As an example:

I can relate to your concern about printers that need to be fixed every month. We had one at our company like yours. Our research indicates that this new machine will not need to be fixed more than once a year and, generally, only serviced once a year.

Association

This technique is used to establish a connection between what the interviewer is selling and other companies or persons that the persuadee would respect. For example:

This printer is being used by the ABC Writing Company and the XYZ Writing Company. They report that they are very satisfied with the quality of the printer.

Bandwagon

This technique goes beyond the association and generalizes to a larger group. The interviewer is saying "everyone is doing this."

The latest statistics indicate that almost 90 percent of writing companies with desktop publishing capabilities use this laser printer. Every writing company in this city uses this printer.

Testimony

The interviewer cites a credible person, and one that the interviewee probably should know, to build the case for the proposal.

Paul Warner, president of Warner Writing Company, indicated that this printer is the best on the market.

Bifurcation

Bifurcation tries to polarize each situation. On the one hand, if you buy a certain product everything will turn out well, and, on the other hand, if you don't buy the product, you will regret it.

Either it's the new printer, or you will lose many of your clients. You either buy the new printer or sell your business.

Questions in the Persuasive Interview

The interviewer will use a variety of question types when conducting the persuasive interview. Questions that focus on agreement with the proposal or topic of the proposal are used most frequently. Questions of agreement refer to the "yes-response" method. Here are several examples:

You agree that this printer is the best, don't you?
Aren't you in favor of purchasing the new printer?
Isn't this the best printer you have seen?

The "yes-response" technique is built on the premise that the persuadee will respond "yes" to these questions and this will lead to selling the product.

Interviewers also use other types of questions. During the beginning of the interview, open-ended questions might be asked to determine the level of knowledge and perceptions that the interviewee has about the product. Questions such as:

What do you know about the new laser printer?
How do you feel about the new laser printer?
What types of experiences have you had with this printer?

In addition to leading and open-ended questions, the interviewer might ask a verification question such as: Am I correct in assuming that you publish three weekly newsletters and publish fifty software programs each year?

Closely related to the verification question is the summary probe question:

Let's see if I understand your basic needs; you feel that the printer needs to be compatible with all three types of your computers, that it must be less expensive than the current ways the printing is done, and you would like to see some documentation on the statistics I have cited, is this correct?

All the types of questions, of course, that we have discussed in this book might be used in a persuasive interview. The interviewer needs to be well trained in the "tools of the trade" to conduct ethical persuasive interviews.

Setting for the Interview

The setting for a persuasive interview is very important. Stewart and Cash point out that the interviewer needs to take into consideration the time of day, the events that precede and follow the interview, size or room, furniture arrangement, seating, noise level, heat and lighting. In many cases, the interviewer might not be able to change some of the conditions such as the lighting in the room. The interviewer can schedule a time that is convenient for both parties and make an appointment so that the interviewee is aware that the individual is coming to display some equipment.

STRUCTURING THE INTERVIEW

After completing your homework on the persuadee's personal characteristics, as well as the beliefs, attitudes and values of the person toward the topic, the interviewer will develop an interview guide. The guide, for the most part, will be designed for the target person. For example, if the analysis indicates that the persuadee will be reluctant to purchase new laser printers, the interviewer will present the strongest argument first. In contrast, if the analysis reveals that the client is very interested in the laser printer, the interviewer could present this argument either first or last. In addition, if the client is highly educated, the interviewer should present both sides of the issue. The level of knowledge of the client also will determine how the interviewer will approach the interview.

The Opening

Robeson, Mathews, and Stevens concluded [6, p. 109] that "roughly 75 percent" of all sales representatives "fail in the attention step." Ideally, the interviewer, in addition to obtaining as much information from others prior to the interview, will have communicated with the interviewee prior to the interview. Perhaps the interviewer will have talked on the telephone to the interviewee to set up the interview. The interviewer also might have sent literature to the interviewee about the laser printer. The interviewer wants to establish credibility with the interviewee prior to the interview. Based on the assessment of the interviewee, the interviewer will select an opening technique that is most appropriate.

The opening should be designed to gain the attention and interest of the interviewee. The opening also should motivate the interviewee to want to participate in the interview. The types of openings discussed in Chapter 2 can be used to gain the attention of persuadees. Goyer, Redding, and Rickey include the following [7, pp. 49-50]:

1. Summarize the problem or need.
   Based on our phone conversation, your printers are adequate for everyday tasks but can not be used for printing newsletters and software documentation. The attitude of the writer is that you need to have a laser printer to increase the quality of printing and to enable you to produce your own newsletters and software.
2. Ask your way in with a question that identifies a "customer" problem or need.
   How long does it take to complete the printing of the newsletter with your present printer?
3. State the benefits that the persuadee may expect if he or she accepts your proposal.
   Research indicates that the laser printer prints three times faster than your present printer and is capable of producing quality graphics.
4. Explain how you happened to learn that a problem exists and suggest that the persuadee should want to discuss it.
   As you know by our conversation, Bill and I play softball for the church team. We were sharing information about our jobs when he mentioned that your printers are obsolete, so I decided to call you to see if I might help you.
5. Refer to the known position of the persuadee.
   I understand that you like the quality of the newsletter and don't feel there is a need to obtain desktop publishing capabilities here.
6. Refer to the background leading up to the problem.
   Enga Widmer in your accounting office indicates that the cost to produce your newsletter and graphics is too large. She said you are losing $2,000.00 a quarter. I'd like to share with you how I might help you.
7. State the name of the person who sent you to see the persuadee.
   James Smith told me that you are interested in improving the quality of the printing of the newsletter.

8. State the name of the company, organization, or group you represent.

   As you know, Happy Printers Company does several of the newsletters for various chapters of the Society for Technical Communication.

9. Request a brief period of the persuadee's time.

   Mr. Jones, I've communicated with your secretary on several occasions and have learned that you have a very tight schedule. I only need ten minutes to introduce you to the Happy Printers Company.

10. State a striking or dramatic fact.

    As you know it was reported in the *International Technical Communication Conference Proceedings* that any printer that is more than two years old is obsolete.

After gaining the attention of the interviewee, the interviewer will build rapport and set the stage for the main part of the interview. Throughout the opening, the salesperson stresses that the purpose is to help the client to identify problems, find the causes and provide solutions.

The Body

The body is the main part of the persuasive interview. In the body the persuader might define a problem and discuss how the situation could be resolved. For example, prior to the interview to sell a laser printer, the salesperson will assess the needs of the client and will arrange the main points to fit the client's needs. Basically the interviewer will follow the steps of Dewey's Reflective Thinking Model as presented in Chapter 8.

As indicated earlier, the interviewer will begin with the strongest point. The interviewer will ask questions to determine level of knowledge of the persuadee and the level of interest in solving the problem. The salesperson's objective is to sell the product, and, thus, it is essential that both parties agree on the nature of the problem. In order to identify the problem, the interviewer will develop questions to obtain the opinions of the client. Through this process the interviewee will define the problem. This might include the time taken to complete the newsletter, the quality of the printing, and the attitudes of workers responsible for producing the newsletter.

Next, the interviewer will suggest criteria to evaluate solutions to the problem. At this stage the interviewer should ask the interviewee what would help to solve the problem. By asking open questions, the interviewer can develop criteria for solutions to the problem. Through this process the interviewer increases credibility with the interviewee and builds a foundation of agreement.

Finally, the interviewer will use the information of the persuadee to propose a solution to the problem. At this stage of the interview, the salesperson might use the "yes response" technique, bandwagon technique, testimony, repetition, reflective and summary questions, and leading questions to persuade the interviewee to purchase the product.

In summary, the salesperson does the following in the body of the persuasive interview [7, pp. 50-51]:

1. Defines the problem.
2. Establishes criteria to evaluate solutions to a problem.
3. Jointly proposes solutions to the problem.
4. Jointly evaluates the proposed solutions.
5. Agrees on the best available solution.

Remember that throughout the interview the salesperson needs to listen sympathetically as clients will disclose how they can be sold.

The Closing

The salesperson moved through the opening and body of the interview, and now wants to close the interview. Massimino indicates that this is the most fearful time during the interview [8, p. 103]. The closing, of course, is the most important part of the persuasive interview, yet hesitation to ask for the sale is the major cause of failure.

Zima points out that following **DO'S** in handing the close [9, p. 386]:

1. Do maintain control over the agenda and the structure.
2. Do maintain initiative.
3. Do state goals, expectations, and standards forcefully and clearly.
4. Do build common ground.
5. Do make clear what will happen if the persuadee does not accept your proposal.
6. Do show enthusiasm about your proposal.
7. Do involve the persuadee in the discussion.
8. Do get the persuadee to agree overtly on each point.
9. Do listen and give your courteous attention.
10. Do get agreement at each point along the way.

Zima also points out several DON'TS in handling the close [9, p. 387]:

1. Don't attempt to rush the persuadee's thinking.
2. Don't argue.
3. Don't preach.
4. Don't make dogmatic assertions.
5. Don't make accusations.
6. Don't present all your arguments at one time.
7. Don't use "you" statements.

Stewart and Cash point out that the closing usually consists of three stages: trial closing, filling out the contract or agreement, and leave taking [5, pp. 230-232].

Trial closing — Throughout the interview the salesperson should be assessing the nonverbal, paraverbal, and verbal messages of the interviewee and should be prepared to close the interview after discussing the solutions. Verbal cues such as:

> The laser printer would help you with several phases of printing. I know it is being used by most of the Fortune 500 Companies. A laser printer would increase your credibility in the publishing field.

The attentiveness on the part of the interviewee such as constant eye contact, smiling, and positive vocal variety should cue the interviewer that it is time to close the interview.

At the beginning of the close, the interviewer might determine if it is time to close by using the "yes response" method. For example, the following might be used to sell the laser printer:

> The Happy Laser would seem to be an ideal printer for your printing needs, wouldn't it?
>
> It is understandable why so many companies are using the Happy Laser, isn't it?
>
> If our figures are correct, it will actually cost you less than the present system, won't it?

Contract agreement — This is the telling phase of the interview. The salesperson has the contract ready for the persuadee to sign. Based on the dialogue that occurred during the interview, the salesperson might use an assumptive close. For example, the salesperson might say, "I assume you want the Happy Deluxe Printer as it provides all the latest technology." Other types of closes, as pointed out by Stewart and Cash, include summary close, elimination of single objection close, and sense of urgency close [5, pp. 230-232]:

Summary close—summarize the need, criteria, or agreement made earlier as a basis for decisions.

Elimination of a single objection close—respond to a single objection that is delaying the sale.

Sense of urgency close—stress why the interviewee should act now.

Leave taking—As in all other interviews, last impressions are built during the close of the interview.

THE MOTIVATED SEQUENCE

The motivated sequence might be adapted to the persuasive interview situation. Monroe and Ehninger use five steps, instead of three, in the persuasive process [10, p. 244]. These include: Attention, Need, Satisfaction, Visualization, and Action. Each persuasive interview is unique so that the amount of time spent on each step will vary based on the salesperson's understanding of the personal

Step	Function	Client's Responses
Attention rapport building	Getting attention, gaining control, building trust	I want to listen. I trust this person.
Need, assess where client stands on the issue	Describe and develop the problem under consideration	Something needs to be done.
Satisfaction	Present benefits of your point of view	This is what must be done.
Visualization	Reiterate accepted benefits with visualization of results	I can see myself enjoying the satisfaction of doing this.
Action	Request tangible proof of acceptance	"I will do (believe, feel) this."

Figure 17. Motivated sequence.

characteristics of the client. Figure 17 shows the steps, functions, and client's responses to the steps of the interview.

After analyzing the client, the interviewer might develop an interview guide using the motivated sequence. Persuasive communication generally begins with a specific purpose statement, central idea statement, and general purpose statement. For example, here is how an interview guide might appear to sell the Happy Printer.

Interview Guide

Specific purpose — To persuade the interviewee that the Happy Printer should increase the quality of publication of the Good Writers Company.

Central idea — Happy Printers will enable the Good Writers Company to publish its own newsletters.

General purpose — To persuade the interviewee to buy Happy Printers.

Introduction

Attention   I. Do you think your present printing facilities are adequate? Did you know that over 300 of the Fortune 500 have purchased the new Happy Laser Printer?

          II. Bill March told me that you are considering up-dating your printing capabilities. He has shown me several of your newsletters and asked me to assess the quality of the printing.

         III. Today I am here to share our product with you and to explain why our product might fit your needs.

Body

Need | I. You need printers that are capable of producing quality visuals, that cost less than 30 cents a copy, and that look neat and professional.

Satisfaction | II. The Happy Laser Printer can solve your problems as this printer is designed to produce quality newsletters and manuals.

Visualization | III. Here is how the XYZ Writers Company uses the Happy Laser Printer. Imagine how your newsletter will look if you used a Happy Laser Printer.

Conclusion

Action | I. Now that we have discussed the pros and cons of the printer, I know you can understand why we are so proud of it.

II. I know you would like the "state of the art" printer in your office, wouldn't you?

Interview Schedule

Next the interviewer should develop an interview schedule.

Attention Step
1. Do you think your present printing facilities are adequate?
2. Would you like to produce your newsletter in-house?

Need Step
1. What do you want out of your printers?
2. You want the best quality for your money, don't you?
3. What are the major problems with the present printing orientation?

Satisfaction Step
1. How can we help to solve your problems?
2. Did you know that the Happy Printer is the best selling printer in the United States?
3. You would like to produce your own publication in-house, wouldn't you?
4. Which of the following graphics do you think were printed on the Happy Laser? (show list)
5. Here are some sample newsletters; they really look professional, don't they?
6. This new printer would meet your needs, wouldn't it?

Visualization Step
1. Imagine how your newsletter will look when you buy this printer; you would be satisfied with this printer, wouldn't you?

Action

1. You do understand why we are so pleased with the printer, don't you?
2. You would like the "state of the art" printer in your office, wouldn't you?
3. You would like to purchase the Happy, wouldn't you?

The interviewer is ready to conduct the interview.

CONDUCTING THE INTERVIEW

Prior to conducting the interview the interviewer will analyze the dimensions of the interviewee, create an interview guide and interview schedule, and develop the opening and closing. The salesperson will need to be prepared to respond to the client's objections. For example, the client might want to delay in making a decision about the new printer. Prior to the interview the interviewer should plan how to deal with objections. Below is an example of how a client might try to delay in making a decision:

> **Client:** I'm sure the Happy Printer is the best that money can buy. But we need to use our present printers until they wear out and until we have used all the paper.

> **Salesperson:** I'm sure you don't want to lose money by switching to the Happy Printer, but we will buy your extra supplies of paper, and we will take your old printers as trade. We have discovered that even small companies want their own printers. Your present printers are quite suited for smaller companies.

In addition to trying to delay in making a decision on the printer, a client might assert that the new printer costs too much money. The vendor will need to show the customer that in the long-run the new printer will save them money, might lead to new clients and increase the prestige of the company. For example a vendor might respond to a client who says "We can't afford the printer, right now," by saying the following:

> **Salesperson:** Cost is a major concern to you, isn't it?

> **Client:** Yes!

> **Salesperson:** I agree that in the short run you might feel that the change in printers would be a bad financial decision. I, however, have data from several writing companies that show that your loss is short lived. In fact, within six months, you will be ahead of the game. Let's examine the following data . . .

If the client is older and in an established firm, tradition might be the biggest hurdle to overcome. Using the same example, the salesperson might compare the change from typewriters to word processors, showing the advantages of word processors over typewriters by referring to how much time they have saved by using word processors and showing how the new printer will increase the quality of the printing and enable the Good Writers Company to produce its own graphics.

Obviously, the interviewer will need to be very attentive throughout the interview. The interviewer needs to be able to use verification questions such as, Am I correct in assuming you are not satisfied with your present printers? The interviewer might use "What-If" questions such as, What if we could delay the payment by 90 days, would you be able to afford the printers?

THE INTERVIEWEE

Although the major focus of this chapter has been on the role of the interviewer in the persuasive interview, attention also should be paid to the role of the interviewee. Most people play the interviewee role more frequently than that of the interviewer. The interviewee needs to assess and evaluate what will be gained by purchasing a product or accepting a plan. In persuasive situations the interviewee should try to answer the following questions:

1. What will I really gain?
2. What will the demands be on my time and resources?
3. What will it cost me in dollars?
4. How will the acceptance of this persuasion affect others with whom I am close?
5. What are the short-term benefits?
6. What are the long-term benefits?
7. What will be the probable outcomes if I am not persuaded?

The interviewee needs to consider all the information thoroughly and make a decision based on facts. The personal relationship with the interviewer should not be a deciding factor in making a decision to buy a product or in accepting a proposal.

SUMMARY

Persuasive interviews occur quite frequently in the "world of work" and in our daily communication with others. Probably everyone has played the role of the interviewee, and many have played the role of the interviewer. This chapter has discussed the important variables of persuasion: definition, dimensions, planning and conducting the persuasive interview.

A PERSUASIVE INTERVIEW FOR REVIEW AND ANALYSIS

This interview takes place between a salesperson and client. The vendor is trying to persuade Dr. Pam Bennett, the Director of a Technical Communication Program to buy XYZ computers for the writing laboratory. Dr. Bennett has invited several vendors to make sales presentations to the writing faculty and demonstrate their software and hardware.

Prior to the interview, the interviewer surveyed technical communication students to find out the types of writing and graphic needs of students. The interviewer knows two faculty members in the department and asked them to describe Dr. Bennett's background in computers, her perceptions of the basic needs of the writing laboratory and her personality. The vendor then prepared for the interview.

As you read the dialogue please answer the following questions. How effectively does the interviewer open the interview? Does the interviewer establish a need for purchasing the XYZ computers? Does the interviewer satisfy the need? How effectively does the interviewer close the interview? What types of appeals does the interviewer use? How would you describe the interviewee? How would you describe the interviewer? How effectively does the interviewer close the interview?

Interviewer: Good Morning, Dr. Bennett. Thank you for agreeing to meet with me to discuss our computer. I've done some research on your students here and have talked to some of your colleagues, so I feel I have some understanding of your needs. I also feel that I know you because of our phone conversations and the memos we have sent to each other. (The interviewer and interviewee smile as they greet each other. They shake hands.)

Interviewee: Thanks! I'm really excited to see the demonstration. I have read the literature and shared it with the other writing teachers, but I'm not sure if we need such an elaborate system.

Interviewer: As you know this is the "state of the art" equipment, and it is used in over 300 writing laboratories in universities throughout the United States. You do want your TC majors to use the best equipment, don't you?

Interviewee: Yes! Of course! We want our students to be familiar and competent with the best equipment. Other companies make the same claim as yours does. How do we know which vendor to believe?

Interviewer: We have conducted several usability studies, field studies, survey studies and have concluded in-depth interviews with several clients. You probably have not had an opportunity to read our report on the various studies. Actually, the scientific research has been completed by professors at five different universities. We are really proud of this. I have a copy of the report for you (handing the report to the interviewee). Please check with other computer firms. We feel we have more documentation for our system than any other company. You also should know some of the people who have conducted the research. We feel we have a credible product.

Interviewee: Thanks! I will read the report tonight!

Interviewer: Now, I would like to explain why our system can satisfy your needs. First the system has the most software for writers. This system would be helpful for your students, wouldn't it?

Interviewee: Yes!

Interviewer: The computer blinks if you make a mistake, so that you can correct it immediately. The correction device would be a nice feature on your computer, wouldn't it?

Interviewee: Yes!

(The interviewer states six other advantages of the computer. After each advantage, the interviewer asks a leading question. Next the interviewer demonstrates the features of the computer, and faculty members have an opportunity to use the computer.)

Interviewer: Thanks for giving me an opportunity to demonstrate the equipment. We are excited about it. The computer is an impressive unit, don't you think? (The interviewer looks directly at Dr. Bennett and other faculty members, smiles, and uses open hand gestures.)

Interviewee: Yes!

Interviewer: This computer would be good for your students, wouldn't it?

Interviewee: Yes!

Interviewer: You want to purchase this equipment, don't you?

Interviewee: I guess so, but I need to read the studies and meet with the writing staff before we make a decision.

Interviewer: This is the best system on the market, and you want your students to have the best computers to work with, don't you?

Interviewee: Yes! We will make a decision within the next two weeks.

QUESTIONS

Participate in a "real world" persuasive interview. You might be the interviewer or interviewee. For example, you could invite a salesperson to come to your home to sell you something such as life insurance, or you could go to a computer business and listen to a sales presentation on why you should buy a computer or certain software. After participating in the program, please answer the following questions:

Interviewer
1. If you were the interviewer, how did you analyze the characteristics of the interviewee?
2. What type of motive appeals did you use?
3. How did you establish your credibility?
4. What types of persuasive tactics did you use?
5. What type of introduction did you use?
6. How did you establish a need for your product?

7. How did you develop the satisfaction and visualization steps?
8. What type of conclusion did you use?

Interviewee

1. If you were the interviewee, how did you prepare for the interview?
2. What type of motive appeals did the interviewer use?
3. How did the interviewer establish credibility?
4. What type of persuasive tactics did the interviewer use?
5. What type of introduction did the interviewer use?
6. How did the interviewer persuade you to buy the product (if he/she did)?
7. How would you rate your performance in this interview?

Case 1

Pretend that you are a vendor and you have been assigned to conduct cold calls to sell a new computer by a well known company. You have limited documentation on the advantages of the new computer over the ones that the companies are using, but your company feels that the computers are more user friendly, take up less space and are more attractive.

Case 2

Pretend that a salesperson has arranged to meet with you in hopes of persuading you to purchase membership in a health club for your writing company. How would you prepare to play the role of the interviewee?

Case 3

Little Art Buick, an excellent salesman in your organization, has been selected to demonstrate a new line of computers to major writing companies. Art, however, has some grooming and dressing habits that need to be overcome. You have been assigned to talk to Art to try to persuade him to obtain some new suits and shave his beard. How would you approach Art? How would you establish a need to buy a new suit? How would you satisfy the need?

REFERENCES

1. M. Karlin and H. Abelson, *Persuasion: How Opinions and Attitudes Are Changed*, Springer, New York, 1970.
2. M. Rokeach and S. Parker, Values as Social Indicators of Poverty and Race in America, *Annals of the American Academy of Political and Social Sciences, 388*, pp. 101-102, 1970.
3. R. Verderber, *The Challenge of Effective Speaking*, Wadsworth Publishing Co., Belmont, California, 1985.
4. J. Rubin and B. Brown, *The Social Psychology of Bargaining and Negotiation*, Academic Press, New York, New York 11975.

5. C. Stewart and W. Cash, *Interviewing Principles and Practices*, William C. Brown Co., Dubuque, Iowa, 1988.
6. J. Robeson, H. Mathews, and C. Stevens, *Selling*, Richard D. Irvin, Homewood, Illinois, 1978.
7. R. Goyer, C. Redding, and J. Rickey, *Interviewing Principles and Techniques*, William C. Brown C., Dubuque, Iowa, 1964.
8. S. Massimino, *The Complete Book on Closing Sales*, AMACOM, New York, 1981.
9. J. Zima, *Interviewing: Key to Effective Management*, Science Research Associates, Chicago, 1983.
10. A. Monroe and D. Ehninger, *Principles of Speech Communication*, Scott, Foresman and Co., Glenview, Illinois, 1975.

CHAPTER 10

Oral Communication in the Workplace

OBJECTIVES

On completion of this chapter you should be able to:
  List types of oral communication
  Identify directions of oral communication
  Describe types of oral communication
  Assess leadership skills
  Analyze types of oral communication

The focus of this book has been on various types of interviews in the "world of work." Of course, other types of dyadic communication occur between managers and subordinates and between peers. In fact, it is estimated that between 50 and 80 percent of a manager's workday is spent in interpersonal communication. Obviously, not all employees will communicate at this level, but face-to-face communication will play a primary role in the workday of employees who choose careers in communication research, technical communication and management. The focus of this chapter is on types of on-the-job oral communication, including directions of oral communication, small group communication, and public communication.

DIRECTIONS OF ORAL COMMUNICATION

Ideally, interpersonal communication should be the primary means of communication among levels of the organization, but because of the complexity of organizations other communication channels must play a role. In this section of the chapter downward, upward, and horizontal communication will be discussed.

Downward

Downward communication is the flow of messages or information from superiors to subordinates in the organization. Downward communication can be both written and oral. If it is oral, it can be face-to-face or over the telephone. Katz and Kahn discuss five types of downward communication [1, pp. 239-240]:

1. To give job instructions. These are directions on how to complete a specific task. Instructions could be given in a face-to-face information-giving interview, an enlightenment discussion, a demonstration speech, a memo, a letter, or a set of written instructions.
2. To complete a job rationale. A manager might explain how a specific task relates to other tasks. Interpersonal communication might help to develop a sense of interdependence among levels of the organization. A manager also might give information to a technical writer on the relationships among the various parts of a manual. This same information could be completed with other forms of oral communication as well as with written communication.
3. To explain policies and procedures. These messages point out the organizational rules, regulations, and benefits. A good example would be to explain how long you have to work before you are eligible for a week's vacation with pay.
4. To provide feedback to workers. Interpersonal communication might consist of informal feedback given by supervisors to subordinates or formal appraisal interviews.
5. To indoctrinate employees. Messages are intended to build employees' commitments by explaining the mission and the overall goals of the organization. The lead writer might try to persuade the writing team that the success of the project is dependent on the level of commitment of each person. Information-giving, information-gathering, problem-solving interviews and group discussions might be used to inform and persuade the other party. A memo might be written to members of the project team and might stress the importance of team work.

Obviously downward communication passes through many levels of the organization. Nichols indicates that as the message moves from one level to another, more information is lost [2, p. 4]. Nichols uses the following example (see Table 7).

Although downward communication should move smoothly as power and authority are behind it, this is not the case. The reasons why downward communication causes problems are that it is generally one-way communication, differences exist in values and perceptions, mistrust, lack of open communication, inappropriate use of language, over-communicating or under-communicating. The primary problem is a lack of face-to-face communication between managers and subordinates. Fisher suggests that supervisors take the following steps to improve downward communication [3, p. 46]:

1. Maintain contact with subordinates and encourage two-way communication.

Table 7. Information Reduction in Downward
Communication

Level of Hierarchy	Percentage of Information Received
Board	100
Vice-President	63
General Supervisors	56
Plant Managers	40
General Foreman	30
Workers	20

R. Nichols, Listening Is Good Business, *Management of Personnel Quarterly*, pp. 2-10, 1962. Reprint by permission of John Wiley & Sons, Inc.

2. Use several channels of communication, including face-to-face conversations.
3. Build trust by letting subordinates know how decisions, ones affecting their pay and career development, are to be made.

Upward Communication

Upward communication refers to messages that flow from subordinates to supervisors. It provides feedback to superiors' downward communication. Through this process subordinates become more goal-oriented as they have the opportunity to express their feelings about their jobs, co-workers and the company. In short, Koehler and Huber indicate that subordinates have an opportunity to talk to the boss [4, pp. 8-9]. They indicate that five factors have a significant impact on the effectiveness of upward communication.

1. Positive upward communication is more likely to be utilized by managerial decision makers than negative upward communication.
2. The timeliness of the communication is important.
3. Upward communication is more likely to be accepted if it supports current policies.
4. Upward communication is more likely to be effective if it goes directly to a receiver who can act on it.
5. Upward communication is more likely to be effective when it has an intuitive appeal to the receiver.

Obviously upward communication can be written or oral. Through face-to-face interviews, meetings and conferences, supervisors and subordinates can establish effective upward communication. Planty and Machaver list several benefits for management [5, pp. 315-317]:

1. Management obtains an improved picture of work, accomplishments, problems, plans, attitudes and feelings of subordinates at all levels.
2. Management can identify individuals, policies, actions or assignments that are likely to cause trouble.
3. Management can get the lower echelons to do a more systematic and useful job of reporting.
4. Management can utilize ideas of subordinates.
5. Upward communication helps managers in downward communication.

Overall, upward communication should help managers and subordinates to develop better interpersonal relationships, and both parties should become better listeners. Planty and Machaver concluded [5, p. 319]: "The most effective method for encouraging upward communication is sympathetic listening in the many day-to-day, informal contacts within the department and outside the workplace."

Horizontal Communication

Horizontal communication refers to the lateral exchange of messages among peers (people on the same organizational level of authority). It reduces the potential for distortion of messages through a long series of communication links. Koehler and associates indicate that horizontal communication establishes several benefits for the organization [6, p. 101]:

1. Providing coordination between departments to maximize productivity.
2. Increasing the morale and confidence of the individuals involved in problem-solving.
3. Sharing information contributes to task effectiveness.
4. Solving intradepartmental and interdepartmental conflict without intervention.
5. Providing social and emotional support for peers.
6. Serving as a substitute for upward and downward communication.

Unlike upward and downward communication, horizontal communication is generally interpersonal. For example, two writers from the same writing group might be involved in a series of information-gathering and information-giving interviews. In addition, a number of writers might meet as a group to share information on the project or attempt to solve problems. Problems such as lack of management recognition and reward and lack of interpersonal skills impede effective lateral communication. Research indicates that effective supervisors spend a great amount of time in contact with lateral groups.

GROUPS

Group communication starts at birth and continues throughout a person's lifetime. During childhood the family is the primary group. The family includes parents, brothers, sisters, children, grandparents, cousins, uncles, and aunts. Relationships developed in our early years will help to determine our various self-concepts, willingness to disclose information to others in interpersonal communication situations and small group communication situations. A person's interpersonal relationships will affect that person's perceptions of others, will affect verbal, vocal, and nonverbal communication in both interviewing and group situations and will affect the personal ability to resolve conflict.

Group communication plays a significant role in the writer's "world of work." This section of the last chapter will focus on definitions of small groups, types of small groups, discussion forms, leadership, communication patterns, and interactions and effective participation in small group discussion.

Small Groups

Small groups are an important part of the technical writer's "world of work." The term *small* refers to the number of participants in a discussion. The participants can interact face-to-face and are interdependent. Typically, when two people are discussing a problem it is called a problem-solving interview. When more than two people are discussing a problem, it is called a problem-solving group discussion. Likewise, when a psychologist is counseling a patient, the interview is called a counseling interview. When a number of patients are being treated at the same time, it is called a help group or counseling group. Here are some definitions of small groups: Fisher defines *a small group as a small number of people who are aware of one another and who see each other as being part of a group* [3, p. 221]. Bormann and Bormann indicate that *group discussions refer to one or more meetings of a small group of people who thereby communicate face-to-face in order to fulfill a common purpose and achieve a group goal* [7, p. 6].

These definitions, as well as others, collectively lead to the following definition: *A small number of people who communicate face-to-face as a dynamic whole with a sense of interdependence to fulfill a specific task and achieve a common goal.*

Types of small groups include: primary and secondary, formal and informal, and problem-solving. Each type of group might play a role in the daily activities of the technical writer. The term "primary group" is self-explanatory as it refers to the most important groups in a person's life. Family is the first primary group. This group plays an important role in developing attitudes, values, beliefs and behaviors and helps to determine other primary groups in which a person belongs. Other groups include peers, friendships, colleagues and church groups. Primary groups exert a strong influence on their members. For example, technical writers might form a softball team which would be classified as a primary group.

Unlike a primary group whose basic purpose is social, secondary groups are basically task-oriented. For example, the Society for Technical Communication is a secondary group. Within this large group several divisions exist that focus on research, management, and new technology. These groups are necessary as various reference groups can focus on specific needs, and, in many cases, face-to-face contact does not occur. Obviously, most organizations have several secondary groups in order to perform various tasks. Secondary groups are more impersonal than primary groups.

Formal and informal groups — Groups also can be classified as formal and informal. In the "world of work" you might be assigned to a certain committee, a formal group to perform a specific task. For example, five writers might be a formal group for a specific project. Within this group several information-giving and information-gathering interviews might occur, as well as appraisal, disciplinary, and exit interviews. The five writers might meet as a group to discuss various aspects of a writing project. Other formal groups might be established between writing and engineering groups. For example, three writers and two engineers might form a group. Another group might consist of two writers, a graphic expert, an engineer, and a vender.

Informal groups, on the other hand, consist of people who self-select into a group because of social needs, common interests, friendship or companionship needs. Examples of informal groups are Parents without Partners, Tall-Girls Club, Weight Watchers and Alcoholics Anonymous. The primary purpose is a social function.

Problem-solving group — The main purpose of many groups is to solve problems. Sometimes problem-solving interviews will lead to resolution of problems, while at other times members of different units will join together to solve a problem. Thus, the problem-solving group is task-oriented, on-going and the goal involves anticipated action. Brooks and Emmert assert that several factors will determine the outcome of the group [8, pp. 275-278]. These include individual personalities, communication skills, group size and group leadership. Basically, group members will follow Dewey's Reflective Thinking Model to solve problems. Questions of fact, questions of value, and questions of policy might be used to guide the discussion.

By following the reflective thinking process, group members experience, according to Bales and Strodtbeck, three stages [9, pp. 485-495]: orientation, evaluation, and control. During the orientation stage members exchange information and clarify, classify, confirm and repeat it among themselves. In the evaluation stage members share opinions and feelings about the problem and analyze the problem. During the control stage, members ask and give suggestions, solutions and possible plans to resolve the problem. In small group situations decisions are generally made by a majority or by a consensus, but in some cases, a formal leader or project director might make the decision. Bales' categories of behavior in groups, presented in Figure 18, can be used as a guide to chart the interactions

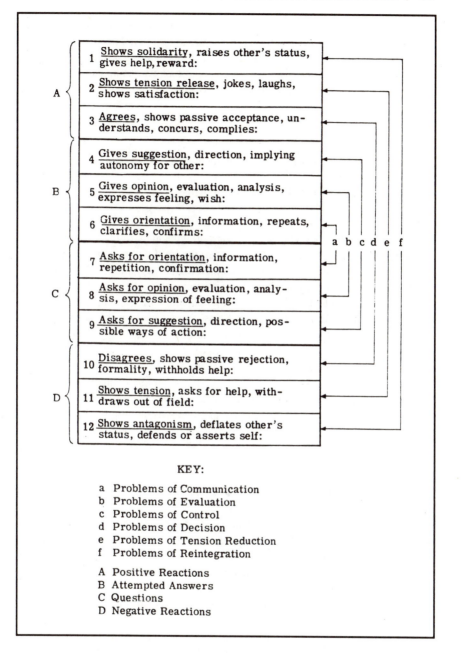

Figure 18. Bales' categories of behavior in groups: Interaction process analysis.
R. F. Bales, *Interaction Process Analysis,* University of Chicago Press,
Chicago, p. 9, 1950. Reprint by permission of University of Chicago Press.

between group members and indicate the types of communication between group members. The behaviors are categorized into social-emotional positive and social-emotional negative comments and task comments. During a conversation, an interview, and group discussion, participants' comments can be charted into one of the three types for one of the categories [10, p. 9].

Discussion Forms

The basic discussion forms include the panel, symposium, and lecture-panel.

Panel — The panel is one of the most popular forms of public discussion. It usually consists of three to five people who are selected prior to the discussion and who have a special knowledge of the problem. Prior to the discussion, members usually have met to plan the agenda or outline which follows the reflective thinking process. Occasionally, the discussion outline may be prepared by the leader and presented to the panel members who may make suggestions for changes before the discussion. During the planning stage the group members will interact with one another. Typically, group members will use both social and task comments in planning the discussion. Bales' model could be used to chart the interactions between group members. For the discussion the panel members assemble themselves in a semicircle in front of an audience as this enables visual and oral contact to occur between group members as well as the audience. The leader generally sits in the center of the group so that eye contact can be maintained with all members and with the audience.

Group members share their information and opinions on different aspects of the problem and interact with one another throughout the discussion. After the panel members have shared their information and opinions, the leader may ask for questions from the audience. This open question period is called a *forum*.

Symposium — The symposium, which is a formal method of presenting information and opinion, consists of three to five people who have knowledge on a specific aspect of the topic. This discussion method would be used by group experts in discussing a topic. For example, if a project team, consisting of writers engineers, graphic designers, and vendors were to present their project to a decision-making team in an organization, the group might begin with a symposium discussion. Each member has a well prepared and rehearsed speech on a specific subtopic. The speeches are usually between five and ten minutes in length depending upon the subject and purpose of the discussion.

Lecture panel — In the third discussion form, the lecture-panel or lecture-forum, a speech is presented by a person who is qualified on the topic. The panel members then interact about the material covered in the speech, or the audience interacts with the speaker.

All of these methods might be used along with the problem-solving interview, information-gathering interview, and information-giving interview in everyday on-the-job communication situations.

LEADERSHIP

Basically a leader can be defined as a person who performs leadership behaviors or who exerts influence on another person in an interview or other people in a group. Ideally, the leader has the ability to think carefully and is knowledgeable about task functions in an interview or group. Leadership is generally discussed as something that occurs in groups, but obviously, as pointed out in Chapter 8, each person or party assumes various roles in the interview. Nelson and Pearson indicate that a leader is an influential person who helps members clarify, attain and maintain goals. A leader must be an effective communicator.

Brilhart points out that an effective discussion leader must possess the following qualities [11, pp. 131-132]:

1. Skill in organizing group thinking.
2. Open-mindedness.
3. Active participator.
4. Democratic and consultative nature.
5. Articulateness.
6. Respect for and sensitivity to others.
7. Temperance and self-control.

In an information-gathering interview, the interviewer might be a task leader, while the interviewee might be the social emotional leader. Likewise, each member of a group might assume some aspect of the leadership role. A leader might be appointed or emerge as a group of people are discussing a problem. Appointed leaders might be selected by someone outside the group or elected by group members. For example, a teacher or manager might assign a leader to read a case study on persuasion and decide how to solve a problem or sell a product. A technical communicator also might be elected as the leader of the local chapter of the Society for Technical Communication. An emergent leader occurs when group members recognize the leadership of a particular person who then will assume the leadership role.

Bales and Strodtbeck indicate that some leaders are good at task-orientation and skilled in problem solving, while other groups would function best with a social emotional orientation [9, p. 493]. In some cases both task and social emotional leaders will emerge. Generally, research supports the notion that males are task leaders and females are social emotional leaders. For example, Maier found that male leaders perform better in unstructured, creative situations [12, p. 459]. Megargee discovered that even if females have personality characteristics for leadership roles, the sex-role attitudes, group composition, and task might intervene to curtail their ability to lead [13, p. 382]. Now let's focus on leadership.

According to Brilhart, leadership refers to any behavior which helps a group to clarify and achieve group goals. Leadership means influence. White and Lippitt define three types [14, p. 32]:

> *Authoritarian*: The leader determines policy, procedures, tasks and or roles of members. The leader makes personal praise or criticism of individual contributions.

> *Democratic Leader*: The leader suggests alternatives, but the group decides specific policy, procedure, tasks and roles of members. Group discussion is encouraged and assisted by the leader. Everyone is free to participate.

> *Laissez-Faire*: The leader supplies information and material when asked. The leader does not take part in direct discussion of the group. The group has complete freedom to determine policy, procedure, tasks and/or roles of group members. Laissez-faire is essentially nonleadership.

White and Lippitt drew the following conclusions concerning leadership [14, p. 85-86]:

1. More work is done under a democratic leader than a laissez-faire setting.
2. More work is done under an autocratic leader than under a democratic leader.
3. Work motivation and originality are better under a democratic leader.
4. Autocracy seems to create aggression and discontent, even though discontent may not appear on the surface.
5. More dependence and less individuality exist in autocracy.
6. More group-mindedness and more friendliness exist under a democratic leader.

These results support their study that a democratic leader is the most acceptable of the three types of leaders.

Leadership is an important variable in group communication as well as interpersonal communication situations. Think about leadership in various types of interviews and groups and answer the following questions:

1. What makes an effective leader?
2. Have you participated in an interview with an autocratic leader?
3. Do you enjoy leadership roles? If yes, why?

COMMUNICATION PATTERNS AND INTERACTIONS

Patterns of interaction will determine who will interact with whom. Leavitt asserts that certain members of a group fall into patterns of interaction called communication networks. A communication network is a schematic diagram that charts the interaction among members. The four types of networks include chain, Y, circle, and all-channel [15, pp. 42-46].

In the chain network, Figure 19, each member communicates with the individual next to him/her for task related communication. This type of network creates a sense of the overall structure of the group. As a result there is not an opportunity to build personal relationships with all group members. For example, a team of writers might be working on software documentation where each writer has a specific task to perform and can communicate only with the next writer when the task is completed.

In the Y communication network, the two people in the middle disseminate information to those on the outside. Members who assume leadership functions are satisfied, but other members experience less satisfaction (see Figure 20).

The circle network eliminates the status differences on the chain and Y networks as group members have relatively equal status. Unless a task leader emerges, there will be a lack of coordination to solve a problem (see Figure 21). If a lead writer or manager is part of this network, this person will assume the leadership.

The all-channel network, according to Brilhart, leads to greater productivity and member satisfaction (see Figure 22). In this network all members have equal status, equal responsibility for task accomplishment, and maintenance of groups,

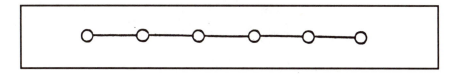

Figure 19. Chain communication network.

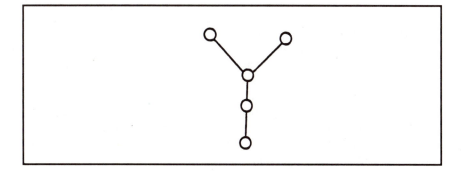

Figure 20. Y communication network.

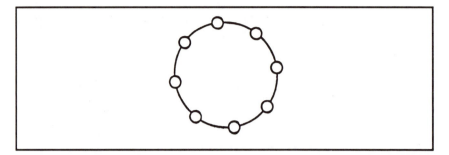

Figure 21. Circle communication network.

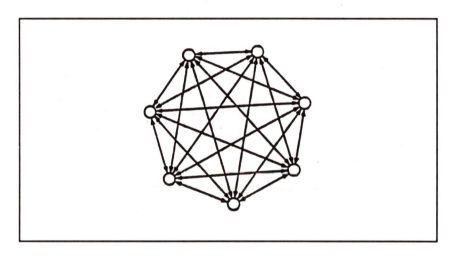

Figure 22. All-channel network.

and interact face-to-face with all other members. Ideally, the all-channel network will create an atmosphere that leads to trust and self-disclosure, and group members will share task and social-emotional leadership responsibilities. The all-channel network will work well with a group of cohesive writers, writers and editors, or writers and subject matter experts.

In summary, the chain and Y networks permit group members to communicate with one or two other members, but all members are not plugged into all other members. The all-channel network enables all members to communicate with one another and results in the highest member satisfaction.

The types of communication which occur among group members might be classified into verbal, nonverbal and paraverbal categories. Bales indicates that interaction is a continuous stream of acts, words, symbols, reactions, gestures and so forth. Communication flows from member to member, might include some or all members of the group and is distributed over time.

An examination of the categories indicates that group members make task and social comments. Research indicates an approximately fifty-fifty balance of questions and answers during a typical problem-solving discussion. The instrumental areas consist of giving information, suggestions, and opinions, and asking for information, suggestions, and opinions. In the social-emotional areas group members can either show solidarity or antagonism. Both task and social comments will determine the overall productivity of the group. The interaction process analysis system also can be used to classify various task and social comments in the problem-solving interview, as well as all other types of interviews.

PUBLIC COMMUNICATION

Public communication refers to a sending of messages to a group of people. It refers to when one person is doing most of the sending, and a number of listeners are doing most of the receiving. Unlike interviewing and group communication, public communication is limited to nonverbal messages from listeners. Typical public speaking events include organizational-wide meetings, orientation sessions, training programs, and social functions. Below is a list of speaking occasions for technical communicators:

1. Lead writer presents the new software package to four writers, four engineers, and four graphic experts who created the manual.
2. Vendor makes a sales presentation to a group of writers at Good Writers Company.
3. Manager presents an informational speech on the need for a new policy and procedure manual.
4. In a speech of special occasion the president of a writing organization presents gold pens to writers for their outstanding performance.
5. Several managers make speeches on the goals of the organization for the next fiscal year.

SUMMARY

The technical writer's "world of work" is filled with interpersonal communication. Much of the communication is one-on-one with a purpose which is termed *interviewing*. In many cases, group communication is necessary as many writers might be involved in the writing process, or writers and subject matter experts are responsible for completing a project together. Less often, but still important, public communication will occur to develop and disseminate information to a large audience.

QUESTIONS

Keep a log of the types of oral and written communication in which you are involved in your present technical communication position and answer the following questions:

1. What percent of your workday is spent in oral communication?
   a. What percent of the oral communication do you spend in interviewing situations? Identify the types of interviews and describe your most recent interviewing experience.
   b. What percent of your oral communication do you spend in group communication situations? Identify the types of groups and describe your most recent group experience.
   c. What percent of your oral communication do you spend in public communication situations? Describe one of your public speeches.
2. What percent of your work day is spent in writing? Describe a significant writing situation.
3. Describe an informal communication situation in your "world of work."
4. How does downward communication operate in your organization?
5. How does upward communication operate in your organization?
6. What are your oral communication needs in your "world of work?"

REFERENCES

1. D. Katz and R. Kahn, *The Psychology of Organizations*, John Wiley and Sons, New York, 1966.
2. R. Nichols, Listening Is Good Business, *Management of Personnel Quarterly*, 1962.
3. D. Fisher, *Communication in Organization*, West Publishing Company, St. Paul, 1982.
4. J. Koehler and G. Huber, *Effects of Upward Communication on Managerial Decision Making*, International Communication Association Convention, New Orleans, 1974.
5. E. Planty and W. Machaver, Upward Communication: Project in Executive Development, *Personnel, 28*, pp. 314-319, 1952.
6. J. Koehler, K. Anatol, and R. Applbaum, *Organizational Communication Behavioral Perspectives*, Holt, Rinehart and Winston, New York, 1981.
7. E. Bormann and N. Bormann, *Effective Small Group Communication*, Burgess Publishing Co., Minneapolis, 1972.
8. W. Brooks and P. Emmert, *Interpersonal Communication*, Wm. C. Brown Co., Dubuque, Iowa, 1976.
9. R. F. Bales and F. L. Strodtbeck, Phases in Group Problem-Solving, *Journal of Abnormal and Social Psychology, 46*, pp. 485-495, 1951.
10. R. Bales, *Interaction Process Analysis*, Addison-Wesley, Reading, Massachusetts, 1950.
11. J. Brilhart, *Effective Group Discussion*, Wm. C. Brown Co., Dubuque, Iowa, 1974.
12. N. Maier, Male Versus Female Discussion Leaders, *Personnel Psychology, 23*, pp. 455-461, 1970.

13. E. Megargee, Influence of Sex Roles on the Manifestation of Leadership, *Journal of Applied Psychology, 55*, pp. 377-382, 1969.
14. R. White and R. Lippitt, *Autocracy and Democracy*, Harper and Row Co., New York, 1966.
15. H. Leavitt, Some Effects of Certain Communication Patterns on Group Performance, *Journal of Abnormal and Social Psychology, 46*, pp. 38-50, 1951.

Part 5
ARTICLE REVIEW

THE INTERVIEW*

EDWARD PRICE BELL

Bell's article provides a point of view concerning the importance of interviewing. This article was published sixty-five years ago, but the points discussed at this time are still as relevant today. After reading the article please answer the following questions:

1. How do the terms *intangible gold* and *silver* and *gems* relate to interviewing.
2. Why is this article relevant to you as a technical writer or technical communication student?
3. How is this article relevant to you as a human being?

*   *   *

It was a real pleasure to me to accept the honor of addressing you tonight. There was something I very much wished to say—a point of view I very much wished to urge in this technical journalistic company.

My subject is "The Interview." I am a great believer in the interview—in the honest interview, in the searching interview, in the interview that exemplifies the elements of both science and art. For no other phase of journalism, in my opinion, is there a wider or more vital field of usefulness.

What is the interview? Why is it important? What type of person is worthy of the interviewer's attention? How is the valuable interview done?

Interviewing in which are both science and art is an intellectual and moral force of a high order. It enlightens and stimulates. It discloses facts and marshals arguments and sounds a trumpet for the pursuit of high ideals. It is educative and evangelic. It bridges the gulf between knowledge and ignorance, between moral ardor and moral apathy, between genius and the common understanding.

Devoted and skillful interviewers may be likened to the great portrait painters of the world. They may be likened also to those who go prospecting and delving in search of precious metals and precious stones. Your portrait painter—what does

*Edward Price Bell, The Interview, *The Journal Bulletin*, pp. 13-18, 1924. Reprinted by permission.

he do? Gives you a lifelike reproduction of physical lineaments. What does your skillful interviewer do? Gives you a faithful picture of a human mind and soul.

Yes; your trained interviewer is a painter. He does not use a brush and pigments: such implements and media are too crude for his work. Only words will serve him. Only words are adequate vehicles of the full message, emotional and intellectual, which he strives to communicate. Definite sentiments, definite ideas, definite facts—words must bear them if they be borne at all.

Devoted and skillful interviewers, I have said, may be likened, not only to portrait painters, but to those who go prospecting and delving in search of precious metals and precious stones. Golden feelings, golden thoughts, golden precepts, all manner of emotional and intellectual jewels, lie hidden in the hills of silence. There they are comparatively useless. It is the interviewer's business to dig them out, to garner them, and to make them the common property of mankind.

Psychic portraiture, one need not say, calls for professional dexterity. Intangible gold and silver and gems are even more elusive than are their material correlatives. You cannot see an emotion—not with the naked eye. You cannot see an idea—not with the naked eye. All sentiments, all thoughts, all ideals, all moralities, the whole range of humanism, are invisible to the naked eye.

It is in the domain of humanism that your expert interviewer labors. From the first to last, his main concern is with the human heart and mind. He knows that emotions issue in ideas, that ideas issue in actions, and that actions determine the destiny of the world. It is his purpose, therefore, to make us understand emotions and ideas—to make us, so to speak, see these unseeable things, these potent invisibilities, that are wont to translate themselves into life and into history.

Emotions and ideas you cannot examine without confronting facts, conditions, realities, or particular versions of facts, conditions, realities. In other words, your interviewee is feeling and thinking about some phase of human life, some political or social matter, some question of literature, art, or philosophy, some scientific discovery or speculation, some momentous event that seems to him to be casting its shadow before.

There are those who fancy that emotions and ideas—abstractions—are colorless. I venture to say to you ladies and gentlemen, if you are looking for rainbows, for beautiful rainbows, for rainbows that span the whole reach of human interest and welfare, seek them in emotions and ideas.

Very wonderful is nature, no doubt—full of mystery and beauty, infinitely soothing to the human spirit. But, as walls do not make a city, so mountains, forests, rivers, lakes, seas, do not make humanity. Give me an exquisite painting of land or ocean, and I shall love it. Give me an adequate picture of a great human heart and mind, with all their nobilities of fervor and vision, and I shall love it inexpressibly more.

Your first-rate interview, then, is a medium or a mirror. It is a pervading substance through which you catch moral fire and mental suggestion or guidance. It is a mirror held up to remarkable personality—a mirror in which you descry the spiritual, ethical, and ratiocinative features of an outstanding statesman, admiral, general, orator, divine, scholar, poet, novelist, playwright, artist, physician, surgeon, lawyer, businessman, journalist.

But why trouble to devise these media, to construct these mirrors, to affect these interpretations? I will tell you why. Because the world thirsts for inspiration and knowledge—for draughts of genius and study—as the bronzed and parched desert traveler thirsts for water. Education, light, moral exaltation, wisdom, sympathy, the civilization inhering in culture—to what besides does the normal human soul turn so eagerly as it does to these?

Well, your great interview is a means to these. It is an enemy of ignorance, or darkness, of spiritual torpor, of malice, envy, and animosity. It calls the great women and men of the world to fight these evils. It asks them to use the hypnosis of their names, the magic of their prestige, to arrest and hold the public attention, in order that they may drive their lessons home. Only those who feel profoundly, who think intensely, who aspire mightily, who struggle indefatigably, and to whom self-immolation is a privilege—only such offer the interviewer openings for the masterpieces of his craftsmanship.

It is the interviewer's duty, in my opinion, as it is the duty of the journalist in general, to steer clear of Machiavellianism in statesmanship, and mischief-making in every form. That rock-spring which the blow of the interviewer releases should furnish water wholesome for all humanity to drink—water in substantial volume, water vigorously moving, water prismatically tinted, and not without its music. "Crime," and 'crime' only, is the word for the act of the interviewer who uses his talent and the machinery he commands to poison the thought-stream of the world.

Machiavellianism, if my experience be a reliable guide, is disappearing from the chancellories of the nations. Statesmen are seeking a wiser way. They have more faith than they once had in honesty, candor, sincerity, the golden rule. But the world is not snow-white yet. The interviewer must be on his guard. He must say to those who would talk to him, and through him, that he is under one obligation which is inviolable—the obligation of serving mankind at large to the best of his ability. Your first rate interviewer, ladies and gentlemen—if we may say so in the privacy of our fraternal company—occupies a highly responsible position.

Now we come to the question of how the valuable interview is done. First, since journalism is a matter of the passing hour, a matter of the day, we must have in mind some current situation. This situation must be important. It must be important in the sense that it involves possibilities and probabilities of significance to a large number of people, if not to a whole nation, or to all nations. And let us not call "all nations" extravagant, for there are few really great questions which are not international in their scope.

Currency of interest and weight of subject are indispensable. Having these, one studies the matter in hand from every material angle, formulates as many questions as seem likely to elicit illuminating answers, and then makes one's approach to the person to be interviewed. This approach, time allowing, is made with most advantage, in my view, by letter. This letter, like all others, should be as brief, clear, and pointed as the writer can make it, should indicate the public service renderable by the proposed interview, and should be accompanied by the interviewer's questionnaire.

Such knowledge of the subject in hand as the interviewer can gain he should take with him to the interview. Proportionate, indeed, to his acquaintance with the subject is apt to be the success of his endeavor; for nothing else encourages an authority to talk so much as does a consciousness on his part that he is addressing a zealous and intelligent student of the question he is expounding. However well informed or gifted the interviewee, there can be no great interview without an able and alert interviewer.

Tactics on the part of the interviewer, in the course of the interview, must be determined by the idiosyncracies of the interviewee. Other enterprises than that of war demand strategic and tactical procedure. In a sense, every one who sets out to do a thing of consequence is a general. Strategy occupies the mind of the general before he commences his action; tactics concerns him and his officers on the field of battle. It is the same with the interviewer.

With the strategy of the high-class interview we already have dealt. It consists merely in thoughtful preparation for logical questioning. Tactical responses must await the interview itself. If the interviewee takes up the questionnaire with alacrity, and talks freely, making himself intelligible on all points as he goes, do not interrupt him. Hold your tongue, however piqued you may be to use it. For interviewers, I suppose are without the experience of a colleague, in cases of collective interviewing, talking too much, and so destroying or seriously diminishing the value of an interviewing opportunity.

If your man talks, and talks plainly, let him talk. But, if he does not talk, you must try to make him talk; you must try to kindle him with your own enthusiasm, to make him feel the importance of what you are about, to quicken his interest with short remarks of your own. Whatever happens, of course, you must understand what is said—must grasp the speaker's meaning in full—else you can hope for only a partial success. Any obscure point in the speaker's statement must be cleared up before the discussion proceeds, or must be returned to for clarification at a later stage. Guesswork, in an interview of the first order, is barred.

Note-taking, while an interview is in progress, I regard as nearly always inadvisable, except for recording certain names, facts, and figures. Sentiments and opinions, I think, are best left to the memory. Notes on such things I find a handicap to comprehension while the talk is going on and a source of confusion afterward. My effort always is to seize the speaker's ideas and master his argument, to note his style, to imbue my mind with his temperament, and to consider his gestures, appearance, and dress.

All these things belong to what one may term the interviewing unity. Style, temperament, gestures, appearance, dress, vocal timbre, any attribute or circumstance attending the interview—every one of them, in my judgment, should be taken account of and blended into the interviewer's conception of what he heard. Notoriously, psychology is a curious thing. Its complex of associations defies analysis. Ideas and arguments may be held in the mind by the recollection of many things essentially non-pertinent to them.

Note-taking at the time of the interview I disapprove, but note-taking as soon as possible afterward I think of the highest importance. Key-words should be set down rapidly. Developments of any aspect or feature of the interview should await the fixing in the memory of salients for final attention. If the course be not followed valuable elements may be overlooked in the finished work. Not all of a long interview starts up instantly in the mind. Such interviews are recalled bit by bit, a word now, a sentence then, perhaps a series of paragraphs as one wakes at night. I think a week, or even a fortnight, not too long a time to give to reproducing an interview of, say, 5,000 words.

Formal authentication, to my mind, should accompany all interviews of the first category. For this there are several reasons. The main reason is that formal authentication means the approval of the interviewee after personal revision. Your reader then knows that in no respect has there been a misquotation. Interviews of unquestionable validity command attention and credence, and thus serve their educational purpose. Furthermore, the formally authenticated interview bears a definite seal upon the accuracy of the interviewer's work, and so safeguards, not only the interviewee, but the journalist who reduced his exposition to black and white.

All the way through, ladies and gentlemen, as you will have observed, I have been contemplating a single type of interview—the honest and searching interview, the interview scientific and artistic, the interview dedicated to the durable service of our fellow-men. Of other types of interview—those types which fly likes sparks in the smithy of our trade—I do not speak. They have their place, their function, their contributory value, in the diversified ensemble of the modern newspaper. But I speak of the more deliberate, the more highly-conceived, the more classic and powerful type of interview—the type which, I hope, will attract every increasingly the ability and energy of educated journalists.

Such are some of the observations that occur to one who has grappled with the problems of the interviewing field. We have seen that the best interviews are serious and vivid moral and intellectual interpretations, representing an ambition to serve civilization. We have seen that the light of great interviews is needed in a dark world. We have seen that such interviews are transmitting media between statesmanship, scholarship, genius, and the masses of men. We have seen that great interviews are true mirrors of brilliant and illustrious personalities. And we have given some consideration to the methods whereby these journalistic achievements are conceived and executed.

Now, if you are not too tired, let us pass from abstraction to concretion. Let us look for a little while at four illustrations of what we have been talking about.

These illustrations, I regret to say—for no journalist likes to emphasize the personal note—these illustrations are work of my own. This work was made possible by the wide outlook of an enterprising, successful, and famous newspaper publisher—Mr. Victor Fremont Lawson, owner and editor-in-chief of The Chicago Daily News, whose long-sustained activities on the intellectual side of foreign news has made the name of his paper familiar to thinking people in every civilized capital on our globe.

These interviews are with Marx of Germany, Mussolini of Italy, Poincare of France, and MacDonald of Great Britain—all of whom when interviewed, were heads of great States, and all of whom were involved in public duties and personal political difficulties as grave and distracting as every harried practitioners of statecraft. Desperately overmatched they were, yet they found time to expound their views upon world problems with a thoroughness and to an extent unknown before in the realm of newspaper interviewing. Not one of these interviews is less than 5,000 words in length, and most of them are more, yet I venture the opinion that whoever reads them will agree they carry very few non-vital words.

Relative to these statesmen, what do their expressed sentiments and convictions show? That, however they may differ, they all are peace lovers, all religious men, all anti-communists, all nationalists yet internationalists, all champions of law and liberty, all classicists and moralists, all missionaries of sacrifice, all pitiless workers, all democrats.

Mussolini, the "dictator"—he a democrat? Read his definition of social science and of liberty. Marx a democrat—he of the socialist government of Germany? Read his confession of the moral and material failure of socialism in Germany in the stress of post-war events. "Imperialist" and "militarist" Poincare a democrat? Read his moving story of what France fought for. MacDonald a democrat? He asserts that socialists of his school are "not only democrats, but the only democrats."

I submit in all deference, ladies and gentlemen, that it is a great picture—this picture of the hearts and the minds of four of the most inspired and radiant figures of our day. To these statesmen I said we were looking for truth, for light, for candor, for that which would be of lasting educational value to the world, and I am convinced that they did their utmost to give us what we sought.

In the Marx interview we see a fine Christian spirit in rough seas. In the Poincare interview we see a great, big mind working and a great big heart aching. In the MacDonald interview we see statesmanship and humanitarianism in their noblest mood. In the Mussolini interview we see the civilian consciousness with a sword in its hand.

My closing word is—and I thank you all profoundly for your attention—my last word is that journalism bears a heavy load of responsibility in this world; that it has great power and the duty of great power; and that in none of its phases or functions can it do more for humanity than through the scientific, the artistic, the enlightened, the sympathetic interview.

INTERVIEWING FOR INFORMATION*

LESLIE LEVINE
Business Relations Analyst
American Satellite Company

Levine's article focuses on the role of interviewing in the technical writer's world of work. As you read this article reflect on its relevance in terms of you as a technical communication student or technical writer, and answer the following questions:

1. Why does interviewing play such a significant role in the technical writer's world of work?
2. Why is preparing for an interview important?
3. Why is research needed to index the importance of interviewing in the workplace?
4. What do you consider the main points of this article?

*   *   *

ABSTRACT

Gathering information is a major task of the technical writer. All too often, however, writers take this important skill for granted. Successful interviewing often is, however, the technical writer's key to writing good technical prose. Whether the writer is seeking the theory behind an engineering design or preparing an annual report, the techniques that the writer uses for successful interviewing will be the same. Further, by developing good interviewing skills, a writer will improve his or her organization and writing techniques. Yet the most important aspect of good interviewing is obtaining accurate information. If technical writers want to be considered professionals in their field, they must become expert interviewers as well as good technical translators.

*Originally published in *J. Technical Writing and Communication, 14,* pp. 55-58, 1984.

Is interviewing important? You wouldn't think so considering the scarcity of reference books on the subject. Nevertheless, one of the first things new technical writers are likely to discover is that their jobs require them to be expert interviewers because interviewing is often the key to good technical documentation.

Based on direct experience with a wide variety of working environments in technical communications, David L. Carson, Director of the Masters program in Technical Writing and Communication at Rensselaer Polytechnic Institute, says that interviewing often plays a larger role in documentation processing than does the writing and editing itself. Further, he states that "some professional technical communicators spend as much as 75 percent of their time gathering information and much of this comes from interviews of some form."

Sharon Powell, Manager of Information Design Development at IBM, Austin, Texas, agrees. According to her, the technical writers on her staff spend at least 40 percent of their time gathering information.

Although job tasks and surroundings may vary, the techniques for successful interviewing are usually very much alike. As a result, any technical writer who hopes to be professional should master the skills and techniques required to conduct effective interviews. Whether the writer works for a large communications firm or is a contributing editor to a popular journal, interviewing will play an important role in the research and writing process.

PREPARATION

Initial preparation of any sort of interview is extremely important. First, an interviewer must always make a formal request for the interview, either by telephone or letter. Second, he should establish the time and place for the meeting. Third, he must establish ground rules with the interviewee. For example, will there be any payment involved? Will the subject be allowed to see the manuscript? Will the interview be recorded or videotaped?

Once these preliminary steps are completed, the writer must prepare for the interview itself. Never should a writer launch into this type of project without first researching any material written by or about the interviewee. If the subject works for a specific corporation or industry, the writer should collect any information that pertains to that company, particularly if the company is involved in a new project. If the writer is familiar with the area of inquiry, not only will the questions be asked in a logical sequence, but the subject, sensing the writer's familiarity with the topic, may be more generous with his time and expertise.

THE INTERVIEW

Once the writer and subject have briefly exchanged pleasantries, the interview should begin. As a general rule, the writer will have only a short time in which to conduct the interview, so organization and good judgment are of utmost importance.

As for the line of questioning, the writer should use the funnel technique. That is, the interview should begin with a few general questions, then move on toward more specific ones. For example, the interviewer might start out by asking the owner of a larger computer company, "How do you think Reaganomics is affecting the computer industry?" He might later ask, "When do you think the gallium arsenide chips will be on the market, and how do these chips compare with silicon chips?" Obviously the second question is more detailed than the first, and answering it requires some marketing knowledge of computer hardware. By first asking a few general questions, the interviewer will hope to relieve any tension that may be in the air.

One problem that will face writers is eliciting information that is controversial, unpleasant, or just hard to get a hold of. When this happens a writer must depend on the art of persuasion. Responses such as, "Yes, I can understand that" or "I wasn't aware of that" or even "You're kidding!" will encourage the subject to proceed with the interview.

Any interview, whether it lasts sixty seconds or one hour, should be recorded on paper and/or tape. Yet as an interviewer records the subject's responses, the writer should face the subject, not the legal pad or the recorder. If writers concentrate too closely on their note pads, the subjects may feel they are being ignored and may, as a result, eventually stop talking.

The writer who chooses to use a tape recorder should take a few precautions. Technology has made incredible strides, but even the simplest of machines can stop functioning when they are most needed. The tape recorder is very temperamental; it may start to chomp on the tape without any warning; or it may lose its energy and slow down. So don't depend entirely on it. Whatever ails a tape recorder, you're always safe if you've jotted down some backup notes during the interview. Also, in order to remember any points of emphasis, jot down any gestures the subject makes, such as clenched fist or a pointed finger. Other precautions might include the following:

- Use a recorder with a self-contained microphone.
- Do not purchase cheap tapes; you'll pay a higher price later.
- Use a tape that exceeds the expected interviewing time.
- Label the tape *before* the interview.
- Test for volume and tone level *before* the interview.
- Avoid background noises.

THE CLOSING

The closing of an interview is just as important as its beginning. You should always leave your subject with a pleasant feeling. So, rather than end an interview with an abrupt closing, such as "In conclusion . . . " the interviewer should ask an open-ended question like, "Is there anything we have overlooked?" Encouraging the subject to close the interview this way provides the writer with the opportunity to gather information that may have been missed during the meeting.

The guidelines I have described should by no means be considered an exclusive list of interviewing tactics. Rather, regard each step as a basic skill, which if applied correctly may enhance the entire interviewing process. Before attempting to interview, however, writers ideally should do some research on their own in establishing good interviewing techniques.

Unfortunately, research in this area is scarce. Most information I have found is located in outdated textbooks. Although the textbooks do provide a few helpful outlines to follow they do not cite specific examples of interviewing techniques commonly used in industry and business today. However, a few journal articles provide some insight into the various types of interviewing and the effectiveness of certain interviewing methods.

For example, Herbert J. Koudry described in his article, *Techniques of Interviewing*, a few guides to be followed by a systems analyst during the course of an interview [1]. Referring to the student interviewing reference guide for Honeywell BISAD, an acronym for Business Information Systems Analyses and Design, Koudry set forth three premises. First, the interview should be used as a fact-gathering technique. Second, it should be well planned and well handled in order to produce reliable facts. Third, the interview should be considered a selling job. "The systems man is selling his ability to find a solution to the business problem." Furthermore, Koudry suggested that as an introduction the interviewer explain to the subject the purpose and objective of the interview and the method by which that subject is selected.

Another valuable source of literature on interviewing is *The Craft of Interviewing* by John Brady [2]. This book is perhaps the most informative and enjoyable publication printed on interviewing in the last ten years. Brady's conversational and anecdotal style successfully demonstrates what the interviewer must do from start to finish in order to produce a professional piece of written work.

In any business setting, whether it be marketing research, popular journalism, or data communications, gathering information is a technical writer's first step towards achieving his or her finished product; an informative, organized, and coherent document.

Anyone who wishes to lay claim to the profession of technical writing must not only perfect his writing skills but must also develop good interviewing techniques. Unless technical writers are familiar with a variety of fact-gathering techniques, their finished products are likely to be incomplete. That is, by relying exclusively on written information, technical writers may be missing what could be valuable knowledge, often communicated through a personal interview. Further, by becoming a proficient interviewer, a technical writer can expand his permanent information network. Whatever motivates technical writers to learn the craft of interviewing, their efforts will always be worth the extra piece of information often forsaken in written literature.

REFERENCES

1. H. J. Koudry, Techniques of Interviewing, *Journal of Systems Management, 213*, pp. 22-23, May 1972.
2. J. Brady, *The Craft of Interviewing*, Vintage Books, New York, 1971.

AN INVESTIGATION OF THE INTERVIEWING PRACTICES OF TECHNICAL WRITERS IN THEIR WORLD OF WORK*

EARL E. McDOWELL
BRIDGET MROLZA
EMMY REPPE

University of Minnesota, St. Paul

In the McDowell, Mrolza, and Reppe article trained interviewers surveyed the interviewing practices of technical writers. This study adds support to the article by Levine. Read this article carefully as it covers the interviewing practices of professional writers. After reading the article, please answer the following questions:

1. What were some of the surprising aspects of the study?
2. If you are a writer, do you agree with the general conclusions of the article?
3. What do you consider to be your strengths in information-gathering interviews?
4. What do you consider to be your weaknesses in information-gathering interviews?
5. How do you plan to overcome your weaknesses?

*   *   *

ABSTRACT

We surveyed 176 technical writers to determine the type of information-gathering interviewing practices they use in their work. Major areas of inquiry were demographic information, involvement with information-gathering interviewing, methods of preparing for interviews, and the dynamics of the interviewing process. This paper reports the results of the survey. The technical writers surveyed write for computer, medical, or other audiences, and on

*McDowell, E., Mrolza, B., and Reppe, E., An Investigation of the Interviewing Practices of Technical Writers in Their World of Work, *RPI Proceedings, 35*, pp. 1-21, 1987. Reprinted by permission of the authors.

the average they conduct three to five interviews per week. Overall, the technical writers surveyed feel that interviewing is an integral part of their work, and that effective interviewing skills are necessary for them to perform their jobs well.

In 1924, Bell likened skillful interviewers to the great portrait painters of the world. Whereas the role of the painter was to create a lifelike reproduction of physical lineaments, he observed, the role of the interviewer was to provide a faithful picture of the human mind and soul [1]. Though today interviewers may be regarded in less metaphorical and more substantive terms, interviewing remains an important form of human communication with wide application in the workplace. In addition to providing a means for selecting potential employees, interviewing is a highly useful method for giving information, gathering information, appraising employees, solving people- and work-related problems, and persuading in the business world.

Interviewing is defined by Stewart and Cash as a process of dyadic, relational communication with a predetermined and serious purpose that involves the asking and answering of questions [2]. Interviewing is an important tool in almost any profession [3]. One area where this can be observed is the field of technical communication, which has been expanding to complement the surge of growth in the "high-tech" industries. In these firms technical writers working on a document, such as a manual, must often collect technical information from technical source people. In many cases, the information-gathering interview between the technical writer and technical expert becomes the primary tool used by technical writers to obtain information for a written project.

Unfortunately, limited attention has been devoted in the technical communication journals to information-gathering interviews. Levine reported in the *Journal of Technical Writing and Communication* that technical writers are likely to discover that their jobs require them to be expert interviewers because good interviewing is often the key to good documentation [4]. In the same article, Carson, Director of the Masters Program in Technical Writing and Communication at Rensselaer Polytechnic Institute, asserted that 1) interviewing often plays a larger role in documentation processing than does the writing and editing, 2) some technical writers spend approximately 75 percent of their time gathering information, and 3) a significant amount of this time is spent interviewing.

Additional evidence supports the contention that information-gathering interviewing plays a significant role in the technical writer's world of work. During the past five years over 200 students, enrolled in a graduate level interviewing course taught in the Department of Rhetoric, University of Minnesota, have interviewed technical writers to learn how they function in the workplace. One of these writers was Gerry Stimmler, a Senior Technical Writer in the Cray-1 Publication Group. Stimmler's comments concerning interviewing are representative of the composite group of writers. He stated that many writers underestimate the importance of interviews for gathering information, and finds that he uses information-gathering interviewing quite often—probably an average of once a day [5].

Further, the use of interviewing skills can extend beyond the completion of written projects. Ridgway notes that technical writers must often depend on customer interviews and surveys to gauge the success of a project, and, therefore, writers need to develop interviewing skills for the collection and analysis of feedback in a systematic and formal manner [6].

The findings presented in this introduction suggest that successful technical writers must be able to do more than just write—they must be competent in the oral interpersonal communication skills they use during their informational interviews. The following study investigates this aspect of the technical writer's world of work.

RATIONALE FOR STUDY

This study was designed to examine the informational interviewing practices of technical writers/communicators, and is important for the following reasons:

1. The informational interview is the primary type of interpersonal communication between the technical writer and the technical source person.
2. Much of the emphasis in the technical communication literature has been on processing information into a format desired for a particular audience analysis, but no previous research has focused on the interviewing practices of technical writers.
3. No previous research has focused on the perceived level of knowledge of technical writers about information-gathering interviewing.
4. This exploratory study may provide insight for developing curricula in technical communication programs.

This study addresses the following research questions:

1. What are the demographics of technical writers?
2. What types of training have technical writers had in interviewing techniques?
3. To what extent are technical writers involved with information-gathering interviewing in their work?
4. How do technical writers prepare for information-gathering interviews?
5. How do technical writers conduct information-gathering interviews?
6. What are the dynamics of the interviewing process?
7. What demographic factors do technical writers perceive as having an influence during the interview?
8. How do technical writers feel about their own interpersonal communication skills?
9. Which is the preferred job title—technical writer or technical communicator?

PROCEDURE

We selected a systematic sample of 180 technical writers/communicators from the Twin Cities Chapter of the Society for Technical Communication (STC) and American Medical Writers Association (AMWA), and alumni of the Technical Communication degree program at the University of Minnesota. We also contacted local businesses to obtain names of additional technical writers, as we wished to represent a cross section of technical writers employed by computer firms, manufacturers, medical organizations, financial firms, and public utilities in the Minneapolis/St. Paul area.

Two researcher assistants in the Laboratory for Research in Scientific Communication trained fifteen students from the interviewing course to assist them in conducting telephone interviews with the sample of technical writers. We used a telephone survey because 1) we felt that direct contact with the technical writers would encourage greater participation, 2) we would be able to ask more questions than would be feasible for a self-administered questionnaire, and 3) we would be able to include some open-ended questions that would allow the technical writers to elaborate on their responses.

The research and student assistants contacted potential interviewees and read them a standard introduction that briefly explained the purpose of the study, and then asked them two contingency questions:

1. Do you conduct information-gathering interviews in your work?
2. Would you be willing to participate in this survey? Participants had the option to complete the survey at that time or to reschedule the survey to a time more convenient for them.

The survey instrument was the Information-Gathering Interviewing Questionnaire (IGIQ). We designed this questionnaire from theories and models of interviewing. We then pilot tested the IGIQ with a sample of technical writers and revised it. Most of the items in the pilot study were open-ended to assess the relevance of the questions and to determine additional pertinent areas of inquiry.

The final draft consisted of fifty-six questions, most of which were closed-ended with "yes" or "no" response categories. Likert-scaled items and four open-ended items were also included. As with most studies, we requested some demographic information in order to better interpret the results with an appreciation for the homogeneity or heterogeneity of the subject pool. We also were interested in determining differences among technical writers with technical communication degrees and those who either held degrees in social sciences or were technical experts themselves; that is, they held degrees in the biological, mathematical, or physical sciences such as engineering. Other areas of inquiry included frequency of involvement with information-gathering interviewing, methods of preparing for interviews, structuring interviews, and the dynamics of the interviewing process. Finally, we asked the technical writers to indicate their preferred job title, as we felt that this was a succinct way to conclude the telephone survey and provide an indication as to how the writers perceive themselves and the nature of their work—for example, do they regard themselves primarily as writers or do they wish to have other aspects of their jobs reflected in their job title?

Statistical analyses of the data consisted of calculating frequencies and percentages for all items on the questionnaire. Chi-square analyses were calculated to determine percentage differences between biological sex groups (male and female), and among the three academic cluster groups for academic majors.

RESULTS

Demographics

Of the 180 technical writers, 176 participated in the survey to give an approximately 98 percent response rate. Fifty-three percent of the technical writers have been employed no longer than five years, and 80 percent have been in their present positions for no longer than five years. The majority (72%) of writers are under the age of forty. Ninety-nine percent of all writers surveyed hold a bachelor's degree. Undergraduate majors were assigned to one of the three academic cluster groups: 1) English, journalism, and social sciences (57%), 2) Biological, physical, or mathematical sciences (24%), and 3) Technical Communication (19%). Nineteen percent hold advanced degrees as well. The majority (64%) write for a computer-oriented audience, while 12 percent write for a medical audience and the remainder write for various audiences.

Training in Interviewing Techniques

Over half of the technical writers surveyed have gained some background in interviewing techniques by methods such as observing interviews (65%), talking with interviewers (63%), reading literature on interviewing (61%), or taking courses in interviewing (56%). Other methods for building interviewing skills include attending seminars (46%), in-house staff development programs (43%), and workshops (34%).

Involvement with Interviewing

On the average, writers conduct one to five interviews per week, while 23 percent state they conduct between six and twenty interviews per week. Interviews are generally conducted face-to-face with interviewees, and 86 percent of the writers also conduct interviews by telephone. Most interviews are conducted on a one-to-one basis, but three-fourths of the writers stated that they do conduct group interviews with two or more interviewees as well. Forty-one percent indicated that they tend to interview different technical source people over time, while 52 percent interview a combination of the same and different people.

Responses to the time factor items indicate that over 70 percent of the writers surveyed believe that Tuesdays, Wednesdays, and Thursdays are the best days of the week for conducting interviews, and most feel that morning hours are better for interviewing than afternoon hours. Some writers qualified their responses by stating that they must frequently work around the interviewee's schedule and, therefore, they are not always at liberty to conduct their interviews at optimal times. Interviews generally last no longer than one hour.

Preparing for Interviews

To prepare for their interviews, 74 percent of the writers review related literature, and 67 percent outline the material that they need to obtain. Less often, writers may consult with the technical source people (35%), consult with other technical writers (21%), or create a tentative form of the document (21%). Sixty-three percent of the writers develop interview guides, which are outlines of the questions they will ask. Questions can be arranged in various sequences, depending on the nature of the information to be obtained. Typical sequences used by technical writers surveyed include topical (84%), problem solving (82%), and process (79%). Writers are less inclined to use a chronological sequence (57%), or a spatial sequence (34%).

Various types of questions are used in information-gathering interviews. Eighty-nine percent of the writers surveyed use primary questions, while ninety-six percent use secondary questions. Closed-ended questions are used by 84 percent, while 87 percent use open-ended questions. Reflective probes are used by 91 percent, and 79 percent use mirror questions. Three-fourths of the writers generally use no more than twenty questions in their interviews. The glossary provided at the end of this paper gives definitions of these question sequences and additional interviewing terms.

Structuring the Interview

The interview itself can have varying degrees of structure. Ninety-three percent of the technical writers surveyed use the semidirective approach for structuring their interviews and about one-third of the writers use directive and non-directive methods as well.

Technical writers use a number of opening techniques at the beginning of their information-gathering interviews. Over 70 percent of the writers use personal inquiry, summary of the problem or topic, mention of common goal, request for advice and request for specific amount of time.

Over 70 percent of the writers use a greeting, impersonal small talk, a request for advice, a personal inquiry, the mention of a common goal, a request for a specific amount of the interviewee's time, or a handshake.

To close their interviews, all writers express their appreciation, and over two-thirds use techniques such as clearinghouse questions ("Can you think of anything else I should know?"), a statement of completion, a plan for the next meeting, and a summary of the interview content. Less often, they may state that time is up or use a personal inquiry.

Interviewing Dynamics

Writers perceive that the dynamics of the interview are very important and that nonverbal and paraverbal factors play significant roles in building interpersonal relationships. Interviews typically take place in the interviewee's office or some "neutral" territory, such as next to a piece of machinery on the shop floor. Most writers prefer a seating arrangement of chairs at right angles to each other at the corner of a desk or table, or a side-by-side arrangement, and they maintain a personal (19" to 4") or social distance (4'1" to 12') between themselves and their interviewees during the interview.

Eye contact, smiling, posture, head nodding and hand gestures account for the most frequently used nonverbal cues during the interview. Arm, body, and leg movements, and attention to time are used to a lesser degree, while only 15% of the writers reported using touch as nonverbal cues.

Writers believe that first impressions are important for the interview, and most try to project an informal image. Their style of dress for interviewing is based on personal preference rather than a company dress code. Writers also believe that it is important to build rapport and credibility during the interview, and they seek to establish good working relationships with interviewees by being pleasant and sociable, showing interest, and demonstrating responsibility. Other methods of reinforcing favorable interpersonal relationships include using a conversational interviewing style, which is an informal, interactive approach to questioning, and sharing a common goal with the interviewee. Most writers are satisfied with their interpersonal communication and listening skills and feel equally comfortable with giving or receiving feedback during interviews. Two-thirds of the writers feel that their own status is equal to that of the technical source people being interviewed, and the majority believe that the technical people are competent in their interpersonal communication skills. About 40 percent of the writers engage in "level 3" communication; that is, they feel they can speak freely with the interviewee.

We asked the technical writers to indicate whether they felt the demographic characteristics of sex, age, and education of interviewees had an influence on the communicative interaction during the interview. For example, a male technical writer might perceive that these characteristics influence the level of communication, the language used, or the nonverbal communication during the interview. One-fourth of the writers believe that the sex of the interviewee influences the communication during the interview; of these, 49 percent find it easier to talk to someone of the opposite sex and 51 percent find it easier to talk to a same-sex individual. They perceive that sex has a stronger influence on nonverbal communication than the level of communication or the language used. One-third of all writers surveyed believe that the age of the interviewee had an influence, of these, 62 percent find it easiest to talk to a person of the same age rather than someone older or younger. An equal percentage feel that age affects the level of communication (59%) and the language used (59%) while a slightly lesser number feel that age influences nonverbal communication (52%). Approximately one-half of all writers surveyed believe that the education of the interviewee influences communication, and the majority of these find it easiest to talk to an interviewee with a bachelor's degree. Three-fourths perceive that education affects the level of communication during the interview. Interestingly, more writers perceive the education of the interviewee to have an influence on communication as opposed to the more outwardly obvious characteristics of sex and age.

Information Recall

Nearly all writers (92%) take written notes of the material covered during interviews, and 24 percent reported that they occasionally use a tape recorder. Other methods of recalling information include relying on memory, using notes given to them by interviewees, and using illustrations sketched during the interviews. Most writers estimated that they speak less than 50 percent of the total time allotted to the interview.

Open Ended Responses

The survey participants answered four open-ended questions regarding their experience with information-gathering interview. These questions along with summaries of the most frequently given responses, are as follows:

1. How do you handle people who give you too much information during the interview?
   • Use questions to redirect, refocus, or narrow the topic.
   • Listen politely; let them ramble.
   • Actively interrupt to ask for relevant information.
   • Request the interviewee to correlate the information with the needs of the audience.
2. How do you handle people who give you too little information?
   • Ask more questions or use specific question types—e.g., closed, open, mirror.
   • Find another source person to interview.
   • Reschedule a follow-up interview.
   • Relax the interviewee with small talk.
3. What are your greatest strengths in information-gathering interviews?
   • Ability to establish rapport.
   • Ability to obtain the necessary information.

• Preparation and organization.
• Ability to use spontaneous probing and follow-up questions.
4. What are your greatest weaknesses?
  • Lack of technical knowledge.
  • Poor preparation/organization.
  • Phrasing questions and ineffective interviewing techniques.
  • Poor listening skills.

Preferred Job Title

The final item on the questionnaire asked the participants to indicate their preference for a job title. Fifty-four percent of those surveyed prefer to be called "technical writer," while 30 percent prefer the title "technical communicator." The remainder stated no preference or provided another title, such as "information developer."

Differences Between Profiles of Biological Sex Groups

Over 60 percent of the males surveyed have worked full time as technical writers for five years or longer. Their average age is forty-four, and 97 percent hold at least a bachelor's degree in one of the three academic cluster groups. In contrast, the average age of the female writers is thirty-four, and only 30 percent have been employed as technical writers for more than five years. Like males, nearly all of the females have at least a bachelor's degree, but more females have degrees in technical communication than do males. Unlike males, 10 percent of the females are employed part-time.

Males have had more in-house training in interviewing techniques than have females. To prepare for their interviews, both outline key information, but females are significantly more likely to research related literature and develop interview guides ($p<.01$) than are males. Like male writers, almost all female writers conduct both face-to-face and telephone interviews, but a higher percentage of females believe that the morning hours of Tuesdays, Wednesdays, and Thursdays are the best times for conducting interviews.

Females use significantly fewer questions overall ($p<.05$) in their interviews, with significantly more open-ended and fewer closed-ended questions. They also have more variety in their question types, using more reflective and mirror questions in topical, problem-solving, process, or cause and effect question sequences, but females are significantly more likely to use a chronological sequence ($p<.03$).

To open their interviews, females are significantly more likely to request a specific amount of the interviewee's time ($p<.04$), and females use significantly more clearinghouse questions ($p<.002$) and statements of completion ($p<.03$) at the conclusion of their interviews than do males. Females also are more likely to establish plans for future meetings with their interviewees.

With the exception of arm movements, a greater percentage of female writers reported using each nonverbal cue more than males, with females using significantly more leg movements ($p<.002$). A significantly greater percentage of females also feel that vocal tone is important during the interview ($p<.03$).

Both male and female writers believe that it is important to develop good working relationships with their interviewees, but males are less inclined to find first impressions as important as females do. About 50 percent of the males wear either a three- or two-piece suit, while the others most often wear a shirt and tie or shirt and sweater for their interviews. Over 60 percent of the females reported that they wear a skirted suit for interviewing. Unlike the male writers, an equal percentage of females find it just as easy to talk to same-sex individuals as compared to those of the opposite sex. Like males, most females find it easiest to talk to someone who is of the same age and holds a bachelor's degree.

Finally, 56 percent of the males and about one-half of the females prefer to be called technical writers, while 24 percent of the males and 36 percent of the females prefer the title technical communicator. The remainder stated no preference or provided another title.

Differences Between Profiles of Academic Cluster Groups

Unlike biological sex, academic cluster was not a good discriminating variable as there were limited significant differences among groups—although there were many marginal differences. Therefore, rather than reporting results for each cluster, we will discuss the technical communication group and note differences among the other groups (English, journalism, and social sciences; or biological, mathematical, and physical sciences).

Like the female group, the technical communication group was younger, averaging thirty-one years of age. They have an average of three years experience as technical writers and all have graduated from the Technical Communication program in the Department of Rhetoric, University of Minnesota.

Over 80 percent of the technical communication cluster have completed coursework in interviewing, have read interviewing literature, and have observed interviews. These percentages are higher than for other academic cluster groups. As with the other groups, about 60 percent of the technical cluster write for a computer-oriented audience.

All academic cluster groups review literature, outline information, develop interview guides, and use a variety of question sequences as they prepare for their interviews. A significantly higher percentage of the biological, mathematical, and physical sciences cluster use the process sequencing for questioning ($p<.01$). All groups use a variety of question types, interviewing approaches, and opening and closing techniques. While all groups report that they use the many nonverbal and paraverbal cues, a greater percentage of writers in the technical communication group use head nodding, smiling, and eye contact. The technical communication group also reported that they use more body movements and perceive eye contact as more important than did the other groups.

Interpersonal working relationships are important to all writers, regardless of academic cluster. A majority of writers in each cluster find it important to use a conversational interviewing style, are satisfied with their interpersonal communication skills, and feel comfortable with giving or receiving feedback; however, only about 40 percent of each cluster communicate at level 3. A greater percentage of writers in the technical communication group indicated that they reinforce shared goals with interviewees and are satisfied with their listening skills. In contrast, a greater percentage of the remaining clusters rated the technical source people as competent communicators, feel that their status as writers is equal to that of the technical people, and find that they talk for nearly 50 percent of the total time allotted to an interview.

Finally, 50 percent of the technical communication cluster prefer to be called technical communicators, which is higher than for other academic cluster groups.

OVERALL ASSESSMENT

The purpose of this study was to determine the types of informational interviewing practices that technical writers use. To accomplish this, we developed our questionnaire from models of interviewing presented by Stewart and Cash [2]. Because this was an exploratory study we did not present any hypotheses; rather, we presented a rationale to explain why we conducted our survey. The results of this study indicate only how technical writers perceive their own communication behaviors. Additional research, such as observing actual interviews between technical writers and technical source people, would be useful to further validate our survey results and to evaluate the technical writers' interviewing skills. Nevertheless, the results of this study provide a general overview of the communication behaviors that typically take place during the information-gathering interviews of technical writers.

Initially, the results indicate that although all of the writers surveyed use information-gathering interviews to obtain information from technical source people, only 56 percent have taken coursework in interviewing and 61 percent have read literature pertaining to interviewing. This suggests that the writers use much intuitive thinking to develop their interviewing skills. Likewise, about 35 percent do not develop interviewing guides or outlines of the material they need to obtain, and a similar percentage reported that they do not review pertinent literature prior to interviewing, even though these factors are regarded as requisites for successful interviewing.

The writers surveyed reported that they use a variety of questions, question sequences, openings, and closings in their interviews. Additionally, they believe that they build positive interpersonal relationships through the use of appropriate language, levels of communication, and nonverbal and paraverbal cues. The majority stated that their greatest interviewing strength was their ability to establish rapport with interviewees. These findings suggest that competent technical writers must be able to adapt good analytical and interpersonal communication skills to a wide range of situations encountered on the job. Such versatility may be especially important for contract and freelance writers who are continually working for new clients. To illustrate this, let us present two examples of situations actually described to us by technical writers and then suggest possible strategies to solve the problems experienced in each.

For our first example, suppose that a technical writer is working on a manual for a complex piece of equipment and finds that he must consult with one of the engineers who designed it. The writer has heard from others that although this engineer is a technical wizard, he is very apprehensive about speaking to other people—he avoids eye contact, stares into his video display terminal, and says very little. In this situation, the technical writer decides that he should present himself as non-threatening as possible. First, he schedules the interview to take place on the shop floor, as he feels his interviewee will be more comfortable there. He then outlines the material he needs to obtain and develops his interview guide. He arrives for the interview dressed informally, shakes hands with the engineer, and gives him a friendly greeting, commenting on a new prototype that the engineer has been working on. After he feels that he has "broken the ice," he begins questioning the engineer, initially using closed-ended questions that can be easily answered in short phrases, and as the interview progresses, he begins to ask more open-ended questions that require longer responses. Because the writer realizes that constant eye contact makes this individual nervous, he varies the length of his own gaze by having the engineer look at diagrams while he asks his questions, or by pointing to the components of the actual machinery on the shop floor. He concludes the interview by asking the engineer if there is anything else about the equipment that he needs to know, thanks to him, and states that he will contact the engineer if he has any further questions.

In our second example, suppose a recently hired female technical writer needs to interview an older male engineer who is known for having a low regard for technical writers in general and has a reputation being very argumentative. In this case, the technical writer decides that she should present herself in a formal assertive manner in order to establish her own credibility as a competent professional. She arranges to conduct the interview in her office, and she thoroughly familiarizes herself with the material she needs to clarify for her manual. She dresses for the interview in a skirted suit and greets the interviewee with a handshake, but instead of using small talk to open her interview she begins by giving the engineer a summary of the problem and reason why she is requesting his advice. She chooses to use a semidirective approach for the interview, and her interview guide consists of a half-dozen primary and open-ended questions to allow her interviewee to do most of the talking during the interview. While interviewing, she uses constant eye contact to demonstrate her interest and head nodding to show that she understands, and she is also alert for possible secondary and reflective probing questions to clarify his responses. She concludes by summarizing the contents of the interview, asks the interviewee if he can think of any other information that she might need, thanks him for his time, and states that she will contact him if additional question arise.

These two examples merely illustrate how technical writers can use interviewing skills to facilitate their job duties. In actuality, there is no set format for conducting the ideal interview; technical writers (and any other interviewers as well) must develop the ability to evaluate their interviewees and then adapt the best interviewing strategies for each particular situation.

Most of the technical writers who participated in our survey do not hold degrees in technical communication; however, this is not surprising since technical communication has only developed into a distinct discipline relatively recently. *Post hoc* analyses reveal that those writers who have taken coursework in interviewing rated themselves higher on interpersonal communication skills and perceive that most communication variables are more important than do those writers who have not received such instruction. This may be due to an increased sensitivity toward the communication process and the variables that affect it. The major weaknesses of the writers regarding informational interviewing included poor preparation, ineffective interviewing techniques, and poor listening skills. These responses suggest that writers may benefit from staff development programs designed to build skills in these areas. Further, the results of this study amplify the need to include training in interviewing techniques as part of the curriculum in technical communication degree programs.

Overall, the results of this study indicate that interviewing is an essential part of the technical writer's world of work and that technical writers need to develop effective interviewing skills to perform their jobs well.

CONCLUSIONS

The results of this study indicate the following:

1. Female writers are younger and have less work experience, but a greater percentage of them have degrees in technical communication.
2. Developing interview guides, reviewing pertinent literature, and outlining information to obtain are the primary methods technical writers use to prepare for interviews.
3. Technical writers consider Tuesday, Wednesday, and Thursday mornings to be the best time for conducting interviews.
4. Over 80 percent of the writers surveyed use open, closed, primary, secondary, and reflective questions.

5. Over 75 percent use topical, problem-solving, cause and effect, and process sequences for questioning.
6. Writers use the semidirective approach most frequently.
7. Writers use greetings, problem summaries, and impersonal small talk most frequently to open their interviews, and use expressions of appreciation, statements of completion, and clearinghouse questions most frequently to close their interviews.
8. Over 80 percent of the writers reported using the non-verbal cues of eye contact, smiling, head nodding, and hand gestures during their interviews.
9. Writers prefer a seating arrangement of chairs at right angles or side-by-side, and maintain a personal or social distance between themselves and interviewees during interviews.
10. Writers consider vocal tone and rate as the most important paraverbal variables.
11. Most writers communicate at levels 1 and 2, while about 40 percent communicate at level 3 during interviews.
12. A majority of writers feel their status is equal to that of the technical source people, use a conversational interviewing style, are satisfied with their interpersonal communication and listening skills, and feel comfortable with giving and receiving feedback during interviews.
13. Notable percentages of writers feel that the sex, age, and education of the interviewees influence the ease of communication, the level of communication, the language, and the nonverbal communication during the interview.
14. Fifty-four percent of the writers surveyed prefer to be called technical writers, while 30 percent prefer to be called technical communicators.

REFERENCES

1. E. P. Bell, The Interview, *Journalism Quarterly, 1*, pp. 13-18, 1924.
2. C. Stewart and W. Cash, *Interviewing: Principles and Practices*, Wm. C. Brown Publishers, Dubuque, Iowa, 1985.
3. J. Bradley, How to Interview for Information, *Training*, pp. 59-62, 1983.
4. L. Levine, Interviewing for Information, *Journal of Technical Writing and Communication, 14*, pp. 55-58, 1984.
5. G. Bowman, A Summary and Analysis of Three Interviews on the Subject of Information-Gathering Interviews, Unpublished paper, 5, 1983.
6. L. Ridgway, The Writer as Market Researcher, *Technical Communication*, pp. 19-22, 1985.

PERCEPTIONS OF THE IDEAL
COVER LETTER AND IDEAL RESUME*

EARL E. McDOWELL
University of Minnesota

McDowell's article on the ideal cover letter and ideal resume provides you with background information on how to plan for the interview. This article is important as technical writers change positions frequently; thus, it is important to develop an appropriate cover letter and resume for each position. As you read this article think about how you have prepared cover letters in the past and present, and answer the following questions:

1. How does your cover letter meet the requirements of the ideal one?
2. How does your resume meet the requirements of the ideal one?
3. You will notice that recruiters and teachers differ on how the cover letter and resume should be organized. Do you agree with the recruiter or the teacher in terms of organizing these variables? Why?
4. Does your latest cover letter contain any spelling errors? Poor grammar? Poor organization?
5. What do you consider to be the most startling conclusion of this article?

*   *   *

ABSTRACT

This study surveyed recruiter, teacher, and student groups to determine the following: attitudes about cover letters and resumes, reasons to reject cover letters and resumes, the contents of the ideal cover letter and where specific information should occur in it, and the importance of various categories of their resume and contents of the ideal resume. The results indicate that 1) limited time is spent in processing cover letters and resumes; 2) the length of a cover letter and resume should be one page; 3) spelling errors, poor grammar, and poor organization are key problems in cover letters and resumes; 4) specific jobs wanted, career goals, and personal information are the most important factors of a cover letter; 5) job objectives/career goals,

*Originally published in *J. Technical Writing and Communication, 17*, pp. 179-191, 1987.

employment history, and educational history are the most important parts of the resume. Specific differences in attitudes among recruiters, teachers, and students are discussed in this article.

The cover letter and resume are both either sales tools or forms of persuasive communication. Each is important in creating a favorable impression that will lead to an employment interview. For example, Janes reported the results of a survey of Fortune 500 companies on cover letters [1]. The primary conclusions were that the cover letter should be short, reveal why the applicant is interested in the position, indicate when the applicant is available for an interview, state various areas of interest, and reveal how the applicant learned about the job.

Previous research has focused on both the cover letter and resume. Mansfield used the first one hundred corporations listed in the Fortune 500 Largest Industrial Corporations to assess the resume cover letter [2]. The cover letter results supported, for the most part, Jane's conclusions. In addition, Mansfield concluded that the letter should indicate specific job or career interests in the company, stress contributions the applicant can make, and refer to specific items in the resume. He stressed that the resume should include such categories as previous employers, descriptions of previous jobs, willingness to relocate, college grade-point-average, awards, reasons for leaving previous jobs, and professional organizations or offices. He also recommended a list including special skills, salary desired, and names and titles of supervisors.

Wells, Spinks, and Hargraves also conducted a study on cover letters and resumes [3]. They concluded that the cover letter and resume should demonstrate good grammar and proper spelling, show how the applicant's qualifications fit the job requirements, and conclude by asking for an interview.

Additional research has focused on the resume. Rivers referred to the resume as your representative—your "agent," so to speak [4]. As Issel asserted [5]:

> A resume is a vehicle for presenting an organized summary of a person's professional objectives, ability, and background. . . . To paraphrase a famous quote, it is not what your potential employer can do for you, but rather what you can do for your employer that will convince him to consider your application.

Overall, Rogers indicated that the resume should include a job objective, educational history, extracurricular activities, college grades, and interests and hobbies [6].

REASONS FOR THIS STUDY

The review of the literature indicates that lucid cover letters and resumes are essential to obtain an employment interview. In this study I was interested in cross-validating and updating previous research. This study is important for two reasons. First, past research has not focused on recruiters' perceptions of cover letters and resumes. Recruiters' perceptions might be different from the perceptions of the sample groups referred to by previous researchers. Second, previous researchers have not asked writing teachers what they perceive as essential and/or important in the cover letter and resume. As a result, we have been unaware of the perceptual differences between faculty members and recruiters. This information should help writing teachers better prepare students to develop appropriate cover letters and resumes for various organizations.

PLAN OF THE QUESTIONNAIRE

The instrument used for this study was the Assessment of College Resumes and Cover Letters Questionnaire (ACRCLQ). This questionnaire is an outgrowth of a review of literature, discussions with teachers of scientific and technical writing, and discussions with students. It is designed to evaluate various parts of cover letters and resumes. The questionnaire consists of sections dealing with attitudes about cover letters and resumes, reasons why cover letters and resumes are rejected, the contents and placement of information in the ideal cover letter, the contents of the ideal resume, and the importance of various categories in the resume.

Specifically, respondents were asked to rate their level of agreement, on a 1 to 5 scale, from strongly disagree to strongly agree, with statements concerning contents of cover letters and resumes and grounds on which to reject them. Next, respondents rated the levels of frequency (from very infrequent to very frequent) at which mistakes occur on cover letters and resumes. Respondents also rated the level of importance of various units of information in the cover letter and indicated whether the information should be placed in the introduction, middle, or at the end of the letter. Participants also ranked the categories of the resume in the order they prefer to see them. Finally, respondents indicated the level of importance of several items under each major part of the resume.

Research Questions

This study addressed recruiter, teacher, and student responses to the following research questions:

1. What are their *attitudes* toward cover letter and resume characteristics?
2. Do the sample groups (recruiters, teachers, and students) have *different attitudes* toward cover letter and resume characteristics?
3. What are the *attitudes* toward reasons to reject cover letters and resumes, and how frequently do specific mistakes occur?
4. Do sample groups have *different attitudes* toward reasons to reject cover letters and resumes and the level of frequency at which mistakes occur?
5. What is the level of *importance* of contents of the cover letter and in which section of the cover letter should the material appear?

6. Do sample groups (recruiters, teachers, students) have *different perceptions of the level of importance* of the contents of the cover letter and of the section where the information should appear?
7. What are the most *important* categories of the resume and what information should appear under each category?

PROCEDURES

A random sample of 200 recruiters who interview potential employees at a midwestern university and a randomly selected sample of twenty-five teachers who are members of the Society for Technical Communication participated in the study. Each recruiter received a questionnaire, and twenty-five questionnaires were sent to each teacher. The teachers from the original sample were then requested to ask other teachers and students to complete the questionnaire. Approximately 44 percent (eighty-seven recruiters) completed and returned the questionnaire. In addition, thirty-four teachers and nineteen students completed and returned the questionnaire.

RESULTS AND DISCUSSION

The tables, for the most part, include only items in which 60 percent of the respondents agreed with the statement. The results, reported in Tables 1 and 2, indicated that limited time is spent in evaluating cover letters and resumes, that

Table 1. Composite Percentages and Chi-Square Results among
Sample Groups on Cover Letters

Composite Percentages	Highest Rated Items
82	Most cover letters are quickly evaluated—only those that screen-through (strong potential candidates) are more fully evaluated.
69	Cover letters may be addressed to the office in which the applicant seeks employment.
69	Filed cover letters are usually scanned or retrieved when new jobs are open.
67	Cover letters that screen-through with a positive evaluation are filed for a few months.
60*	Cover letters should be one page.

*$x^2 < .05$

Note: Results show that cover letters should be short because little time is spent on them.

Table 2. Composite Percentages and Chi-Square results among
Sample groups on Resumes

Composite Percentages	Highest Rated Items
86*	Resumes should be one page.
85	Resumes are quickly evaluated—only those that screen through (strong potential candidates) are more fully evaluated.
68	Resumes may be addressed to the office in which the applicant seeks employment.
67*	Resumes are skim-read.
65	Resumes that screen-through with a positive evaluation are filed for a few months.

*x^2<.05
Note: Results show that resumes should be brief because little time is spent on them.

both are read by recruiters and/or potential employers, and that both are needed to provide sufficient information about job applicants.

Significant chi-square results occurred among sample groups in rating the preferred length of cover letters and resumes and in evaluating the necessity of each to assess potential employees. For example, 29 percent of recruiters indicated that a cover letter is sufficient to evaluate job applicants while 24 percent of students and 8 percent of teachers believe that it is only adequate. In addition, 64 percent of recruiters, 40 percent of students, and 39 percent of teachers believe that a cover letter should be only one page long. All other items were rated approximately the same by sample groups.

Overall, these results support the Wells, Spinks, and Hargrave study. That is, approximately 80 percent of the participants in both studies believe that the resume should be one page long.

The items focusing on reasons to reject cover letters and resumes are presented in Tables 3 and 4.

As shown in Table 3, spelling errors, poor grammar, and poor organization are primary reasons to reject cover letters. A further breakdown of these composite results reveals that 100 percent of the teachers, 72 percent of the recruiters, and 36 percent of the students believe that spelling errors, poor grammar, and poor organization are sufficient reasons to reject cover letters. In all cases, a greater percentage of teachers believe that these are appropriate reasons to reject cover letters than do recruiters or students.

The other results are somewhat lower than those reported in Rogers' study. For example, Rogers reported that 87 percent of recruiters would not be interested in candidates whose resumes contain spelling errors, while this study indicates that

Table 3. Composite Percentages and Chi-Square Results among
Sample Groups in Rating Reject Cover Letter Items

Composite Level of Agreement Percentages	P	Estimated Frequency Percentage	P	Items
86	*	45	*	Spelling errors
84	*	52	*	Poor grammar
84	*	52	*	Poor organization
78		47		Little evidence of performance levels
72		63		Credentials not matched to company needs
69		46		Overemphasize own needs

$*x^2 < .05$

Note: Results show that cover letters are most often rejected because applicants do not meet company needs.

Table 4. Composite Percentages and Chi-Square Results among
Sample Groups in Rating Reject Resume Items

Composite Level of Agreement Percentages	P	Estimated Frequency Percentage	P	Items
85	*	43		Poor grammar
83	*	35	*	Spelling errors
81	*	38	*	Poor organization
76		36		Overpromise
73		46		Credentials not matched to company needs
72		31		Unsupported statements or claims
67		38		Unexplained time gaps in record
67		26		Data too selective or narrow

$*x^2 < .05$

Note: Results show that resumes are most often rejected because applicants do not meet company needs.

only 76 percent would be rejected. Other findings indicate that a majority of participants from sample groups perceive that overpromise, unexplained time gaps, irrelevant data, data too selective or narrow, data too broad, an overly aggressive tone, or too few credentials are sufficient reasons to reject cover letters and resumes. These findings, however, should be viewed with caution, as there are large percentage differences between the number of participants in various groups. For example, 62 percent of the respondents were recruiters, while only 14 percent were students and 24 percent were teachers. Thus, these results might not be representative of student and teacher population groups.

Next, participants rated the level of frequency at which these mistakes occur in cover letters and resumes. These findings, also reported in Tables 3 and 4, reveal that, for cover letters, poor grammar and poor organization occur about 50 percent of the time, and spelling errors occur about 40 percent of the time, while each of these items occurs somewhat less frequently in resumes. Again teachers, more often than recruiters, perceive that these occur frequently. For example, 72 percent of teachers and 40 percent of recruiters perceive that spelling errors occur frequently in cover letters. Approximately 40 percent of recruiters and students perceive that poor organization and poor grammar occur frequently, while 65 percent of teachers indicate that these occur frequently.

In addition, the results indicate that between 25 and 50 percent of the composite sample perceive that overpromise, credentials not matched to company needs, unexplained time gaps, unsupported statements or claims, data too general, or data too selective occur frequently on cover letters and resumes. Overall, the findings reveal that there is a need for writing teachers to focus more on mechanics and contents of the cover letter and resume.

Units of Information in the Cover Letter

Participants also rated the level of importance of various units of information in the cover letter. The findings, reported in Table 5, indicate that more than 60 percent of the participants perceive that nine items should be included in the cover letter.

These findings add empirical support to the generalizations about cover letters in Mansfield's article. Teachers, for the most part, rated the items significantly higher than did the members of the other sample groups. For example, 93 percent of the teachers and 54 percent of the recruiters believed that the cover letter should mention the enclosed resume. Overall, large percentage differences occurred among sample groups in rating the level of importance of the majority of cover letter items.

Next, participants were asked to decide whether mention of the resume should be located in the introduction, middle, or end of the cover letter, or whether they believed that location was not important. The findings reveal that most respondents believed that mention of the enclosed resume could appear in the

Table 5. Composite Percentages and Chi-Square Results among
Sample Groups on Contents of an Ideal Cover Letter

Composite Level of Importance Percentage	P	Introduction	Middle	End	Items
92		46	30	2	State specific jobs or type wanted
89		36	33	4	State career goals
81	*	10	45	12	Offer information about self that is not on the resume but that is relevant to the job requirements or the potential employer
79		3	11	48	Suggest time when available for work
78		70	6	1	State wish to apply for job
72		13	57	0	Suggest contributions that applicant can make to potential employer
60	*	36	7	21	Mention the enclosed resume
62	*	9	43	4	State own understanding of requirements for the position
60		7	40	7	Show how items from the resume are relevant to the job requirements of the potential employer

*$x^2 < .05$
Note: Results indicate that over 60 percent of the participants believe the above nine items should be included in the cover letter.

introduction or at the end of the letter, while information focusing on specific jobs and career goals should be presented in the introduction or middle of the letter. Other results suggest that statements about why the applicant was applying for a job should appear in the introduction, and information about self and understanding of the job requirements should appear in the middle of the letter. Overall, large percentage differences exist within and among participants in the recruiter group, teacher group, and student group concerning the location of various materials of the cover letter.

Categories of the Resume

The final part of the questionnaire focused on categories of the resume and the importance of various items under each category. The results, reported in Tables 6 and 7, indicate that job objectives/career goals, employment history, and educational history should be categories of the resume. Fewer than 25 percent of respondents thought pastime activities/participation in organizations, references, and personal accomplishments should be included. The rankings indicate that recruiters consider job objectives/career goals and employment history the most important categories, while teachers consider educational history more important than employment history. Specifically, 59 percent of teachers as opposed to 50 percent of recruiters believe educational history is important. This seems to imply that teachers prefer a chronological resume, and recruiters prefer a functional resume. Significant chi-square differences occurred among sample groups in ranking these items, but other significant differences occurred for other independent variables in their rankings.

Results from questions about the contents of the resume indicate that at least 60 percent of the respondents think that thirty items should be included in the resume. Items under job objectives/career goals, educational history, and employment history received the highest ratings. Teachers, for the most part, rated the items under educational history higher than recruiters, but recruiters rated the items under employment history higher than teachers. There were no significant differences among groups.

Table 6. Ranks and Chi-Square Results of Categories of Resumes among Sample Groups

Categories	Recruiters	Teachers	Students	Composite	P
Pastime Activities	6	5	6	6	
References	4	6	5	5	
Job Objectives/					
Career Goals	1	2	2	1	
Employment History	2	3	3	3	
Personal					
Accomplishments	5	4	4	4	
Educational History	3	1	1	2	*

$*x^2 < .05$

Note: Results indicate that career goals, employment history, and educational history should be categories of the resume.

Table 7. Contents of an Ideal Resume

Categories	Items	Level of Importance Percentage
Pastime Activities	Professional organizations	85
Participation in Organizations	Civil service organizations	68
References	Supervisors	86
	Academic instructors/advisors	83
	Professional peers (not employed with)	
Job Objective/ Career Goal	Specification training and development interests	83
	Description of responsibilities wanted	72
	Sketch of short term goals	70
	Sketch of long terms goals	68
Personal Data	Willingness to move	77
	Geographic preference	62
	Citizenship	60
Employment History	List all employers	82
	Details of actual responsibilities	89
	Dates worked (inclusive)	82
	Specific training and development program	85
	Titles of positions held	83
	Name of immediate supervisor	77
	Indicate full-time, part-time, temporary	76
Personal Accomplishments	Noteworthy honors, awards, commendations	90
	Unusual capabilities and talents	83
	Published works	77
Educational History	Major field(s) of study or specialization	93
	Specific credentials received	92
	List of all post-secondary schools attended	89
	Dates attended	87
	Minor field(s) of study or specialization	80

Note: Results indicate that 60 percent of respondents think the above items should be included in a resume.

Post Hoc Analyses

The study also included *post hoc* analyses (based on dependent variables) to determine differences between the sample groups (recruiters, teachers, and students) and differences within recruiter groups based on experience (0-5, 6-10, 11-15, 16-20, 20+ years, and on sex). It also included factor analyses to determine items that loaded on various parts of the questionnaire. In addition, the study included items on specific factors designed to create new variables.

Results showed that recruiter's sex made a significant difference in rating "Cover Letter and Resume Mechanics" and "Cover Letter and Resume Frequency" factors. Marginal differences also occurred between all sample groups in rating "Cover Letter State and Credentials" and "Personal Health and Outside Activities" factors.

An examination of the means indicates that in all cases male recruiters rated cover letters and resumes lower than females. For example, males indicated that cover letters and resumes contain more spelling, grammar, and organization mistakes, and indicated that these mistakes occur more frequently than did female recruiters. In addition, male recruiters were more critical of overpromise, crowded data, and poor headings than were females. Males also believe that "Personal Health and Outside Activities" should be included in the resume.

Significant differences also occurred among sample groups in rating "Resume Read," "Personal Health and Outside Activities," and "Personal Qualification and Work Experience" factors. In addition, marginal differences occurred in rating the "Resume Credential Frequency" factor. Specifically, recruiters indicated they read resumes more fully than teachers and students believe they do. Recruiters also assess personal qualifications and previous work experiences more completely than teachers perceive they do. These findings, reflected in Table 8, support the inductive analyses reported in the first part of this section.

Limited differences occurred among the various experience levels within recruiter groups. Significant differences in rating "Cover Letter Addressed," "Resume Data and Credentials," and "Cover Letter and Resume Frequency" factors between the 20+ and 6-10 groups. The 20+ group rated these factors more critically than did other groups. For example, members of this group indicated that the data on cover letters and resumes were too selective, had an aggressive tone, used poor headings, and had too few credentials.

The findings also revealed that between 20 and 30 percent of the respondents believe that the cover letter and resume should be longer than one page. Although these results add support to previous research, there is still a need for writing teachers to address questions focusing on the ideal length of cover letters and resumes. The results of this study reveal that much within-group variance exists in rating questionnaire items. They also suggest that communication networks should be established between recruiters and teachers to help develop the ideal length of the cover letter and resume. It may be that recruiters from certain

Table 8. Significant Analysis of Variance for Independent Variables

IV	Factors	F	P
Biological Recruiter Groups	Cover letter and resume mechanics	5.191	.02
	Cover letter and resume paper	8.947	.004
	Cover letter data and credentials	3.339	.06
	Personal health and outside activities	3.045	.07
	Resume read	6.446	.002
Sample Groups	Personal health and outside activities	3.864	.02
	Pastime activities	2.211	.08
	Personal qualifications and work experience	3.182	.05
Experience Groups	Resume data and credentials	3.357	.02
	Cover letter and resume paper	2.736	.05
	Cover letter addressed	2.174	.09

Note: Results support the inductive analyses reported in the first part of this section.

companies are more interested in educational history than recruiters from other companies. Some recruiters might want a list of references while other recruiters will request a list of references only if the company is considering hiring the applicant. By gathering information from various companies, teachers can help students to target their cover letters and resumes for specific companies. Thus, the student might develop several types of cover letters and resumes.

The data also revealed that between 35 and 50 percent of cover letters and resumes contain spelling errors, poor grammar, and poor organization. Assuming these figures are approximately accurate, writing teachers need to focus on eliminating these errors. Overall, this study suggests that responsible writing courses include instruction on developing the ideal cover letter and an ideal resume.

CONCLUSION

In a competitive job market it is essential for students to present themselves as favorably as possible to potential employers. The cover letter and resume are important in this regard since they very often serve as the initial contact with a potential employer. Well prepared cover letters and resumes increase the likelihood of obtaining an interview and, subsequently, being seriously considered for a position. For these reasons, it is clear that teachers should help students in developing cover letters and resumes congruent with recruiters' perceptions of what these documents ideally should contain. Research of this type can assist teachers in maintaining such congruency in their instruction.

In summary, the results of this study reveal that:

- Recruiters spend limited time in processing cover letters and resumes.
- Cover letters and resumes should each be only one page long.
- Spelling errors, poor grammar, and poor organization are key problems in cover letters and resumes.
- Specific jobs wanted, career goals, and personal information are the most important factors of a cover letter.
- Job objectives/career goals, employment history, and educational history are the most important items on the resume.

ACKNOWLEDGMENTS

The author wishes to express his gratitude to Dr. Thomas Pearsall, Head, Department of Rhetoric, University of Minnesota, for his contributions in designing the questionnaire and editing the article.

REFERENCES

1. C. K. Janes, The Cover Letter and Resume, *Personal Journal, 48*, pp. 732-733, 1969.
2. C. Mansfield, We Hear You Mr./Mrs. Business . . . The Resume and Cover Letter, *The ABCA Bulletin*, pp. 20-22, 1976.
3. B. Wells, N. Spinks, and J. Hargrave, A Survey of the Chief Officers in the 500 Largest Corporations in the United States to Determine Their Preferences in Job Application Letters and Personnel Resumes, *The ABCA Bulletin*, pp. 3-7, 1981.
4. P. Rivers, Resumes: Up Close and Personal, *Security Management, 25*:2, pp. 81-82, 1981.
5. C. K. Issel, The Resume—A Sales Tool, *Technical Communication, 1*:2, pp. 7-9, 1974.
6. E. Rogers, Elements of Efficient Job Hunting, *Journal of College Placement*, pp. 55-59, 1979.

Other Articles on Communication By This Author

E. E. McDowell, J. Frissell, and V. Winkler, Profiles of 1981 Technical Communication Students, *Journal of Technical Communication, 29*:2, pp. 11-18, 1982.
E. E. McDowell, L. D. Schuelke, and C. Chung, Evaluation of a Bachelor's Program in Technical Communication—Results of a Questionnaire, *Journal of Technical Writing and Communication, 10*:3, pp. 195-201, 1980.
E. E. McDowell, A Quasi-Unstructured Approach to Interpersonal Communication, *Communication Education, 28*, pp. 239-244, July 1979.

EXIT INTERVIEWS: DON'T JUST SAY GOODBYE TO YOUR TECHNICAL COMMUNICATION STUDENTS*

EARL E. McDOWELL
University of Minnesota, St. Paul

Recently the exit interview has received more attention in interviewing textbooks, but it still is not being utilized as well as it could be. The primary problem is that supervisors or directors of personnel do not like to conduct exit interviews. Thus, companies do not know why employees are leaving. The exit interview also can be used to determine how students feel about a class or a college program. The following article covers how exit interviews can be used to gather information about students' perceptions of the various aspects of their academic major. Please answer the following questions:

1. Have you ever participated in an exit interview?
   a. If yes, were you the interviewer or interviewee?
   b. How did you feel about the experience?
2. If you have participated in an exit interview, how would you respond to the ten questions listed in the study?
3. Would you like to participate in an exit interview for this course?
4. If you are a student, how would you evaluate your academic program?

*   *   *

The exit interview provides employees with an opportunity to tell their reasons for leaving a company. The interview consists of information-giving and information-gathering and also provides the interviewer with an opportunity to counsel the former employee. Both directive and nondirective approaches are used in most exit

*E. McDowell, Exit Interviews: Don't Just Say Goodbye to Your Technical Communication Students, *ITCC Proceedings, 35,* pp. RET 51-53, 1988. Reprinted by permission of Society for Technical Communication.

interviews. The direct method enables the interviewer to ask the relevant questions to determine why the interviewee is leaving. The nondirective method provides the interviewee with the opportunity to tell his/her perceptions of the company. There are both voluntary and involuntary reasons for leaving a company.

Sherwood (1983) indicated that the formal exit interview is one of the best ways to find out where personnel operating and employee relations problems exist, as well as what attitudes employees hold about their jobs, management, and the company itself [1]. The interview is moderately scheduled and should be conducted in private. Wehrenberg asserted supervisors can identify the cause of employee attrition, analyze the symptoms, and seek the most effective, long-term solutions [2].

PURPOSE OF THIS STUDY

The purposes of this study were 1) to obtain graduating students' perceptions of the Technical Communication program, 2) to inform students of positions available in various departments, and 3) to record a forwarding address and phone number. The belief was that students would speak freely as the fear of reprisal is gone and as Zima pointed out it provided both parties an opportunity to create a favorable lasting impression [3].

In this study students were asked to assess the following areas:

1. Competence of their advisors.
2. University distribution requirements.
3. Technical communication competency areas.
4. Courses they liked best.
5. Courses they liked least.
6. Technical elective.
7. Level of satisfaction with internship experience.
8. Relationships with other students.
9. Quality of instruction.
10. Preparation for job market.

PROCEDURES OF THE STUDY

A sample of forty undergraduate and graduate Technical Communication students from the Department of Rhetoric, University of Minnesota, participated in the exit interview study. Students were interviewed shortly after they graduated from our program. Three trained Technical Communication students conducted the interviews. Initially, we developed the Exit Interview Questionnaire (EIQ). The questionnaire was designed to gather demographic information, provide reasons for selecting technical communication as a major, evaluate advisors and registration process, assess the internship experience, assess the Technical

Communication program, and overall determine philosophical attitudes about the program.

The opening of the interview set the tone for gathering information. The interviewers outlined the reasons for the interview and indicated the topical areas. In the opening graduated students were told that faculty members in the Department of Rhetoric were interested in their assessments of the Technical Communication program as their assessments would help us to improve the overall quality of the program in a variety of areas. Students were assured that their statements would be confidential.

The body of the interview consisted of a variety of open-ended and closed-ended questions. The open-ended questions provided former students with an opportunity to share as much information as they wanted to on the various topical areas. The closed-ended questions forced students to make specific assessments of the various areas. During the closing students were given a list of current job openings, and we recorded their present address. Each interview lasted about 45 minutes.

The primary purpose of this study was descriptive and designed to answer the following research questions:

1. How helpful was your advisor in assisting you in deciding on your appropriate course work? How knowledgeable was your advisor about current requirements for the technical communication major?
2. What two competency areas were most important?
3. What three technical communication courses did you like best? Least?
4. How important was your technical elective?
5. How satisfied were you with your internship experience?
6. How satisfied were you with the quality of instruction?

RESULTS

The results of the study indicate that twenty-two (55%) females and eighteen (45%) males participated in the study. Approximately 65 percent were under thirty and 35 percent were thirty or over.

Other results of the study produced mixed reactions to the questions focusing on advisors. For example, 75 percent of advisors were rated as very helpful or helpful and very knowledgeable or knowledgeable, while 25 percent were rated negatively in both areas. In addition, about 50 percent felt their technical elective was important, while 40 percent felt it was unimportant and 10 percent were undecided. Overall, students rated the methods of instruction very positively.

There were also different preferences in terms of the importance of various competence areas and courses liked best and liked least. As Table 1 indicates students felt the *Writing and Editing, Internship,* and *Oral Communication* were the most important competency areas. Students felt that *Philosophy and History of*

Science and *Communication Theory and Research* were the least important. Information in Table 2 indicates that students, for the most part, were very satisfied or satisfied with the various dimensions of their internship experience. They were most satisfied with supervision and appraisal and least satisfied with type of work and responsibilities. Former students who were dissatisfied with these areas complained about performing routine tasks rather than being given challenging tasks to perform.

In Tables 3 and 4 are lists of the five courses students like most and like least. These results support an earlier study by McDowell, Schuelke and Chung [4]. It is interesting to note that although students indicated that they felt the *Writing and Editing* competency area was the most important only the Documentation course was selected from this area as one that they liked best. In addition, two courses from the *Oral Communication* area, Scientific and Technical Presentations and Interviewing: Dynamics of Face-to-Face Communication, were selected as ones that were liked best.

Table 1. Level of Importance of Technical Communication Competency Areas

Competency Area	Important (percent)	Unimportant (percent)
Writing and editing	95	3
Oral communication	90	0
Visual communication	77	0
Organizational communication	63	10
Communication theory and research	50	19
Philosophy and history of science	23	30
Internship	90	0

Table 2. Level of Satisfaction with Internship

Internship Experience	Satisfied (percent)	Dissatisfied (percent)
Working conditions	50	13
Relationship with employees	40	13
Type of work	60	27
Supervision	70	17
Responsibility	53	30
Appraisal	67	20
Overall satisfaction	60	17

Table 3. Five Technical Communication Courses
Liked the Most

Writing in your profession
Scientific and technical presentations
Interviewing: Dynamics of face-to-face communication
Rhetorical theory
Documentation

Table 4. Five Technical Communication Courses
Liked Least

Human communication
Grammatical editing
Senior seminar
Dissemination and utilization of information
Transfer of technology

Other information that was gathered in the questionnaire indicates that 92 percent felt the present program is very adequate or adequate. Approximately 83 percent are interested in pursuing a graduate degree, but only 30 percent plan to do this at the University of Minnesota. Only 20 percent of the students have much more contact with other Technical Communication students, indicating that they worked full-time. Over 80 percent felt they would like more contact with other majors.

Post hoc analyses were completed between biological sex groups and age groups to determine if there were differences between male and female students and students under thirty and students thirty and over. No significant differences occurred between groups on any of the dependent variables.

DISCUSSION

An interpretation of the results of the study suggests that a majority of the students are satisfied with the present undergraduate Technical Communication program. The study, however, reveals that some faculty members need to be more knowledgeable about our program. Because the Department of Rhetoric consists of faculty members from different academic disciplines, and some are involved exclusively with the program while others teach primarily service courses, it is understandable that those primarily involved with the Technical Communication Program would be more helpful and knowledgeable.

Another finding of much importance was the courses that are liked best and liked least. Students responding to open-ended questions provided suggestions to improve the courses they liked best and those they liked least. The internship experience seems to be what they liked best, yet students wanted to be involved in challenging tasks. We obviously will report this finding to companies who list internship opportunities. Students also indicated that they felt their internship experience provided them with a good knowledge of the job market.

Overall, this exit interview study has provided valuable information concerning our Technical Communication Program. Instead of giving information to students, we sought information from them. This was a positive experience for both interviewers and interviewees.

The exit interview also would be a valuable information-gathering technique to determine why a technical writer decided to move from one company to another. Some questions that might be asked are:

1. Why have you decided to leave?
2. What might we have done to persuade you to stay?
3. Under what circumstances would you consider returning to work here?
4. Would you recommend our company to another technical writer?
5. How well did we prepare you for your new job?
6. Which do you feel is more important in our company, how well you perform or whom you knew? Why?
7. How would you describe your co-workers?
8. How would you describe your supervisor?
9. Do you think our writers share your views?
10. Is there anything I haven't asked you that you want to comment on?

CONCLUSIONS OF THIS STUDY

1. Students believed that the internship experience is the most important part of the program.
2. Students believed that the *Writing and Editing* and *Oral Communication* competency areas are the most important.
3. Students liked the following courses best: Writing in Your Profession, Scientific and Technical Presentations, Interviewing: Dynamics of Face-to-Face Communication, Rhetorical Theory, and Documentation.
4. Students liked the following courses least: Human Communication, Grammatical Editing, Senior Seminar, Dissemination and Utilization of Information, and Transfer of Technology.

REFERENCES

1. A. Sherwood, Exit Interviews: Don't Just Say Goodbye, *Personnel Journal*, pp. 744-750, 1983.
2. S. Wehrenberg, The Exit Interview: Why Bother?, *Supervisory Management, 25*, pp. 20-25, 1980.
3. J. Zima, Interviewing: Key to Effective Management, *Science Research Associates, Inc.*, Chicago, 1983.
4. E. McDowell, L. D. Schuelke, and C. Chung, Evaluation of a Bachelor's Program in Technical Communication—Results of a Questionnaire, *Journal of Technical Writing and Communication, 10*, pp. 195-210, 1980.

APPENDIX A

Employment Interview Digest

We already have covered the employment interview, but you might want to review some important concepts before you participate as an interviewee or interviewer. For example, if you are playing the role of the interviewee, you should review information you have on the company, as well as how you plan to create a favorable first impression and how you will create a favorable lasting impression. If you are playing the role of the interviewer, you should review federal, state, and local laws concerning discrimination in types of questions that you ask. In addition, you are concerned about creating a favorable first impression and last impression.

This review process should reinforce the contents of the employment interview chapter. Have fun as you review the material.

EMPLOYMENT INTERVIEWING DIGEST

CONGRATULATIONS! You were just called in for a job interview at Orange Computer Corporation. The job you applied for—Personnel Manager—has a starting salary of $50,000 a year, a well as the following benefits:

Company car
Personal health club
30 personal days a year
Business trips to Hawaii

Now you must prepare for your interview. What should you do to prepare?

INTERVIEWEE TOPICS

In the first part of this review, you will be playing the part of the job applicant going to an employment interview. The topics you will review are the following.

Ways to Prepare for an Interview
Creating First Impressions
Personal Qualities
Last Impressions
After the Interview

Ways to Prepare for an Interview

1. *Research the organization.*   Find out everything you can about the company to which you are applying for a job. The following publications will be helpful: *College Placement Annual Directory, Dunn and Bradstreet's Middle Market Directory and Million Dollar Director.*
2. *Analyze the job description.*   Carefully read the description of the job for which you are applying. Be sure you understand what the job involves. If you have questions keep them in mind so you can ask them during the interview. Think about how your experience and personality qualify you for the job.
   Examples:
   Do you have the necessary background for the job?
   Are the job functions and duties clear to you?
3. *Determine your work needs.*   Think about what you want and need in a job. Determine whether your personality will fit into the company's culture.
   Examples:
   Will there be chances for advancement?
   Can the company meet your salary requirements?
   Does the work offer a challenge?
   Is a dress code required? If yes, are you comfortable with it?
4. *Research the interviewer.*   Be sure you know the interviewer's name and how to pronounce it correctly. Also know the interviewer's title, department and office location before your appointment day.
5. *Select attire to wear to the interview.*   Clothing should be conservative and appropriate to the company to which you are applying. Keep jewelry and accessories simple and to a minimum. Neatness and cleanliness are a must.
6. *Decide on one or two questions you will ask the interviewer.*   Be prepared with one or two questions in case the interviewer offers to answer questions. Other questions may arise naturally through your interaction with the interviewer.
   Examples:
   What kind of training program do you have?
   What are the company's major benefits to employees?

Creating First Impressions

During the opening of the interview you need to create a favorable first impression with the interviewer. Nonverbal communication—how you behave—is one of the factors that determines the first impression you make. Below are a list of some of the important types of nonverbal communication.

1. *Eye Contact.* Good eye contact tells interviewers that you are interested in them and what they have to say. Good eye contact shows that you have self-confidence and trust. Poor eye contact occurs when either party repeatedly turns away, or keeps breaking eye contact. Staring also is unacceptable.
2. *Firm handshake.* Make your handshake firm by exerting a comfortable steady pressure. Handshakes between people of the same sex and/or the opposite sex are appropriate greetings and partings in today's business world. A politely offered, firm handshake communicates your self-confidence to the interviewer.
3. *Facial expressions.* Facial expressions should be expressive, e.g., warm and inviting rather than poker-faced. Avoid worried expressions—smiles and responsiveness will convey your self-confidence to the interviewer.
4. *Posture.* Posture should be relaxed, but active enough to let the interviewer know you are interested. Facing the interviewer and leaning slightly forward will communicate your involvement and self-confidence. Keep your arms and legs uncrossed to convey openness. Avoid "fidgeting."
5. *Appropriate dress.* Appropriate dress is a must for your interview. Today, a conservative suit is usually appropriate for both men and women at the interview. Women's interviewing suits, however, should consist of a skirt (not pants) and a jacket. Keep jewelry and accessories simple and to a minimum.
6. *Seating arrangement.* Seating arrangements for the interview are generally determined in advance by the interviewer. Several arrangements are popular: a small table with a chair on each side (one for the interviewer and one for the interviewee); the interviewer behind his or her desk with the interviewee's seat squarely on the other side of the desk; or the interviewer seated at his/her desk with a chair for the interviewee at the corner of the desk.

Personal Qualities

Now think about what personal qualities the interviewer might consider important in a job applicant, so that you can project those qualities during the interview.

1. *Special abilities* refer to those abilities which may be unique in your field. For example, perhaps, in addition to being an excellent technical writer, you are also a talented artist. Consequently, you bring all the necessary qualifications to your job, plus a bonus. You can write computer manuals and also provide exceptionally good graphics for them. If the company hired you, they would be getting "two for the price of one."
2. *Ambition* is a strong desire to succeed or achieve. This personal characteristic is likely to benefit the company, particularly if the ambitious employee shares the same goals as the company.

3. *Maturely directed energy* is energy expended toward accomplishing necessary day-to-day tasks and long-range goals. Time management is important here. Be sure your experience and skills in time management appear on your resume and/or in your cover letter. Figure out, in advance, how to sell abilities like these during the interview.
4. *Ability to communicate*—Companies look for applicants who can write and speak well. They are interested in how well you can organize and present materials both verbally and visually. Employers are also interested in how well you can work with others in different situations; for example: in one-on-one situations, as a team member, and in other group settings. Be sure your resume reflects your communication skills. Also be aware of both your verbal and nonverbal communication during the interview.
5. *General intelligence and knowledge*—You are born with your intelligence, your capacity for reasoning. You have added to your store of knowledge since birth through study and observations of others. Let the interviewer know, through your resume and during the interview, about the educational background and work experiences that highlight your intelligence and knowledge.
6. *Integrity* is a quality of being honest, upright, sincere, and of sound moral principles. Integrity is considered an important personal quality by interviewers. Think of ways to convey your integrity to your perspective employers.

Last Impressions Count Too

You feel confident that you have made a good impression on Mr. Rich so far, but the interviewer's last impression of you also is very important.

1. *Prepare some questions to ask* when the interviewer gives you the opportunity to do so, or when you simply want answers. Sample questions are:
   What type of training programs does the company offer?
   What are the companies major benefits to employees?
2. *Say something positive about the company.*
   For example: **"I'm excited about the possibility of working with your company, because it is so innovative in the computer software field."**
3. You can end the interview by *asking some friendly, personal questions.*
   For example: **How long have you been with the Orange Computer Corporation?**

Things to do After the Interview

1. *Analyze the interview* by thinking over the main topics covered. Think about how you would improve your communication should you have a second interview with the same or different company.

2. In your *thank-you letter* you have the opportunity to restate what you have to offer the company and give positive reasons why you would like to work for them. Your prompt thank-you letter indicates that you are "on top of things."
3. Now you have more information about the job opening and can decide whether *your goals "fit" with those of the company.*
   For example: **Do you think your personality will fit into the company culture?** If you want to advance in the organization, **are you sure the opportunity will be forthcoming?** Perhaps, you found out that extensive travel is required and you do not enjoy traveling.

INTERVIEWER TOPICS

Now you are going to play the part of an interviewer. The topics are listed below:

How to Prepare to Interview
Interview Schedules
Planning the Opening
Types of Questions
Question Sequences
Closings

CONGRATULATIONS! YOU GOT THE JOB. You are now the Personnel Manager at Orange Computer Company. During your first week on the job you have to interview an applicant for the position of technical writer in the Sales Division. You sit down in your new leather chair behind your new mahogany desk and prepare to interview the applicant.

How to Prepare to Interview a Job Applicant

1. Be familiar with current federal, state, and local laws, court decisions and interpretations relating to discrimination in employment procedures.
2. Determine up-to-date requirements and write a job description which is an accurate statement of what, how, and under what conditions the employee will be expected to perform. Determine qualifications necessary for the job.
3. See if the applicant's education and work experience match the job requirements. Look for missing information, unusual work patterns, and areas you might probe during the interview.
4. Examine the applicant's transcript to determine his/her educational experience and areas of specialty.
5. Create an interview guide, a very general outline of topics and subtopics to be covered in an interview.
6. Decide on the type of questions which will accomplish your purpose.
7. Develop an opening that establishes rapport and orients the interviewee.

8. In the closing keep the tone consistent with the tone of the rest of the interview and make sure there is a mutual understanding between you and the interviewee on what items were dealt with during the interview.

Interview Schedules

The best way to start planning an interview is by making an outline of topics and subtopics to be covered in the interview—*an interview guide.* You can use the interview guide to prepare an interview schedule—a list of questions to ask during the interview.

1. *Nonscheduled interviews* contain primarily open-ended questions and probes that are not usually planned ahead of time. The interviewer asks questions in reaction to the applicant's answers to prior questions, not in any predetermined order.
2. *Moderately scheduled interviews* contain both open-ended and closed-ended questions, but are mainly made up of open-ended questions planned by the interviewer ahead of time.
3. *Highly scheduled interviews* contain questions which have been prepared in advance. No probing or deviation from the planned list is made.
   Questions are usually closed-ended.
4. *Highly scheduled standardized interviews* contain primarily closed-ended questions. Each interviewee receives identical questions. This is the most structured interview.

Planning the Opening

During the opening part of the interview, you want to establish rapport with the applicant and orient him/her about the open job.

1. *Briefly explain the job and the qualifications for it.*
   Example:
   "You are being interviewed for the technical writer position now open in our Sales Division. The job requires writing instructions for user-installation of our products. The qualifications for the job are a Bachelor's Degree in the communication field and at least one year of work experience as a writer and/or editor."
2. *Ask an easy to answer, open-ended question* which will not put the applicant on the spot.
   Example:
   "Tell me how you became interested in writing."
3. *Rapport* (mutual trust and goodwill) can be established by introducing yourself, asking a personal question, and then commenting on the weather or a recent news event. The interviewer must come across as sincere. Good eye contact, smiles, and other friendly nonverbal actions will help.

Example:

Hi, I'm Joan Benson. How are you this morning? It's a beautiful day, isn't it?

4. *Tell the applicant how the interview will flow.*

Example:

"Let me tell you what we'll do in this interview. I'd like us to learn a little about each other so, first, let's talk about your background—training, work experience, career interests and so on. Then I'd like to give you time to ask questions you might have about our company and what we have to offer. Okay?

Types of Questions

You need to use a variety of questions in the employment interview.

1. *Open-ended questions* are broad questions which give the interviewee freedom in deciding how to answer.

   Example—Highly open:

   "Tell me about yourself."

   Example—Moderately open:

   "Tell me about your writing experience."

2. *Closed-ended questions* restrict the possible answers the person answering the questions can give. In highly closed questions the respondent must choose an answer from a list provided by the questioner. Bipolar questions—questions which only offer a choice between two options—are one type of commonly used closed-ended question.

   Example—Highly closed:

   "How satisfied were you with your internship experience?"

   very satisfied_____ satisfied_____ not satisfied_____

   Example—Moderately closed:

   "How many years have you been working on your degree?"

   Example—Bipolar:

   "Do you like or dislike the desktop publishing system we use?"

3. *Neutral questions* allow the interviewee to decide on an answer without pressure or direction from the interviewer, even in bipolar situations.

   Example:

   "Are you willing to travel?"

4. *Leading questions* make it easier or more tempting for the interviewee to give one answer over another. The interviewee can perceive the answer the interviewer wants.

   Example:

   "You would be willing to travel, wouldn't you?"

5. *Nudging probes* are brief questions or requests intended to get the interviewee to elaborate on something they have said.

244 / INTERVIEWING PRACTICES FOR TECHNICAL WRITERS

Example:

"Tell me more."

6. *Clearinghouse probes* are follow-up questions for finding out whether all available and/or important information has been given by the interviewee.
Example:

"Do you want to add anything else about your internship experience?"

7. *Reflective probes* are questions to clarify vague or unclear answers and inaccuracies.
Example:

"Did you say you have had writing experience?"

8. *Hypothetical probes* are questions used to ask the interviewee how he/or she would handle a particular situation should it occur.
Example:

"What would you do if you learned your production manager was drinking on the job?"

9. *Reactive probes* test the interviewee's reaction to a particular real situation. Both sides of an issue are given in reactive probes.
Example:

"What kinds of things do you like best about your job?"

"What kinds of things do you like least about your job?"

(The above two questions together make up a reactive probe.)

10. *Confrontive probes* are questions for clearing up contradictions and confusion.
Example:

"Earlier in our interview you said you've never used the WordStar word processing program, but now you say you once used it for several months. How do you explain these different answers?"

Closings

Listed below are some methods for closing interviews.

1. *Offer to answer questions.* Allow time for the interviewee to ask questions so he/she feels the interview has been productive. You may encourage questions by asking one.
Example:

"Do you have any questions about our benefit package?"

2. *Use a clearinghouse question* to determine whether or not the interviewee has more concerns.
Example:

"I think we've covered everything. Is there anything else you'd like to ask before we close?"

3. *Signal the end of an interview* by using nonverbal and verbal cues.
Example—Nonverbal:

Put down your pencil and close the applicant folder. Stand up.

Example—Verbal:

"Well, our time is up."

"I have another appointment waiting, so we'll have to close for today."

4. You may *use an unrelated personal inquiry* to close an interview.

Example:

"Your new home sounds wonderful. When will you move into it?"

5. *Declare completion* by simply stating that the interview is complete.

Example:

"Well, I think I have the information I need to consider you for the technical writing position."

6. Tell the applicant you *appreciate his/her* time and show satisfaction with the interview.

Example:

"I've really enjoyed meeting you. Thanks for coming in today."

7. *End with concern for the applicant health, future, etc.*

Example:

"Take care, and I will be in touch with you soon."

8. *Summarize the interview.* The interviewer repeats key information about the position and the interview content and confirms its accuracy with the interviewee.

Example:

"It's understood, then, that the Technical Writer position involves writing instructional pamphlets."

9. The interviewer may *plan the next meeting* if additional interviews are required prior to the hiring decision.

Example:

"I would like you to come back next week at this time, if possible, to talk with our Sales Manager and to tour our production area."

10. *Explain how the applicant will be informed as to whether or not he/she will be hired.*

Example:

"We have several more applicants to interview before making a decision and will inform you by letter, one way or the other, in about two weeks."

Hopefully this review will help you perform both the role of the interviewer and interviewee. Remember, you should speak about **30 percent of the time when you are the interviewer and about 70 percent when you are the interviewee.**

Author Index

Subject Index